IMAGES
of America

BAY AREA RADIO

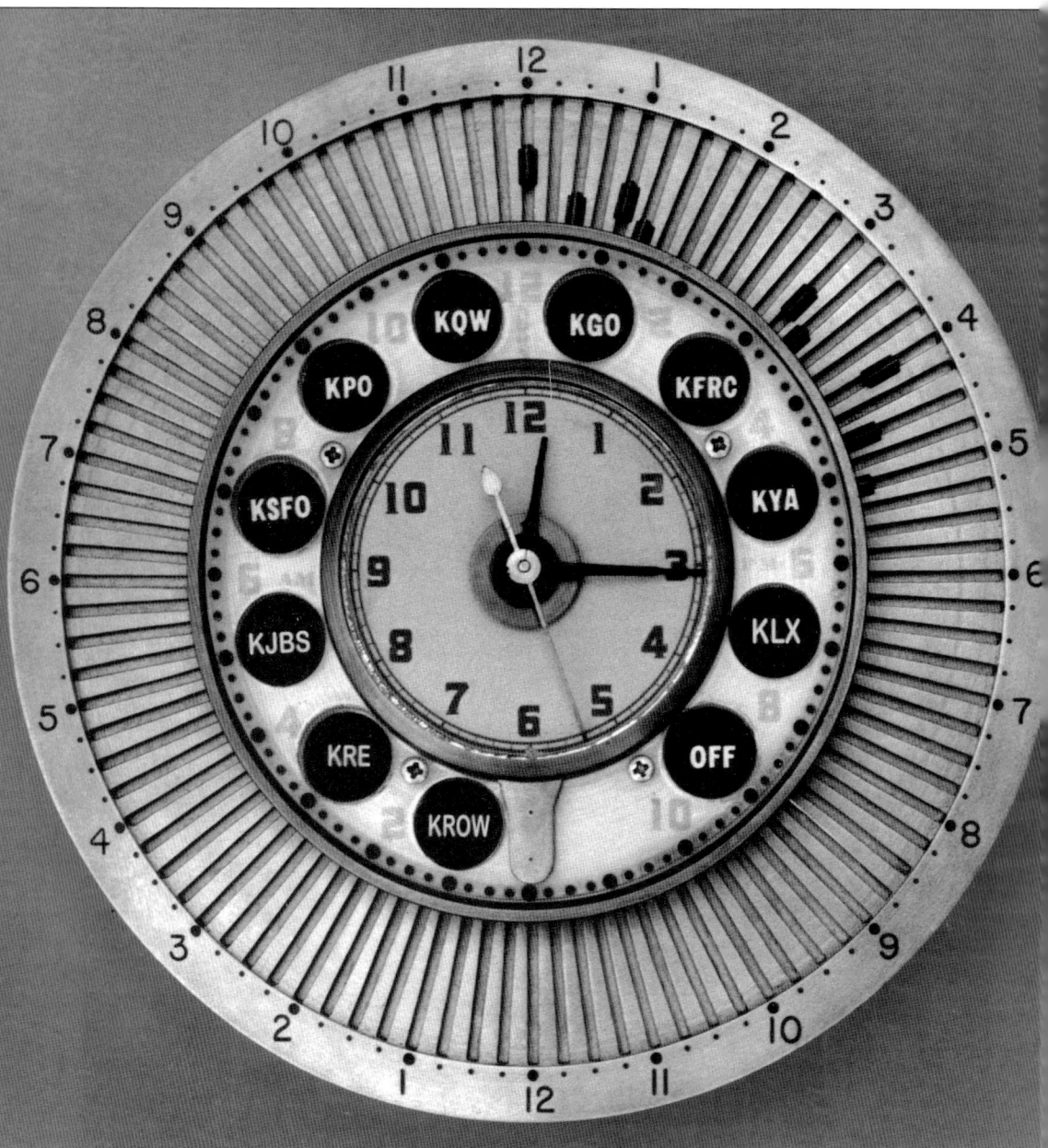

This is a typical radio dial from the late 1930s, with buttons for each of the San Francisco area's radio stations. (Perham Collection, History San Jose.)

ON THE COVER: A live broadcast of *Standard on Parade* originates from the National Broadcasting Company studio A at 111 Sutter Street in San Francisco on June 18, 1933. Meredith Willson conducts the NBC Orchestra. Larry Blake (left) and Barton Yarborough are at the microphone. The variety program was heard Sunday nights over the NBC-KGO Pacific Coast Network. (Author's collection.)

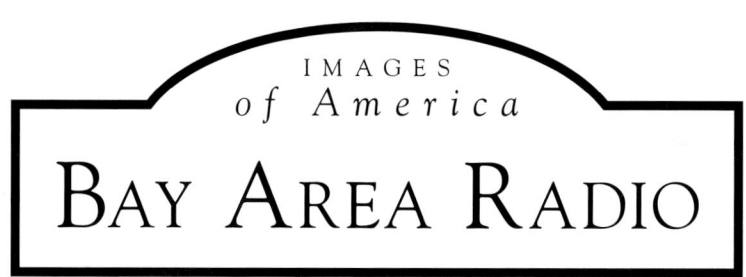

IMAGES
of America
BAY AREA RADIO

John F. Schneider, in association with
the California Historical Radio Society
and its Bay Area Radio Museum

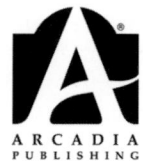

ARCADIA
PUBLISHING

Published by Arcadia Publishing
Charleston, South Carolina

Printed in the United States of America

Library of Congress Control Number: 2011935791

For all general information, please contact Arcadia Publishing:
Telephone 843-853-2070
Fax 843-853-0044
E-mail sales@arcadiapublishing.com
For customer service and orders:
Toll-Free 1-888-313-2665

Visit us on the Internet at www.arcadiapublishing.com

*To the mothers and fathers of the younger generation,
and to their bewildering offspring*

CONTENTS

ACKNOWLEDGMENTS

When I reflect on it, I am amazed at how many people have contributed their time and assistance over the past 40 years towards the body of information that this book represents and who have encouraged and supported me in my long and passionate pursuit of documenting the history of Bay Area radio. I am certain I must be leaving out some important names, and so I apologize in advance if I have forgotten to recognize you for your valuable assistance.

This book would not be possible without the support and cooperation of the California Historical Radio Society (CHRS). The following CHRS members were largely responsible for this support: Mike Adams, Jaime Arbona, David Jackson, Steve Kushman, Bart Lee, and Len Shapiro.

Others who assisted in the collection of photographs and other information for this book include: David Alexander, Paul Bourbin, Jim Bowman, Darryl Compton (Broadcast Legends), Charles Dumm, Jim Eviston, Keith Farr, Jim Gabbert, Gordon Greb, Bruce Hunter, Rich Kolm, Art Leberman, Kevin Mostyn, Bill Newbrough, Jim Reed (History San Jose), Richard Rodriguez (McCarthy family), Bill Ruck, Caryl Heyde Saunders, Bruce Sedley, Penny and Michael Wilkes (Dumm family), George Zema, and Suzanne Teuber (Jamond family).

The following people supported my original research in the collection of materials for "Voices Out of the Fog" from 1969 to 1972: Paul C. Smith, Bill Andrews, Carleton and Patricia Morse, Preston Allen, Dave Amaral, Les Avery, Murray Bolen, Carl Christiensen, Russ Coughlan, Al Cormack, Dave Crosatto, Ron Denman, Bill Doubleday, Wesley I. Dumm, E.F. Fitzmaurice, Eugene Frickstad, Don Hambly, Patrick Hilliard, Bob Hansen, Arman Humburg, Richard Johnstone, Philip Lasky, Bruce Lathrup, Vic Paulsen, Erwin Rasmussen, Dr. Louis L. Sherman, Charles C. Smith, Roswell Smith, Eugene Warner, Cyrus Trobbe, Art Westlund, Harry Wickersham, and Charles Williams.

I am also indebted to the following people who supported the expansion and conversion of my original manuscript into an Internet resource as early as 1995, leading to what is now part of the Bay Area Radio Museum's web page: Steve Gore, David Jackson, Fred Krock, Harry Larkin, Cecil Lynch, Greg Oppenheimer, and William Reed.

—John Schneider
November 2011

INTRODUCTION

Hundreds of books have been written about radio history. Most of these were written from a national viewpoint, concentrating on the eastern half of the nation. But a true picture of what it was like to listen to the radio during its golden years should be told at the local level, because that was the perspective of the listener. Local and regional programs were heard just as often as the big national shows.

It is hard to express to young people today the extent that radio changed the nation and the world starting in the early 1920s. Perhaps the only equivalent event in our time is the creation of the Internet. Before radio, the only means of instantaneous communication were the telephone and telegraph. A long-distance phone call was a rare and expensive proposition, so brief and often cryptic telegrams were the primary means of interpersonal long-distance communication. Newspapers were the only mass source of news dissemination, but they needed hours or even days to deliver urgent news. And, except for phonograph records, all entertainment was performed live in front of the few people who were privileged enough to be in the audience.

Radio changed all of that, especially with the formation of the national networks. News of the nation and the world was instantly flashed to the entire country, often as it was happening. The public could "listen in" to live broadcasts of important events, such as presidential inaugurations or political conventions. The best entertainers and musical performers in the world were for the first time being heard by millions and not just on scratchy records. The great sporting events of the day were now accessible to all and in real time. Radio also transformed politics by letting the public hear the words and voices of the candidates directly instead of reading them in the paper or hearing them spoken from the back of a railroad car. FDR knew instinctively how to use radio to speak directly to the people with his "Fireside Chats," and the sound and impact of a politician's voice quickly became a key factor in winning elections.

Radio created entire new genres that we take for granted today but which had previously never existed. Radio drama, comedy, and variety programs were first influenced by the dramatic stage and vaudeville, but they soon took on new forms unique to the medium. Brand new program concepts were developed, like game shows and amateur talent contests. The creation of radio sound effects became a new art form. News announcers, commentators, and sportscasters all had to invent the skills of describing events in real time and finding ways to make them interesting and relevant to the listener.

In the development of the art and science of American radio broadcasting, few cities were as important as San Francisco. During the prewar years, most important radio activities on the West Coast were centered in the Bay Area. Inventors and tinkerers at Stanford University and elsewhere were among the early developers of the science and art of radio. San Jose was the location of the nation's first broadcasting station (experimental as early as 1909, licensed in 1921 as KQW, and now known as KCBS). In broadcasting's infant years, San Francisco had more pioneering radio stations than any city in the country. It was the networks' West Coast production headquarters prior to World War II, when programs originating in San Francisco were heard nationwide over NBC, CBS, and Mutual. In the 1940s, San Francisco became the news collection and dissemination headquarters for the war in the Pacific, and powerful San Francisco shortwave stations carried information and entertainment to the occupied countries and US servicemen in the Pacific theater.

And yet, with all of this history, there was very little published information about San Francisco's contribution to broadcasting available in 1969, when I was a student in the Department of Broadcast Communication Arts (BCA) at San Francisco State University. My efforts to learn about local radio history uncovered almost no information, except for a few bare clues to indicate that the city had a rich and glorious past. Eventually, my search for this information morphed into a two-year college-credit quest with the support of BCA instructor Paul C. Smith and resulted in a manuscript called "Voices Out of the Fog," documenting Bay Area radio's first 50 years. During a two-year period, I collected dozens of photographs and interviewed nearly 40 active and retired broadcasters—most of whom are sadly no longer with us. In the process, I assembled a body of information that would have otherwise been lost to time.

After graduating and accumulating what was perhaps one of the world's largest collection of publisher rejection letters, the manuscript collected dust on my bookshelf for 20 years. But, when the Internet first surfaced as a worldwide communications resource, I realized it would be the natural vehicle to share the story I had collected years before. And so, a nascent web site was born in 1995. Eventually, with the support of David Jackson's Bay Area Radio Museum (BARM), it became a part of what is today the California Historical Radio Society's popular BARM website. People from around the world who are interested in broadcast history now have a convenient resource to understand San Francisco's contributions to the beginnings of today's radio industry.

In early 2011, Arcadia Publishing expressed an interest in adapting this website into a new book in its popular Images of America series. In addition to my original collection of images, a public call for photographs uncovered over 300 new photographs, many of which have been included in this book. Many of these have not been seen publicly for more than 50 years. In that respect, this book represents the most complete collection of Bay Area radio images ever assembled.

On the following pages, you will be introduced to a few of the thousands of people who participated in early Bay Area broadcasting, as well as the many of the places and technical achievements that made San Francisco a fascinating place to work in radio and created millions of hours of great radio programs for both local and national enjoyment. Stay tuned!

—John Schneider
November 2011

One

THE FORMATIVE YEARS
1905–1922

San Francisco saw some of the world's first experiments in the transmission of the human voice. As early as 1902, teenage radio inventor Francis McCarty experimented with voice transmission using a modified spark transmitter. Stanford University student Cyril Elwell obtained the rights to the Danish Poulsen arc transmitter and formed the Federal Telephone and Telegraph Company. He perfected the arc for Morse code transmission and later supplied transmitters to the US Navy.

Elwell's work may have inspired Charles D. "Doc" Herrold, another Stanford student and experimenter, who opened the Herrold School of Wireless in San Jose in 1909. Within a year, Doc Herrold and his assistant Ray Newby had built an arc transmitter capable of voice transmission, and it caused so much interest among early ham radio operators that, by 1912, the Herrold station was playing weekly phonograph "concerts" using the call sign FN—the first documented case of radio "broadcasting." In 1914, Herrold's wife, Sybil, took over with her *Little Hams Program*. She promoted the music stores on the air that lent her records and held weekly giveaway contests.

Herrold's station was shut down in 1917, when the government ordered all stations off the air during World War I. After the war, his arc technology was obsolete, incapable of operating on the newly assigned broadcasting frequencies. Undaunted, he went back on the air with the call sign KQW. But, unable to finance the station, he soon turned the station over to the First Baptist Church. KQW changed hands several more times until it was bought by CBS in 1949, becoming today's KCBS. For this reason, that station rightfully claims to be the oldest radio station in the country. Forgotten and penniless, Herrold died in a Hayward rest home in 1948.

Several other local tinkerers also opened stations when the ban was lifted, and by 1921, the Bay Area had more broadcasting stations than anywhere else in the country. These were experimental stations with one foot in broadcasting and the other in ham radio, and most of these stations disappeared as quickly as they came on the air. These included Lee de Forest's 6XC in the California Theatre, KDN in the Fairmont Hotel, the *Examiner's* KUO, KJJ in Sunnyvale, KLP in Los Altos, KZM in Oakland, and the Emporium Department Store's KSL.

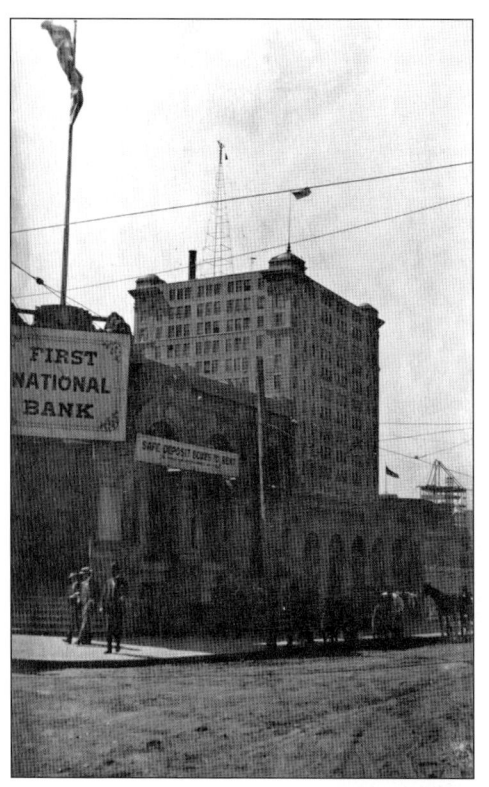

Here is an early indication of wireless activity in San Francisco. This photograph, taken in 1907 by Dr. Stanley Cosby (UC Berkeley, 1916–1935), shows the Merchants Exchange Building at California and Montgomery Streets. The back of the photograph indicates "wireless on top." The building housed the local office of the United Wireless Telegraph Company, operators of marine wireless station PH in the Palace Hotel. When that station was destroyed in the 1906 San Francisco earthquake, a new station was built on Russian Hill. The company probably used this antenna to monitor the Russian Hill transmitter. (William Reed.)

In 1902, young Francis McCarty broadcast his voice across Stow Lake in Golden Gate Park. In 1905, he formed the McCarty Wireless Telephone Company and astounded reporters by talking from the Cliff House to a receiver a mile down the beach. But, McCarty died in a horse cart accident in 1906, two days before his 18th birthday. McCarty's brothers continued for a while under the name of the National Radio Company. (Bart Lee.)

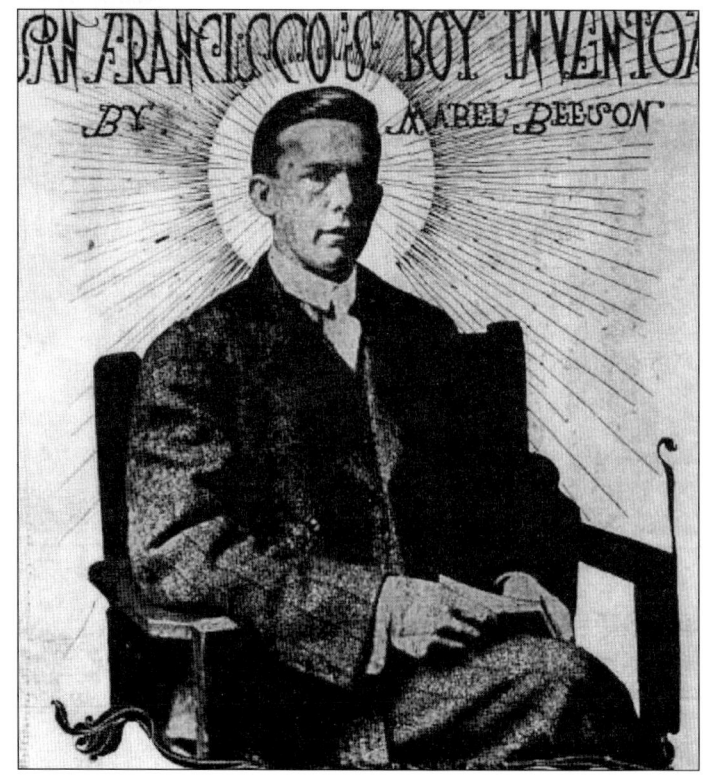

Doc Herrold opened the Herrold College of Engineering and Wireless in San Jose in 1909. It was located on the third floor of the Garden City Bank Building at the corner of South First and San Fernando Streets. A massive "carpet aerial" soon spread like a spider web from the building to neighboring structures. The beginnings of radio broadcasting would take place in this building. (History San Jose.)

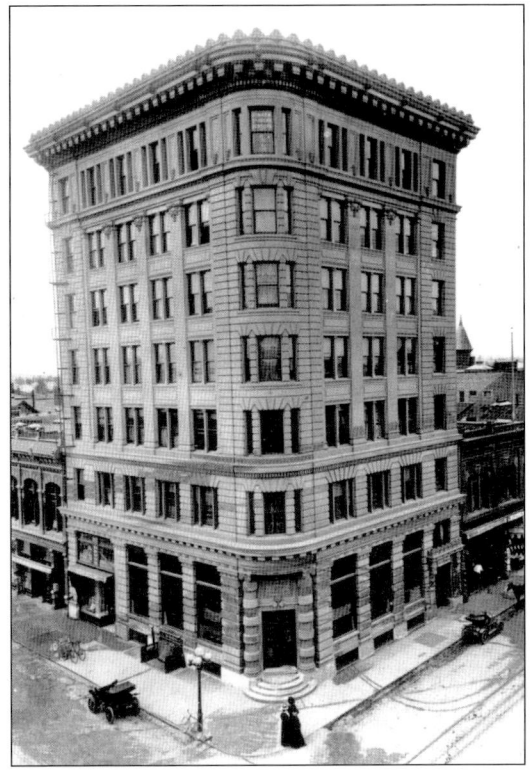

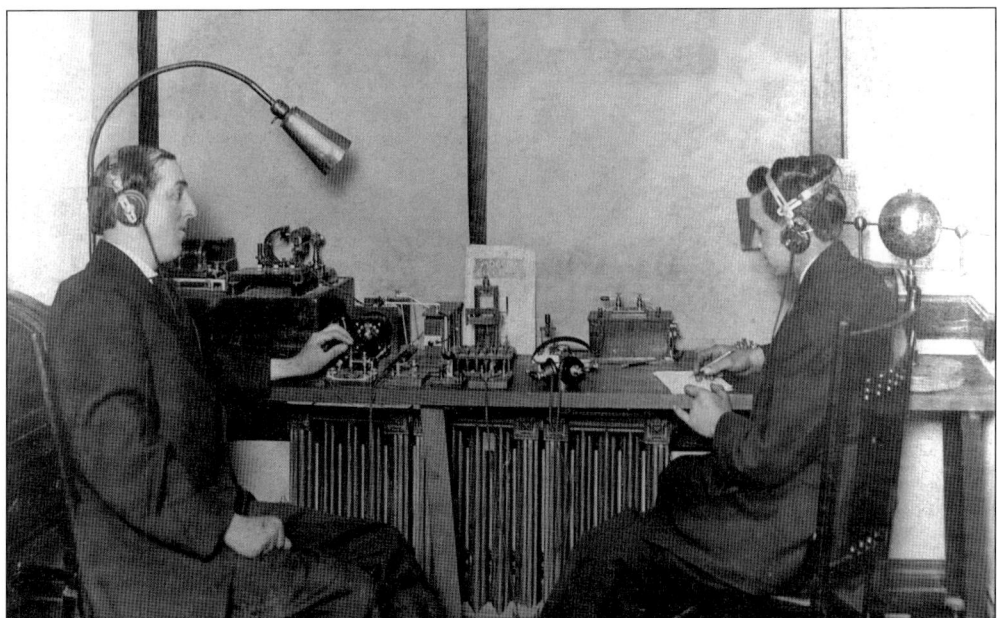

Doc Herrold (left) and student Ray Newby (right) are shown operating a small Morse code spark transmitter in 1909. The two later connected a microphone to the transmitter and sent out poor-quality voice. A search for better quality resulted in the development of an arc transmitter that was used to broadcast voice and music on a regular scheduled basis from 1912 to 1917. (History San Jose.)

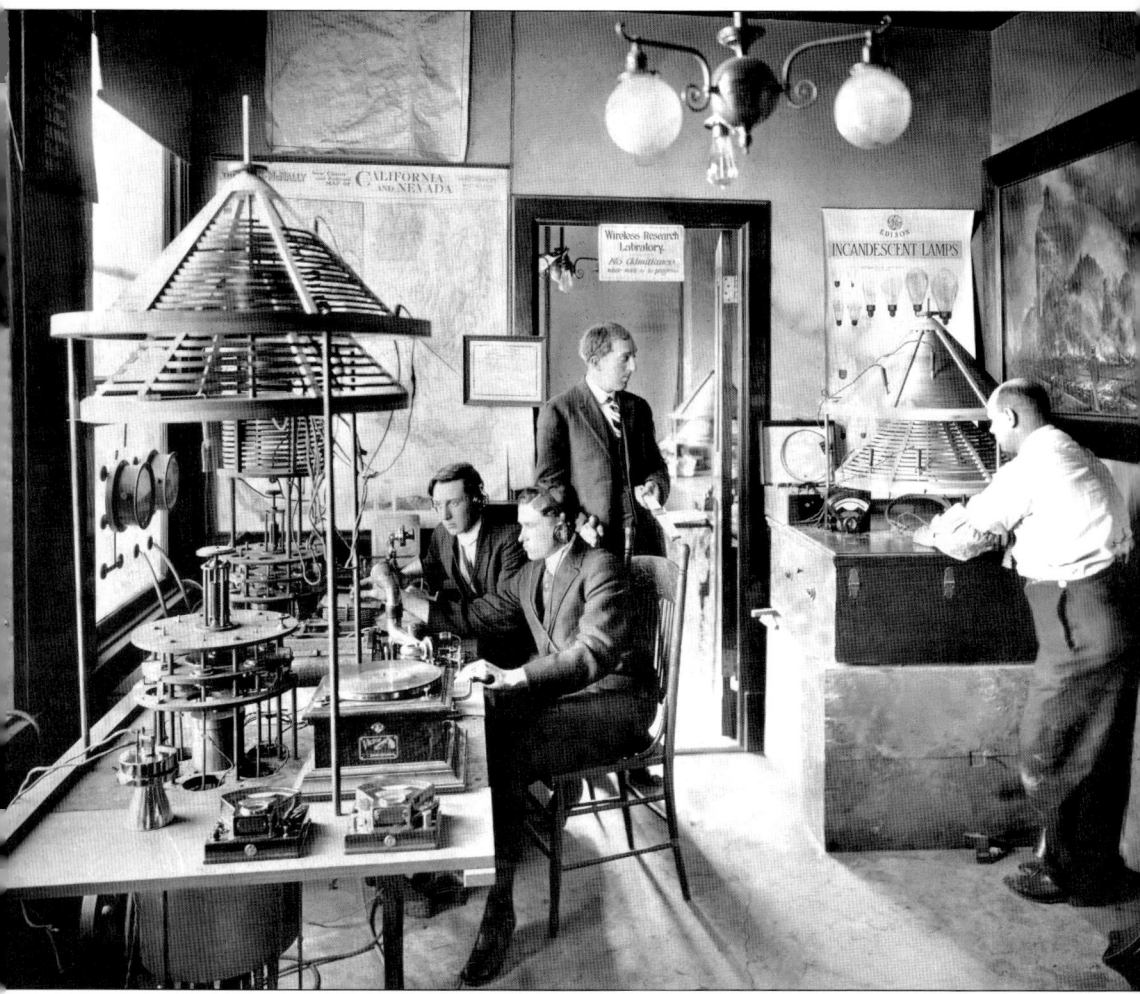

Doc Herrold's "Arc Fone" radio transmitter is seen here in operation at the Herrold College of Engineering and Wireless sometime around 1912. Emile Portal and Ken Sanders are at the microphone, Doc Herrold is standing in the doorway, and technician Frank Schmidt is at the right. The transmitter worked by modulating an oscillating electric arc immersed in alcohol. The specially designed microphone on the table was connected between the transmitter and antenna and needed to be water-cooled to keep from overheating. The phonograph on the table was modified with a special horn to acoustically couple into the microphone for music broadcasts. This early radio station, known as FN or simply "San Jose Calling," was conducting weekly broadcasts eight years before the recognized start of radio broadcasting in the United States. In 1915, it broadcast daily programs to the Panama Pacific International Exposition in San Francisco as an early radio demonstration. Herrold's station shut down during World War I on government orders, but it came back on the air in 1921 as KQW. That station eventually became today's KCBS. (History San Jose.)

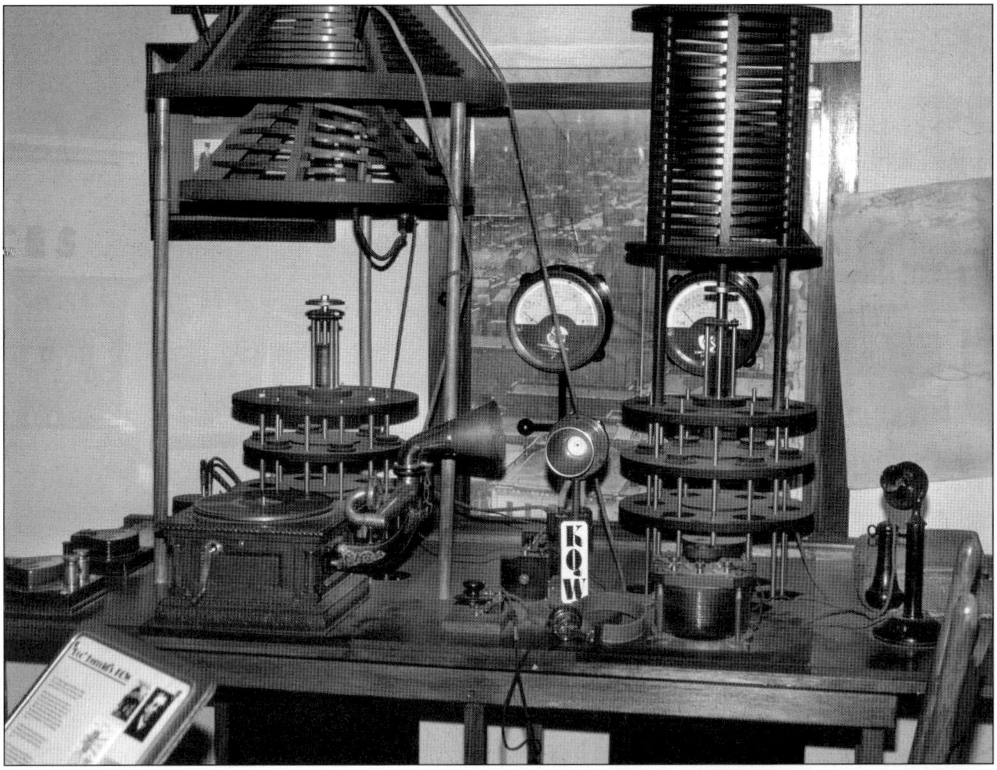

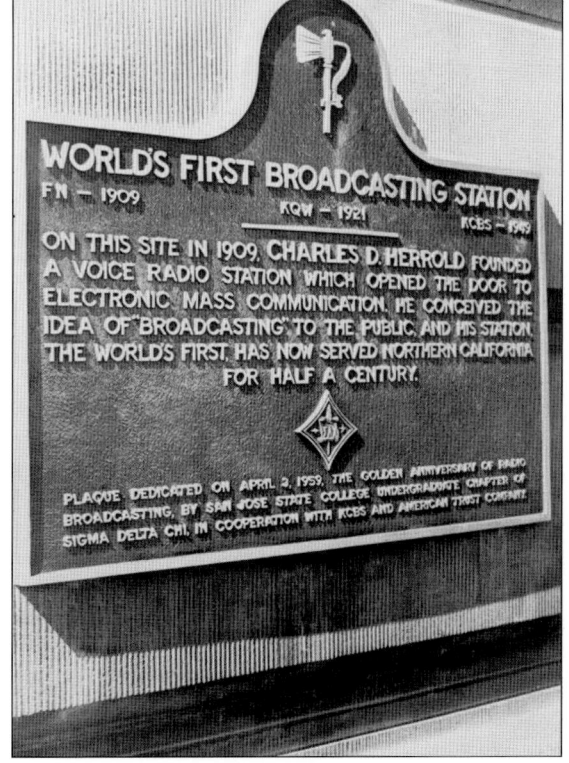

This recreation of the original Doc Herrold station was on display at the Foothill Electronics Museum at Foothill College for many years. Some of the components were original and others were reproductions. The water-cooled microphone on the table was original. The museum closed in 1991, and these artifacts went into storage, but they were placed on display again in a History San Jose window gallery in 2010. (Photograph by the author.)

This commemorative plaque was dedicated in 1959 to recognize the 50th anniversary of Doc Herrold's first radio broadcasts in San Jose. It was placed at the exact site of the original Garden City Bank Building, the location of Herrold's radio school, by radio station KCBS and Sigma Delta Chi, the journalism society chapter at San Jose State College. Two other plaques have since been added. (Author's collection.)

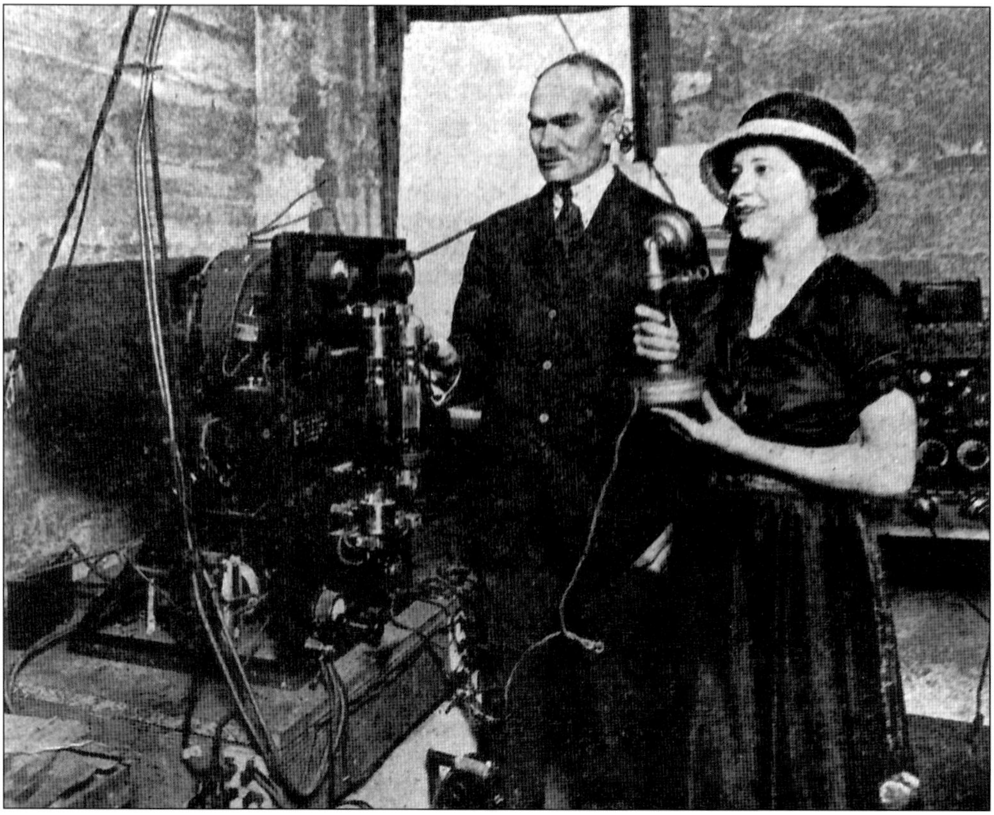

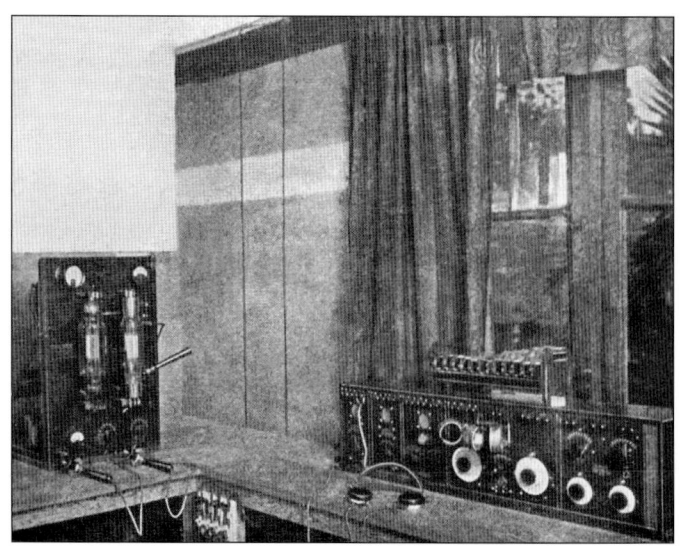

Lee de Forest operated station 6XC from the California Theatre at Fourth and Market Streets beginning in January 1920. He had previously operated this same 500-watt transmitter as experimental station 2XG in New York. Here, he is seen demonstrating his transmitter to Mary White, one of the many entertainers who performed on the station. More than 1,500 broadcasts were made from the theater before the transmitter was moved to Oakland in 1921. (Author's collection.)

In 1921, the Atlantic-Pacific Radio Corporation became the representative for the De Forest Company and 6XC was moved to Oakland, becoming KZY, the "Rock Ridge Station." KZY signed on Christmas Day in 1921 from the home of company president Henry Shaw. Here is the KZY radio room with the 6XC De Forest transmitter and a De Forest Interpanel receiver. The station was closed in June 1922. (Paul Bourbin.)

The *San Francisco Examiner* started KUO in April 1922. The studio and transmitter were in the Hearst Building at Third and Market Streets (below), and the towers stood 150 feet above the 12-story building. The transmitter—nicknamed "Big Bertha"—was the most powerful in the area, rivaling only KLX in Oakland for signal strength. "Sparks" Gaal (right) was the operator and sole KUO staff member during its entire existence. KUO began with great enthusiasm, but the newspaper soon lost interest in the station. By 1924, it was broadcasting on an irregular basis—mostly weather and farm reports, news, sports, and stock quotations. KUO operated until 1927, sending weather and marine information to the San Francisco pilot boat. The *San Francisco Examiner* would again enter to the radio business in 1934 when it would purchase KYA. (Right, *San Francisco Examiner*; below, author's collection.)

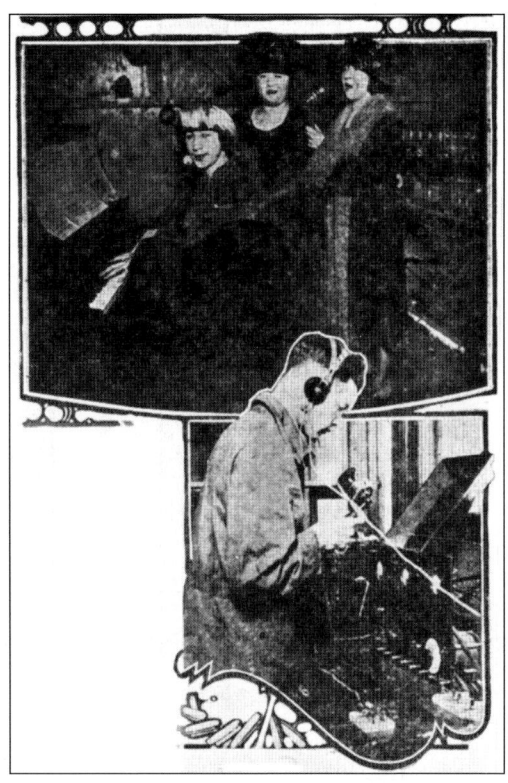

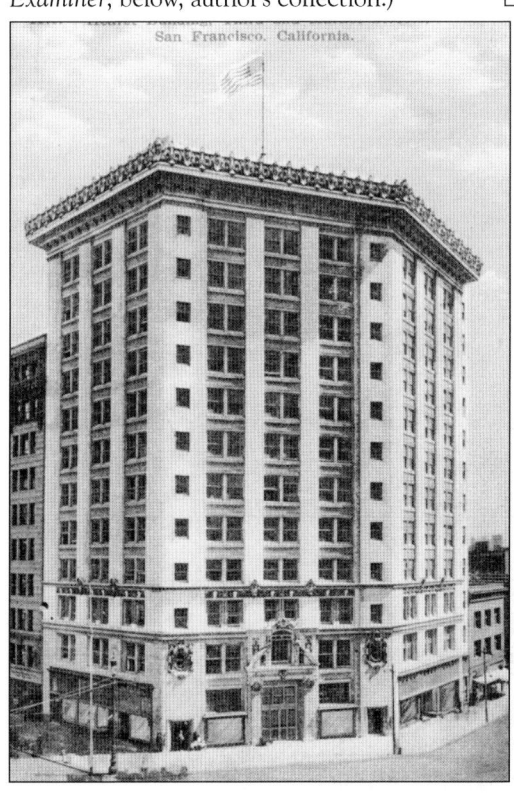

San Francisco. California.

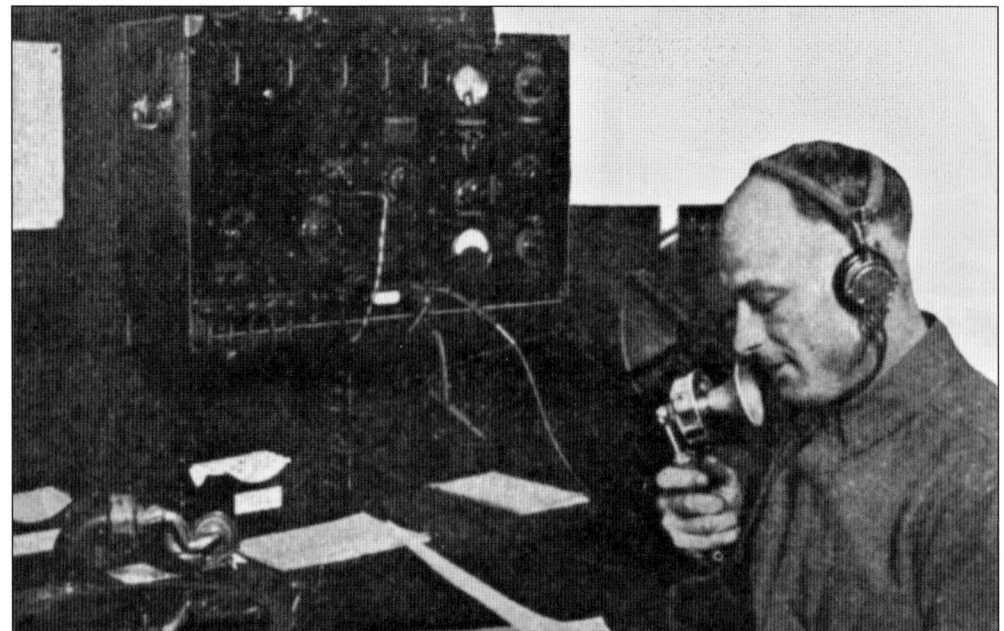

From 1921 to 1923, the Army Signal Corps operated an amateur station at the San Francisco Presidio to communicate with local hams and other Army bases. The station also broadcast music and information programs to the general public. Known first as 6XW and then later by the call letters AGI, this station was operated by Sgt. Richard C. Travers (shown here). He broadcast a concert of phonograph records every Sunday evening. (Author's collection.)

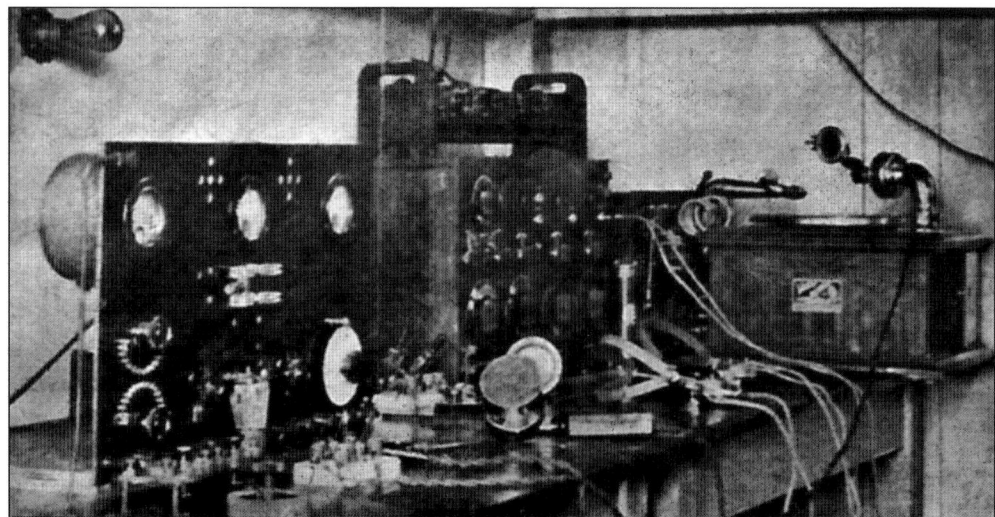

The Leo J. Meyberg Co., an electrical distributor, established 6XG (later KDN) on the roof of the Fairmont Hotel in 1921. Operator Alan Cormack would go to the station every evening and broadcast programs from this little five-watt transmitter, which was mostly a phonograph with player piano rolls. KDN left the air in 1923, but Cormack went on to a long career as a radio engineer with KFRC and KCBS. (Paul Bourbin.)

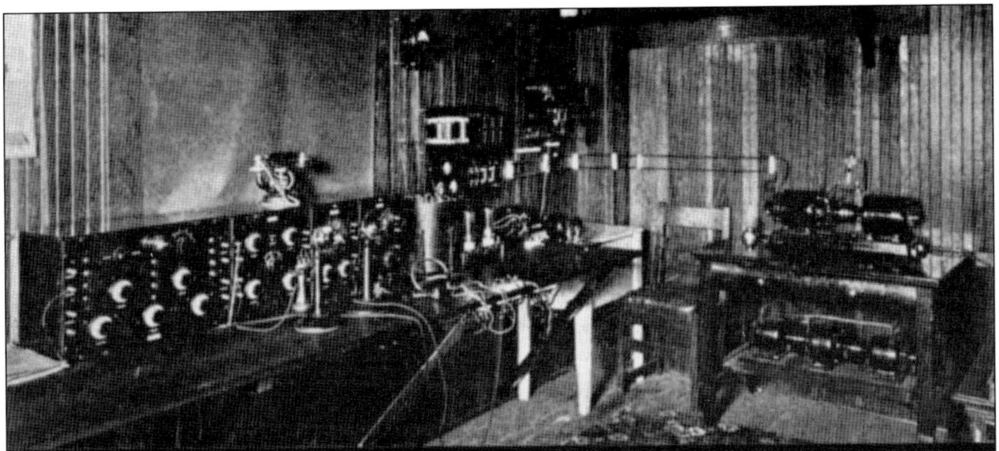

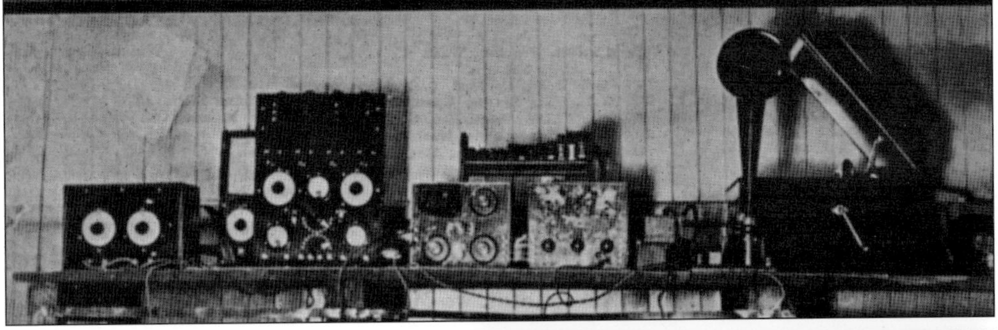

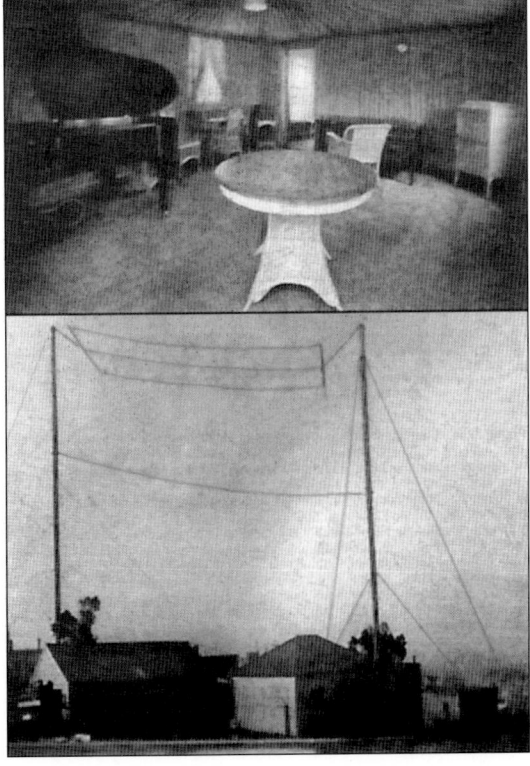

Here are two more of San Francisco's first radio stations. 6XAC, later KLP (above), was operated in 1921 and 1922 by the Colin B. Kennedy Company, the manufacturer of the well-known Kennedy line of receivers. 6UV, later KYY (below), was a tiny station operated from 1920 to 1922 by A.F. Pendleton of the Radio Telephone Shop at 175 Steuart Street near the San Francisco waterfront. (Both, Paul Bourbin.)

In 1922, the Mercantile Trust Company became the first bank to open a radio station. KFDB began broadcasting in November 1922 from Telegraph Hill in San Francisco. Daytime programs were devoted to agricultural news and market reports, and KFDB also broadcast a daily concert hour at night. Here, we see KFDB's transmitter house and studio building. KFDB operated for just a year before ceasing operations. (Both, *Pacific Radio News.*)

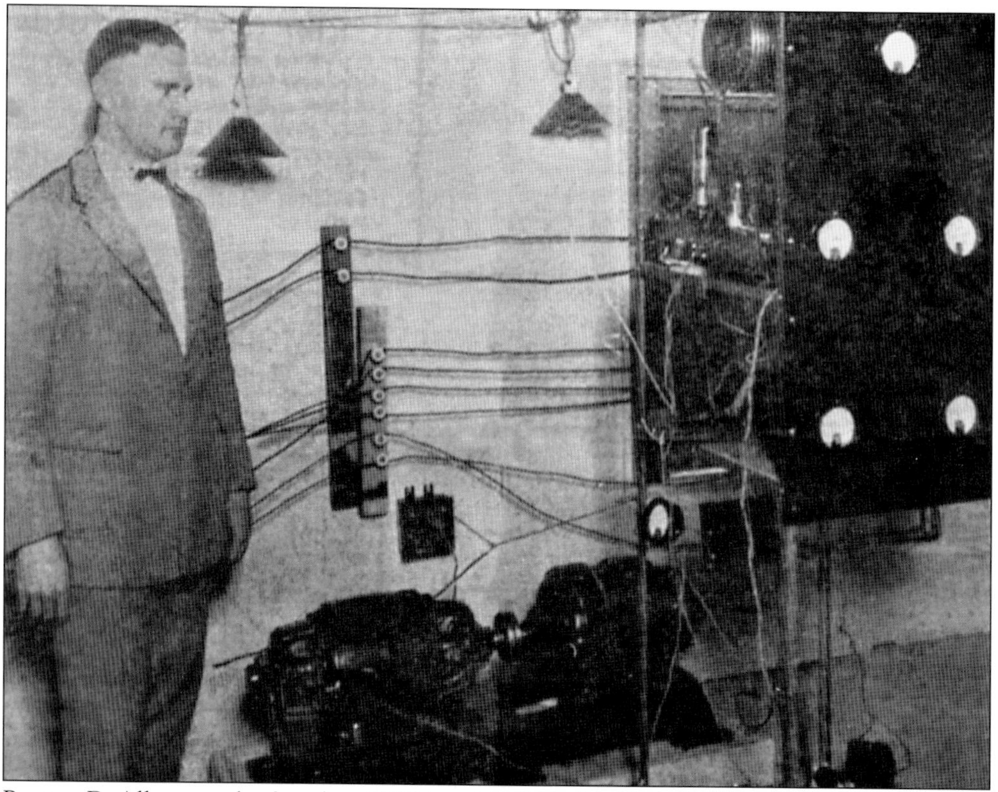

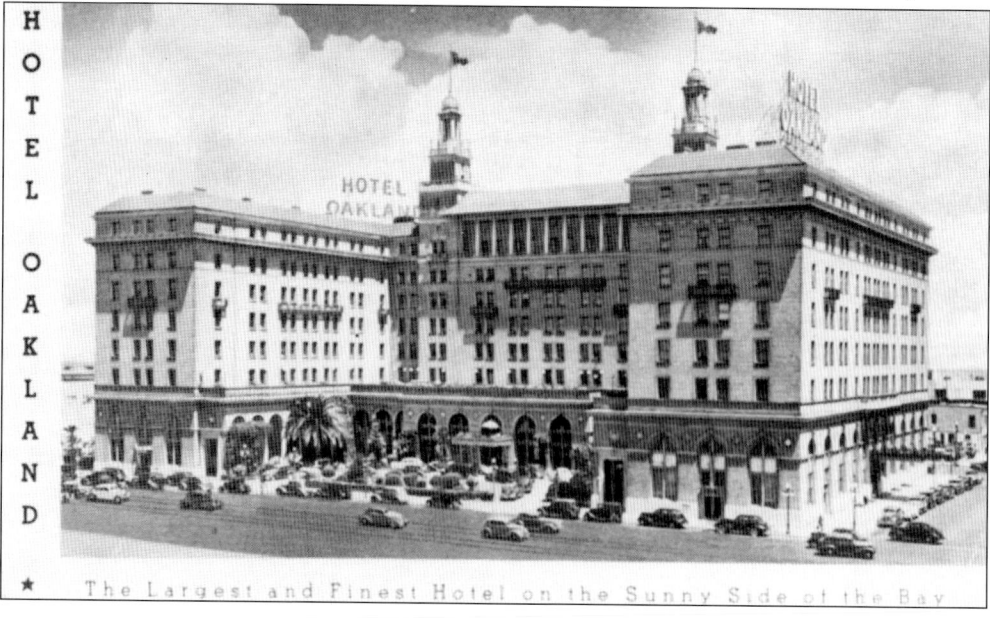

Preston D. Allen was the founder of KZM and KLX at Oakland, and he managed KLX from its inception until called to duty by the Navy before Pearl Harbor. This 1922 *Oakland Tribune* photograph shows him examining the 50-watt transmitter "Powerful Katrinka" in the Hotel Oakland. This transmitter was used by both KLX and KZM until the *Tribune* built its own KLX facility in the Tribune Tower in 1923. (Above, *Oakland Tribune* photograph; below, author's collection.)

HOTEL OAKLAND

★ The Largest and Finest Hotel on the Sunny Side of the Bay

Two

Broadcasting Grows Up
1922–1929

The year 1922 was the nation's big radio boom. Previously just the domain of teenage "hams," radio was suddenly discovered by the public in massive numbers. As many as $60 million in radio sales were recorded that year, spawning the overnight development of an entire receiver manufacturing industry. The number of stations in the country grew from 67 in March to over 500 by the end of 1922.

Listening to the radio in 1922 was a different experience than it would be just a few years later. Most radio receivers were either crystal sets or crude one-tube affairs that required headsets. There was just one channel assigned for broadcasting—360 meters (833 kHz)—and all stations were required to share time on that frequency. There were already a number of radio stations in the Bay Area, and a voluntary transmission schedule was determined by the Pacific Radio Trades Association. Some stations were on the air several times daily, while others broadcast just a few hours a week. The schedule was published in the radio columns of the local newspapers. Most stations broadcast phonograph music "concerts" with occasional live music and news reports. Some of the local stations being heard in 1922 were KPO (Hale Bros. Department Store), KRE in Berkeley (Maxwell Electric Company), KLS in Oakland (Warner Brothers' Store), KLX (*Oakland Tribune*), KQW in San Jose (First Baptist Church), and KFDB on Telegraph Hill.

But radio quickly outgrew its one-channel restriction as more and more people wanted to broadcast. Finally in 1925, the government opened up the AM radio band, giving most stations their own frequencies. Nonetheless, some smaller stations were still required to share channels.

A number of important Bay Area stations had their beginnings in the mid-1920s. General Electric (GE) built its powerful station KGO in January 1924, one of three GE stations designed to cover the entire country. In September of that year, KFRC turned on its signal from the Whitcomb Hotel. The Tenth Avenue Baptist Church in Oakland inaugurated KTAB (now KSFO) in August 1925, and Seattle's Pacific Broadcasting Company opened KYA at the Clift Hotel in December 1926.

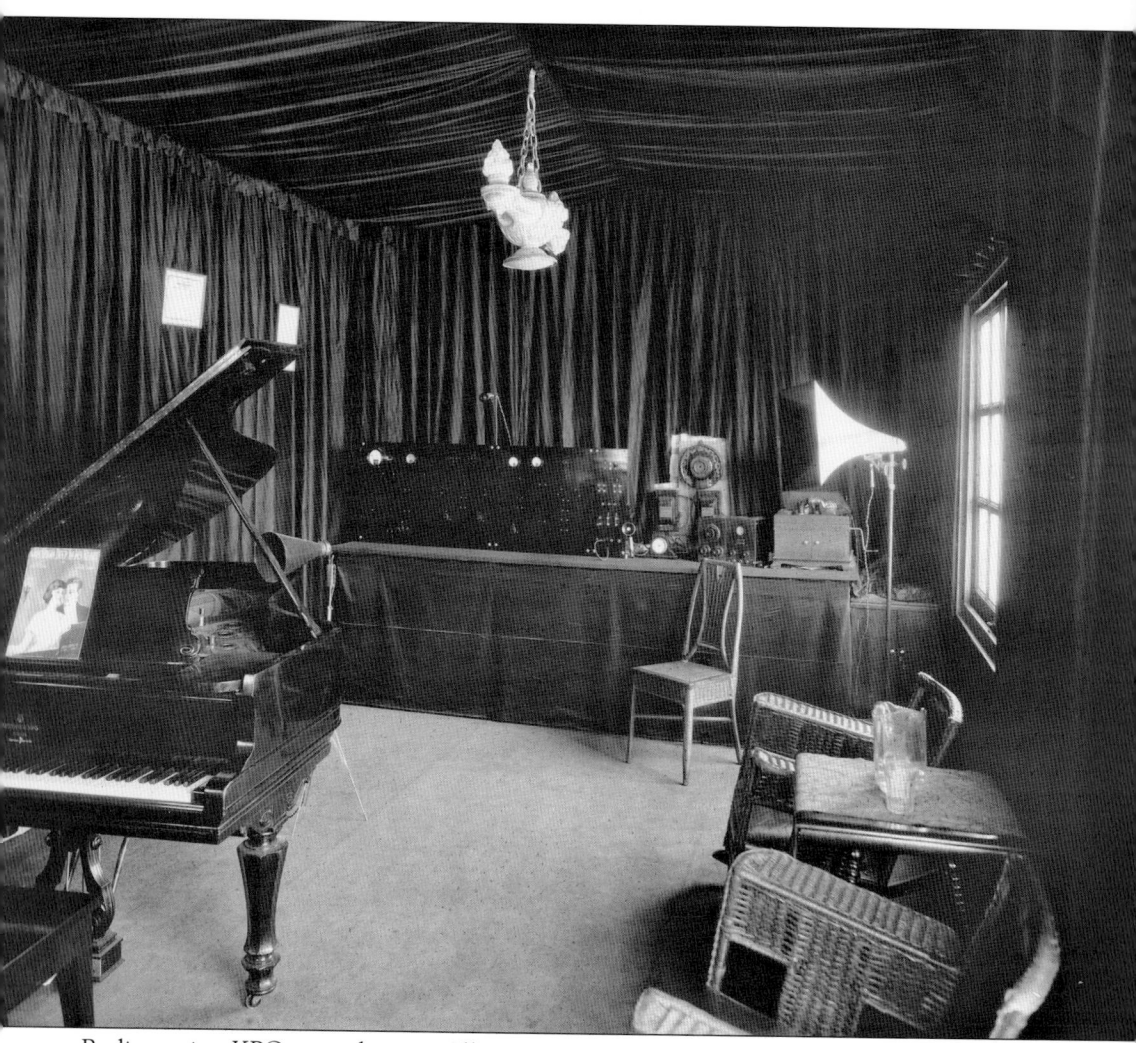

Radio station KPO started as a small operation built by Joe Martineau on the sixth floor of Hale Bros.'s Department Store. After completing his tour of duty as a Navy operator, Martineau approached Francis, Marshall, and Reuben Hale and proposed to build a broadcasting station for them. They agreed, and he built KPO at a cost of just $2,400. It made its debut at 9 a.m. on April 17, 1922. This is the station that Martineau built. A piano and a phonograph were the main source of programming. The transmitter was the large black panel in the rear, and the light bulb above it indicated when the station was on the air. To the right of the transmitter are a carbon microphone and a Westinghouse RC receiver, which was used to monitor for ships in distress. KPO later became KNBC and finally today's KNBR. (Bill Newbrough.)

After KPO signed on, the Hales quickly saw the publicity value of radio and decided to make it the best station in the area. Thus, KPO was reborn on January 16, 1923, as a Class "B" 500-watt station. The KPO antenna was a T type—four wires spread six feet apart and 114 feet in length. It was supported by two 125-foot towers on the roof of the Hale Bros.'s Store on Market Street. This gave the antenna a total height over the street of 220 feet. The studio and transmitter were on the sixth floor of the building. The Western Electric transmitter and audio panel seen below were in the same room as the first photograph on the previous page. The studio and 1600-volt generators were located in adjoining rooms. (Both, author's collection.)

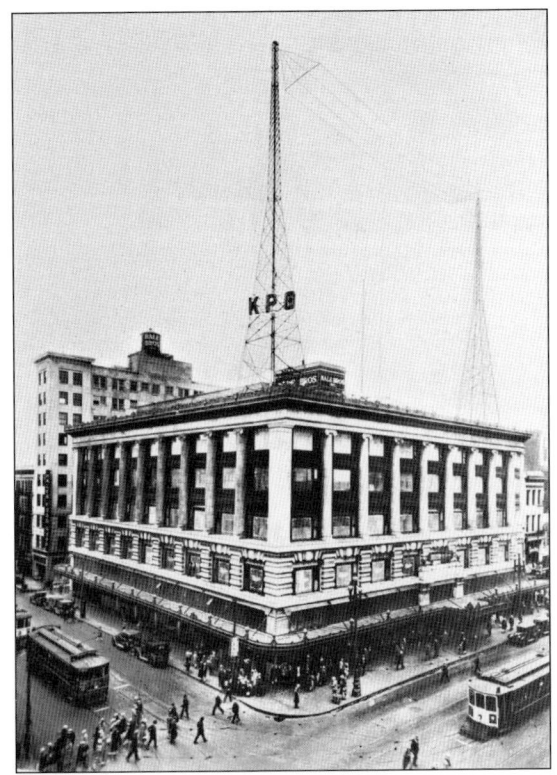

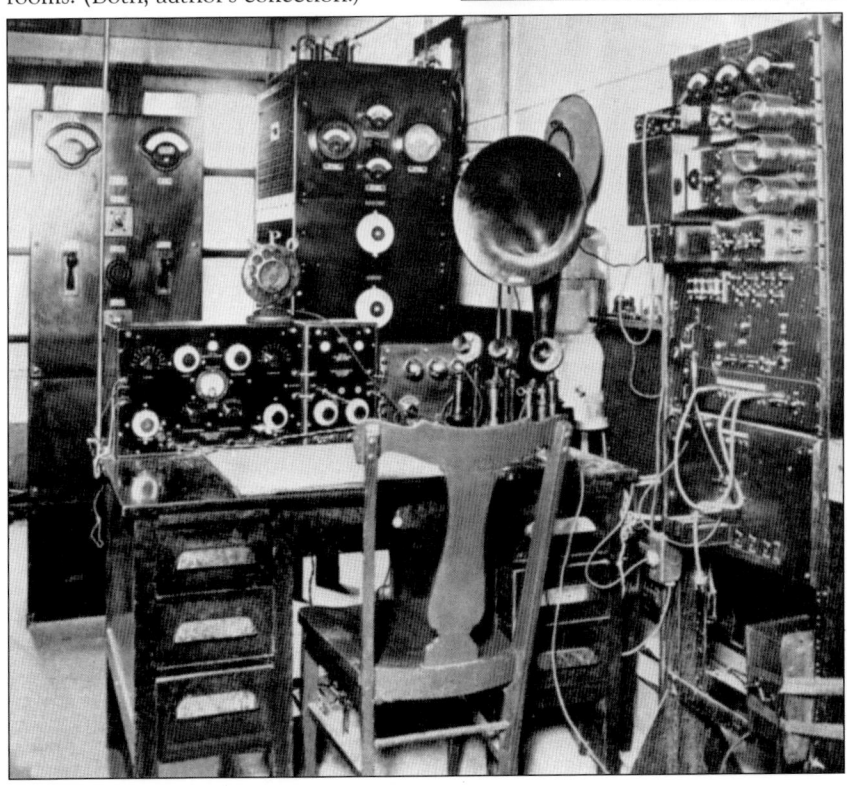

Announcement to Radioland!

KPO

"HALE BROS. and THE CHRONICLE"

¶ THIS is an announcement of special importance to the vast and enthusiastic audience of this station. Conforming to the stated policy originally promulgated by Hale Bros., when K P O first went on the air, two years ago, of ever keeping abreast of the art and opportunity of further service, this station is pleased to announce that hereafter K P O will be known as "Hale Bros. and The Chronicle."

¶ IN joining forces with the San Francisco Chronicle, K P O establishes a connection of stellar importance, offering further opportunities of service to its a...ience.

¶ TWO years ago K P O was dedicated to the public service with the magic transmission of music, song and speech into your homes. Ever conscious of its sacred public trust, and ever vigilant in its broadcasting of only that class of programs fitted for home reception, K P O won its popularity with the vast audience of Radioland. Its name and fame cover the continent and reach far over the seas.

¶ TONIGHT K P O is rededicated to its identical policy and standard, and with The Chronicle joining Hale Bros. in the sponsorship of the station, K P O sets out for further fields of conquest and additional achievements. With the staunch, enthusiastic and enterprising support of such a great metropolitan newspaper as The Chronicle, combined with that of Hale Bros., Inc., K P O is indeed happy.

¶ K P O has fittingly been termed by national radio authorities, and by the tremendous number of testimonials from dear friends in Radioland, as the most aggressive, enterprising and popular station west of Chicago. It modestly accepts such distinction.

¶ AS a California station, owned and operated by resident Californians, and as the major station of San Francisco, K P O will continue on its mission of education and entertainment, giving cheer to the millions of citizens comprising its audience as a public institution rather than as an instrument financed and supported by private individuals.

¶ THIS is Radio K P O---Hale Bros. and The Chronicle. Thus the printed word joins the spoken word in your behalf.

"K P O ⚓ Hale Bros. and The Chronicle"

On March 4, 1925, this full-page announcement in the *San Francisco Chronicle* announced that the *Chronicle* was joining forces with Hale Bros. to operate KPO. The station was now announced as "KPO—Hale Bros. and the *Chronicle*." On the same day, KPO joined in the first coast-to-coast network broadcast for the inauguration of Pres. Calvin Coolidge and was the westernmost link of a transcontinental network of 28 stations. By 1929, KPO was broadcasting with 5,000 watts and had installed an elaborate studio complex on the sixth floor, with two large studios and a master control booth. A pipe organ was featured in the large studio. (Both, *San Francisco Chronicle*.)

Modern Studio Facilities Completed for KPO's New Station

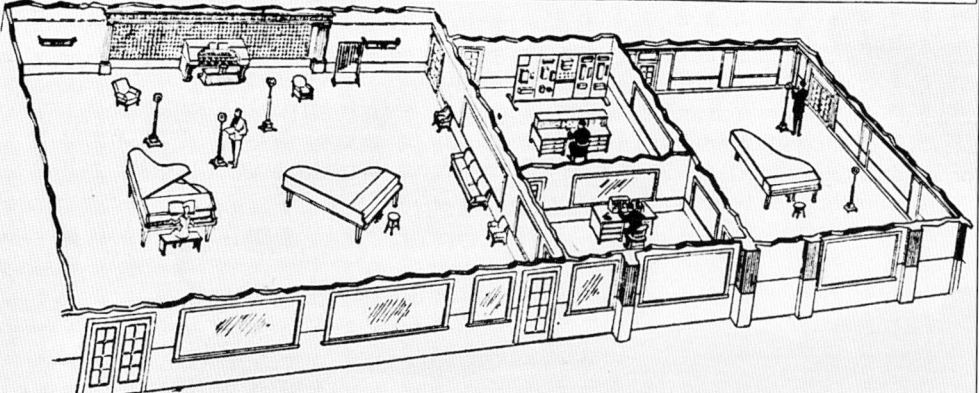

KPO's new studio suite, representing the most modern ideas in broadcasting facilities, is virtually completed and will soon be ready for use. Two large studios, an announcer's booth, and a master control room are included in the suite. The announcer's booth is centrally located, and so designed that the announcer is able to see into every other room. A signal-light system and loudspeakers placed in each room permit the announcer, operator and performers to keep in instant touch with each other while the station is in operation. The new arrangement will improve the broadcasting from the Hale-Chronicle's station, allowing a quicker and smoother operation of each program, and preventing noise or interruption from spoiling its quality. In the above drawing of the new KPO studio layout, the studios are at the extreme right and left. The announcer's booth is shown in front between the two studios, with the master control room behind it. The operator in the control room can also see into each room of the layout. He will virtually control the broadcasting from the studios, shifting from one microphone to another as desired, and monitoring the volume output in his amplifiers. All programs originating outside the station will come to the control room to be transferred to the station's transmitting apparatus in the ninth story of the Hale Brothers' addition building.

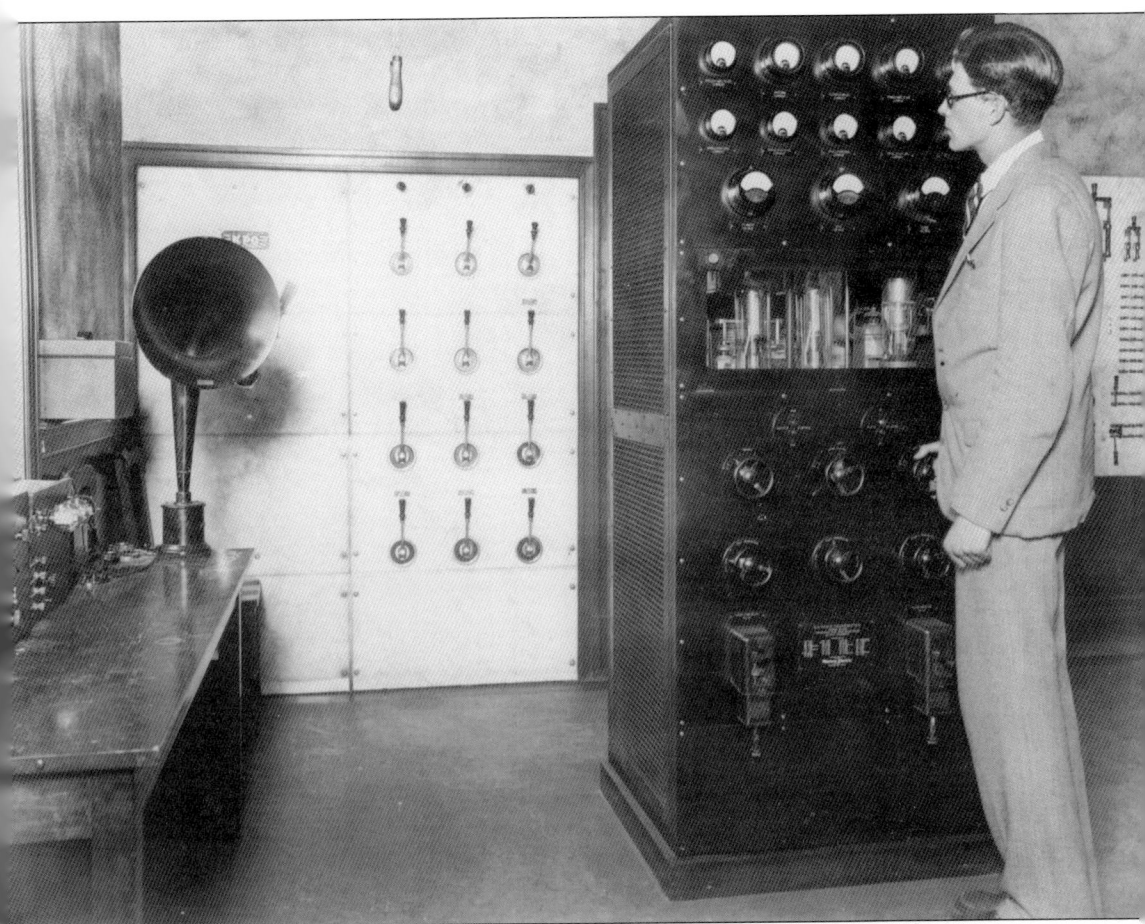

KPO installed its third transmitter in August 1925, this time raising its power to 1,000 watts, which was considered high power at the time. Here, we see the KPO radio transmitter room in the Hale Bros.'s Department Store. In the foreground is the new factory-built Western Electric 6A transmitter with its many electrical meters and water-cooled tubes. This was the finest equipment that money could buy in 1925, at a time when most radio stations were still building their own equipment. In the background, the marble-faced electrical control panels were said to be the only ones of their kind in the country. On the table to the left is a receiver with a horn speaker, used for monitoring the station's signal. The KPO employee inspecting the transmitter is probably Claire Morrison, KPO's first full-time announcer. (Bill Ruck.)

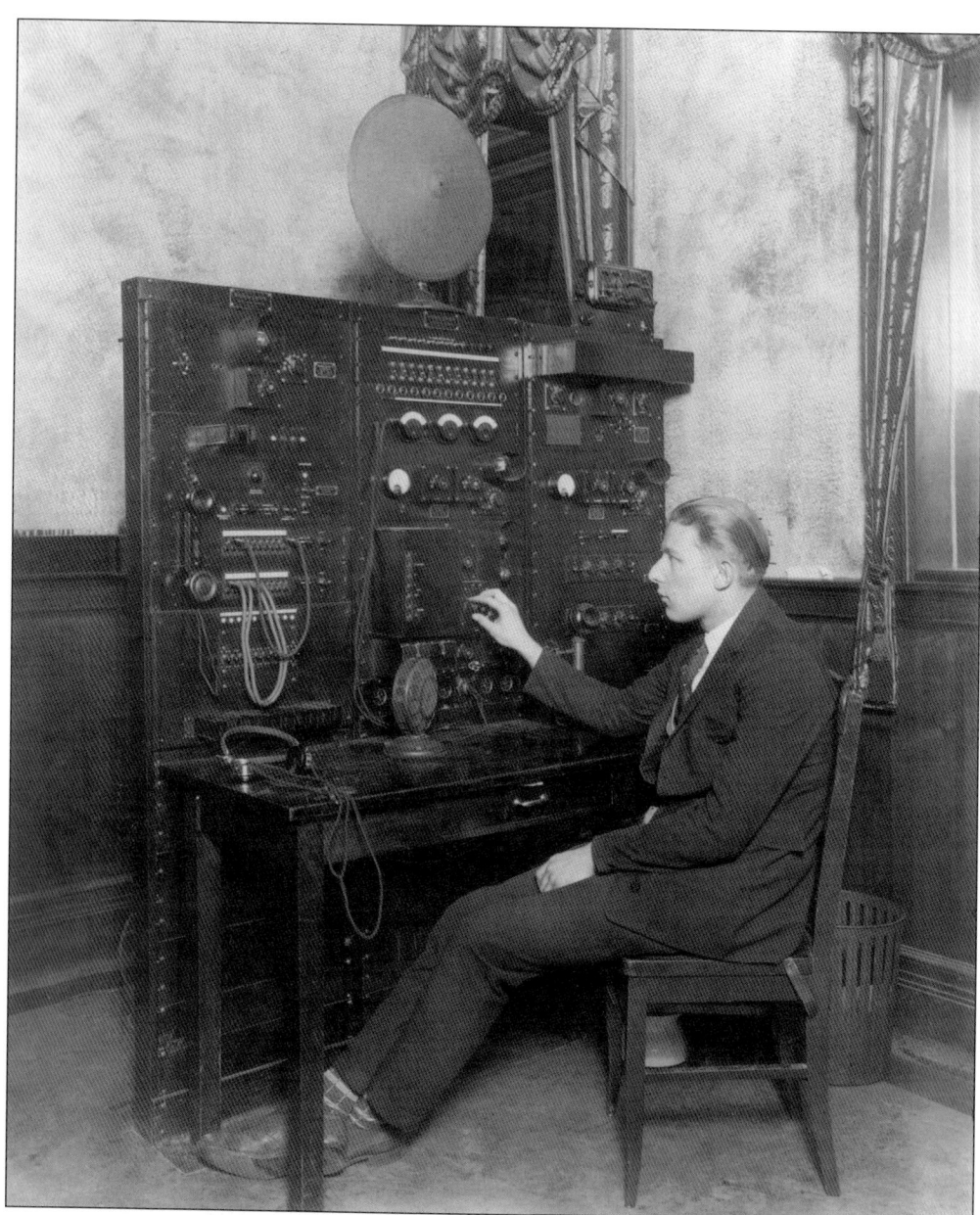

Here is the new Western Electric audio control panel that was installed at KPO in 1925. The operator in this position was responsible for routing the appropriate studio microphones to the transmitter, and also for maintaining a consistent audio level without over-modulating the transmitter. The amplifiers and patch cords in these panels connected the station with outside points for network and remote broadcasts. The telephone intercom and signaling lights were used by the operator to communicate with the studio and remote locations. He could also make on-air announcements if necessary using the microphone on the table. The paper cone speaker on top of the panel was the finest "high fidelity" sound reproducer available in 1925. At its right is a telegraph sounder, which was used for "order wire" communications with stations in other cities during the earliest network broadcasts. In 1925, network broadcasts were still just one-time temporary hookups and were known as "chain" broadcasts. (Bill Ruck.)

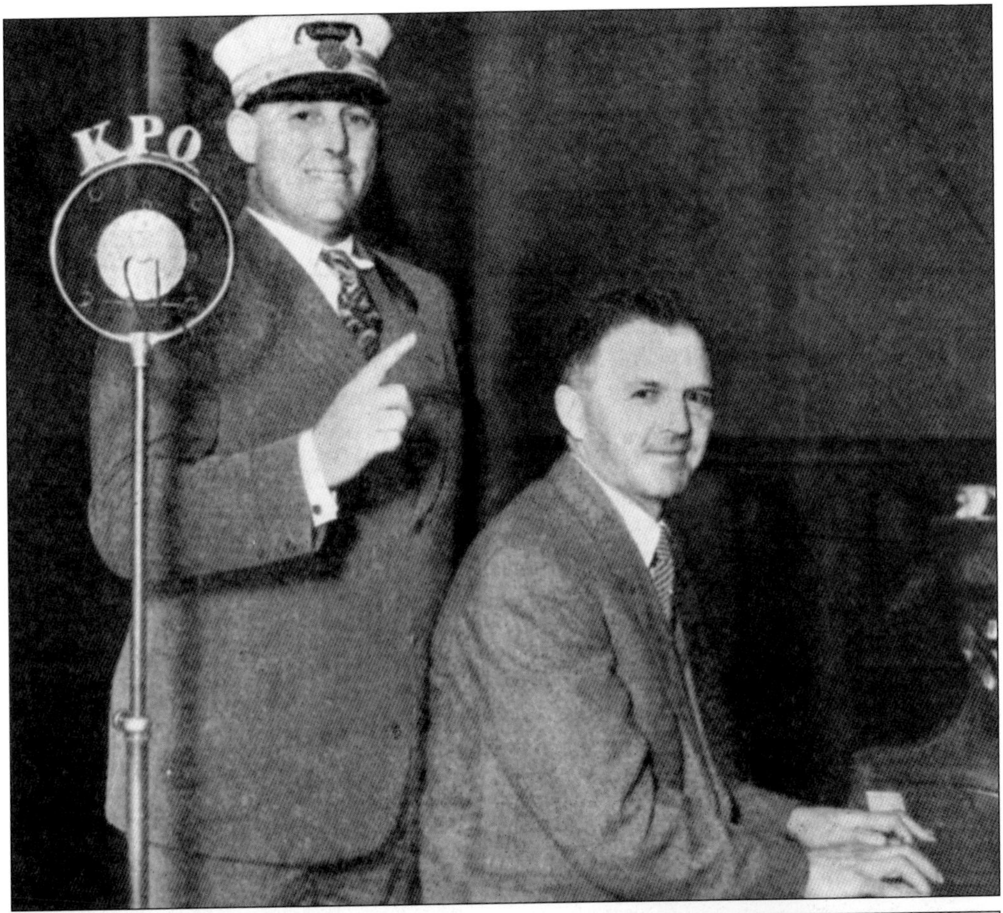

Hugh Barrett Dobbs was a physical education instructor who was hired by KPO in 1925 to do a morning exercise program. Soon "Dobbsie" was hosting *The Sperry Flour Happy Hour*, which became the *Shell Ship of Joy*. The program gained local popularity and later was a regular feature on the NBC Pacific Coast Network. The Ship of Joy was a mythical cruise "from Good Cheer Dock to the Isle of Happiness," gushy sentimentalism by today's standards. Part of each program was the wishing well ceremony. The audience would be asked to place hand over heart and "send out a wish to somebody—somewhere—who may be in sickness or trouble." NBC canceled the program in 1939, and Dobbsie then took it to Seattle where it continued for a few more years. (Above, CHRS Archives; right, author's collection.)

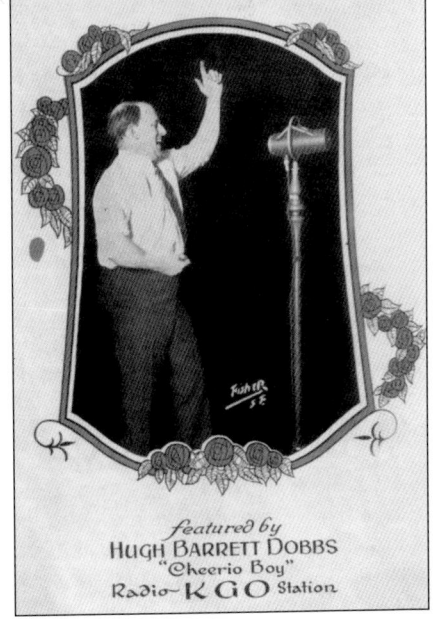

featured by
HUGH BARRETT DOBBS
"Cheerio Boy"
Radio-K G O Station

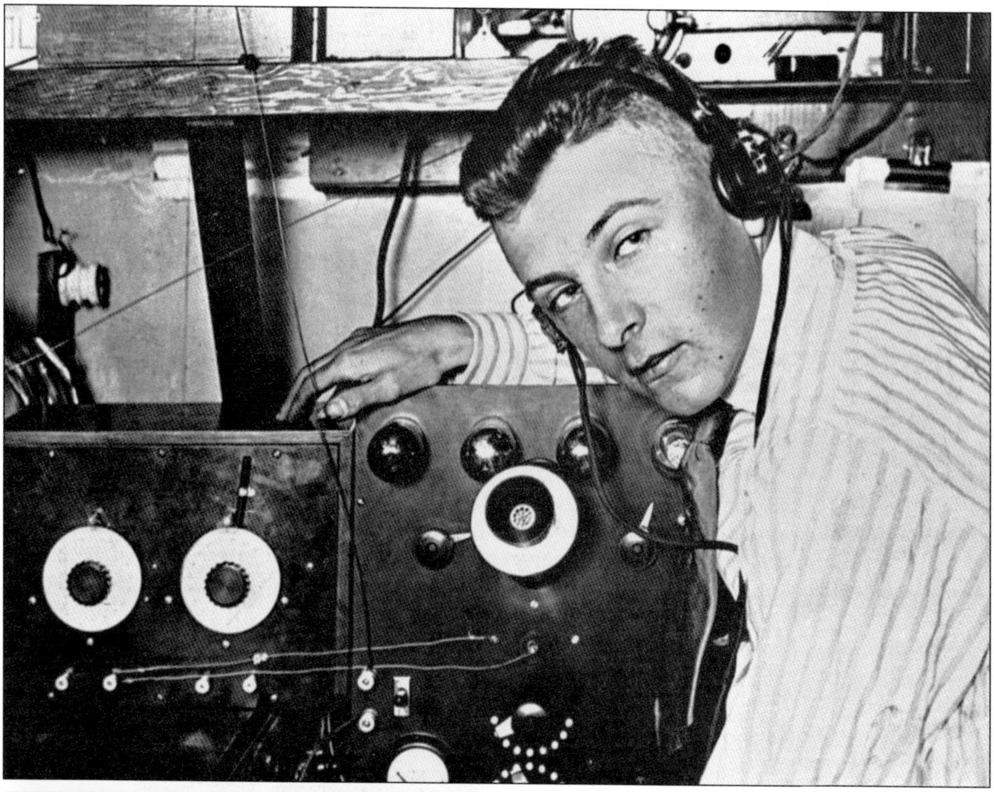

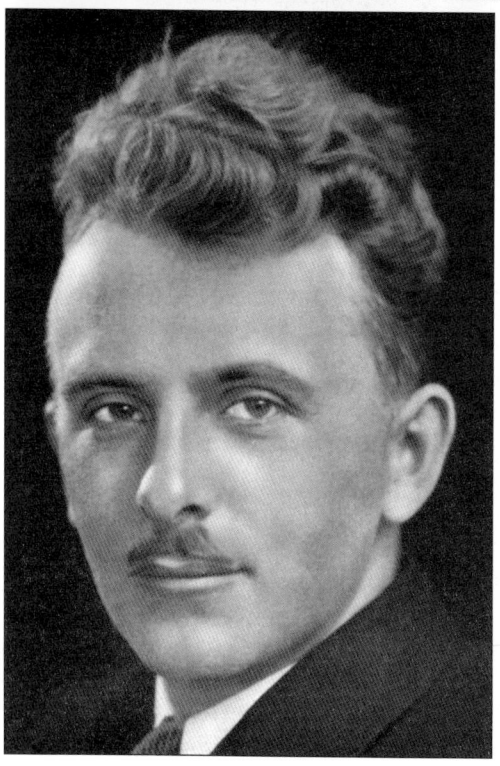

Harrison Holliway's life always revolved around radio. In 1920, he set a world record for voice distance on the ham radio when he talked to Vancouver, British Columbia (above). In 1922, he helped start KSL, a short-lived station at the Emporium Department Store. Then in 1924, he and friends Harold Peary and Alan Cormack established KFRC. They sold it in 1925 to the City of Paris Department Store, which then sold it to automobile dealer Don Lee in 1926. KFRC soon became one of the best stations on the Coast, and Holliway was its manager and announcer. His intuition and creativity helped develop some of the West's most successful radio programming. He rode the station's success through the Columbia-Don Lee Network years, and then became manager of KFI in Los Angeles before passing away suddenly in 1942. (Both, Harrison Holliway Scrapbook, courtesy of Murray Bolen.)

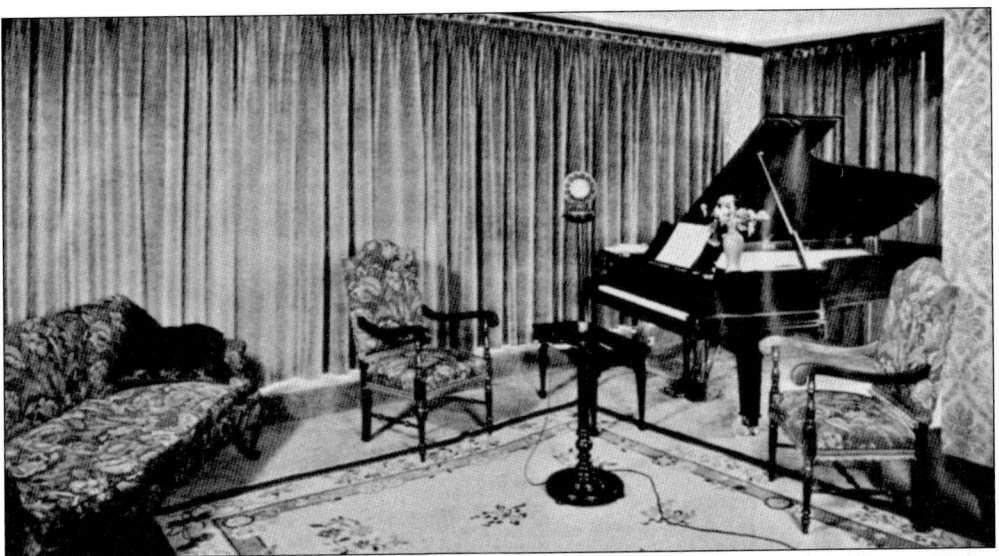

KFRC's first studio was located on the street level of the City of Paris Department Store, behind a large plate-glass window that allowed passing pedestrians to view the broadcasts. It was typical of most 1920s radio studios with heavy draperies, a piano, and a single microphone. (*Modes and Manners* magazine.)

This is the Don Lee Cadillac Building on Van Ness Avenue after its construction in 1912. It was designed by Charles Peter Weeks and William Day, architects for several San Francisco icon hotels. KFRC's studios and offices were on the mezzanine floor until 1958. The transmitter and master control were on the eighth floor with the antenna on the roof. The building is now a national historic landmark. (Jess Oppenheimer.)

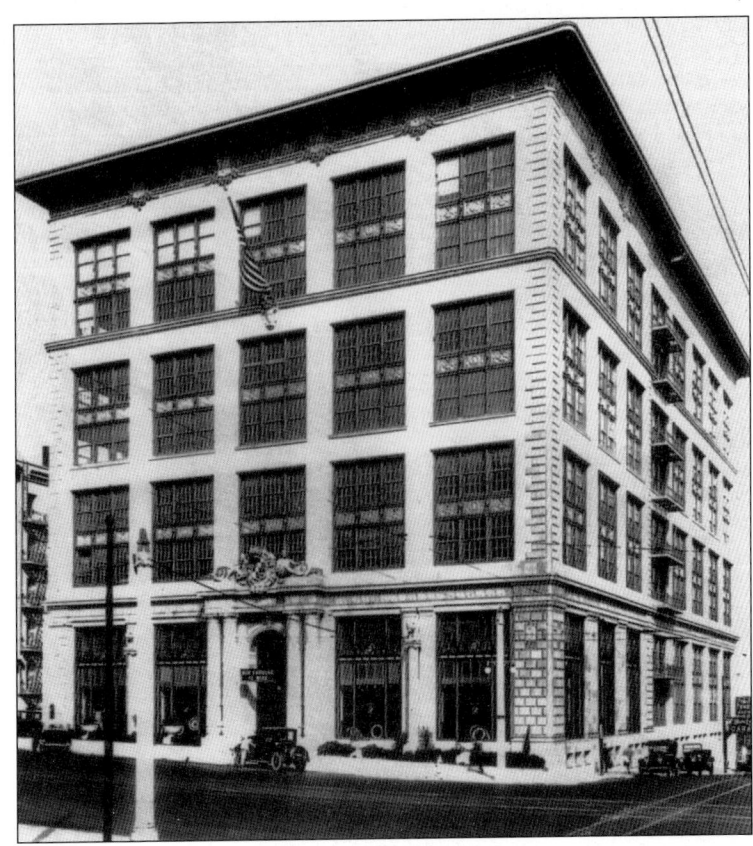

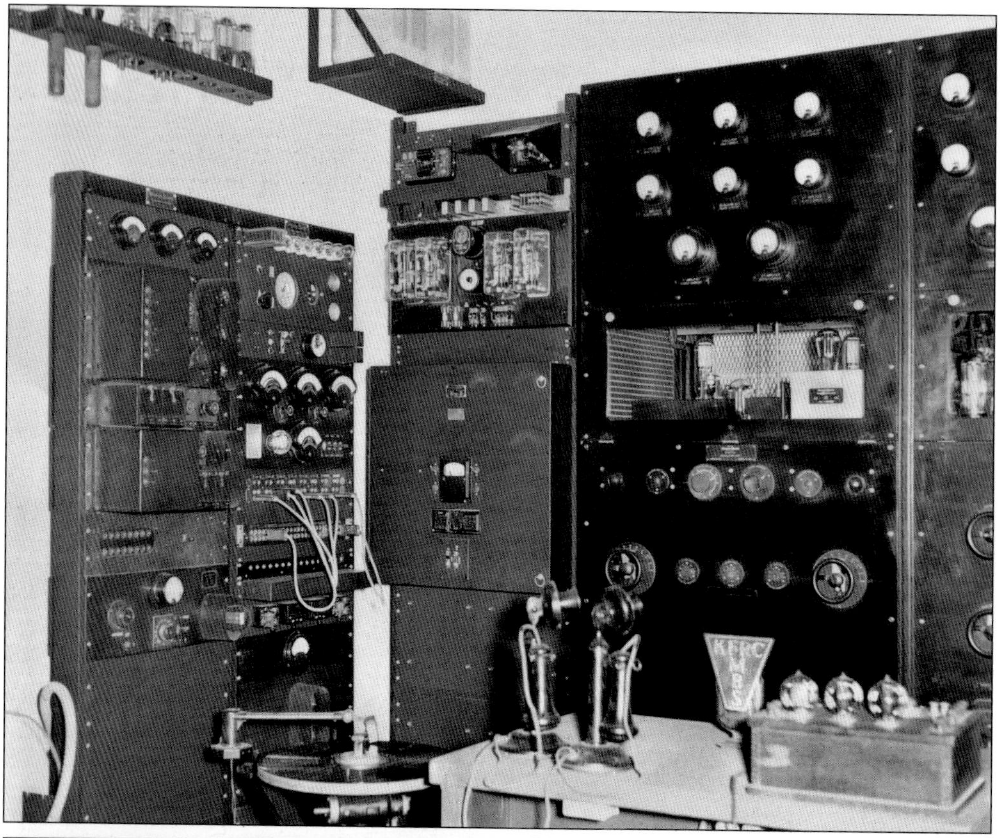

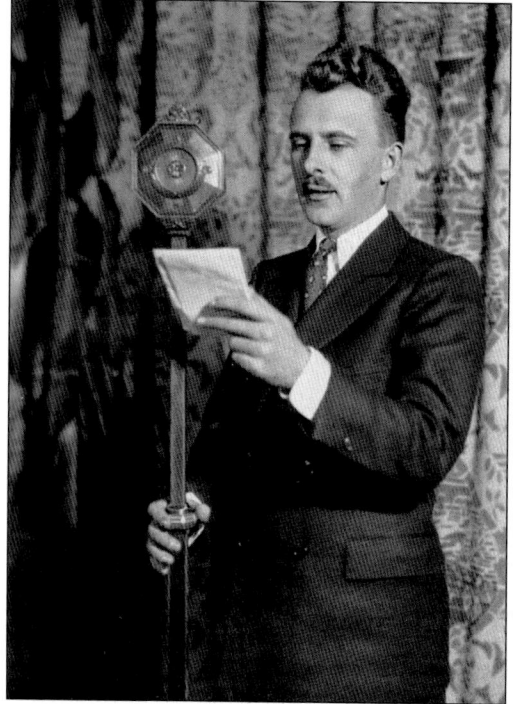

Here is KFRC's 1,000-watt Western Electric transmitter, as it existed in the Don Lee Cadillac building during the 1920s and 1930s. The cabinets to the left housed the audio control and monitoring equipment. This entire assembly was later donated to the Perham Foundation and was formerly exhibited at the now-closed Foothill College radio museum. (Perham Collection, History San Jose.)

Besides managing KFRC, Harrison Holliway was the announcer and emcee of the hit show *Blue Monday Jamboree*, performed each Monday evening in the big studio of the Don Lee Cadillac building. The two-hour music and comedy variety show was heard over KFRC and KHJ and became a sensation throughout California. Here, Holliway announces the program into an ornate Western Electric condenser microphone. (Harrison Holliway Scrapbook, courtesy of Murray Bolen.)

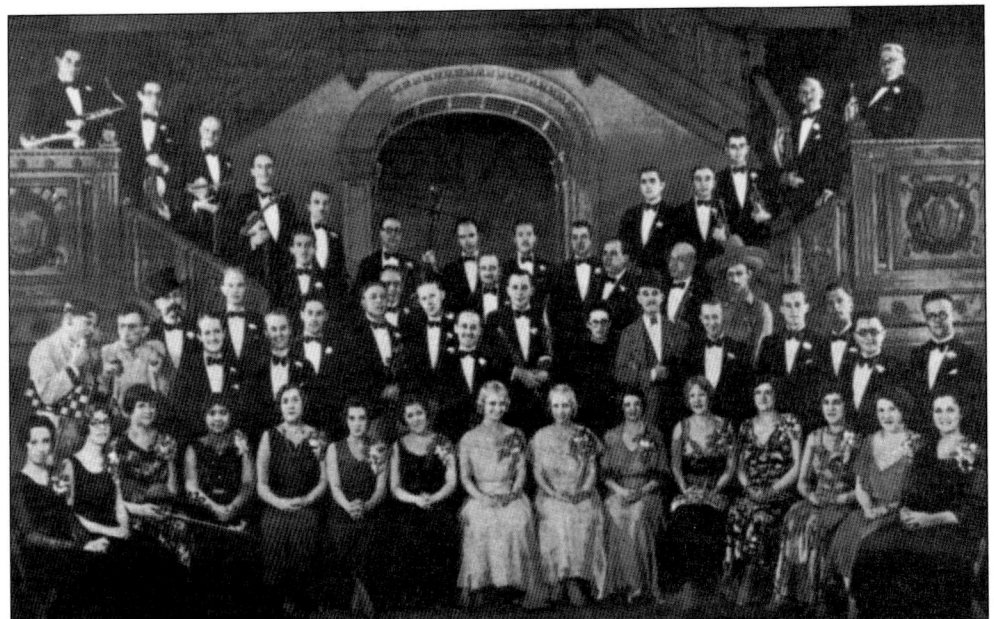

The entire *Blue Monday Jamboree* cast poses on the steps, which led up from the automobile showroom floor to KFRC's mezzanine studios in the Don Lee Building. Some of its better-known stars were Al Pearce, Tommy Harris, Edna O'Keefe, Edna Fischer, Juanita Tennyson, Monroe Upton, Harris Brown, and Murray Bolen. This was music director Meredith Willson's first radio job—the beginnings of an amazing musical career. (Author's collection.)

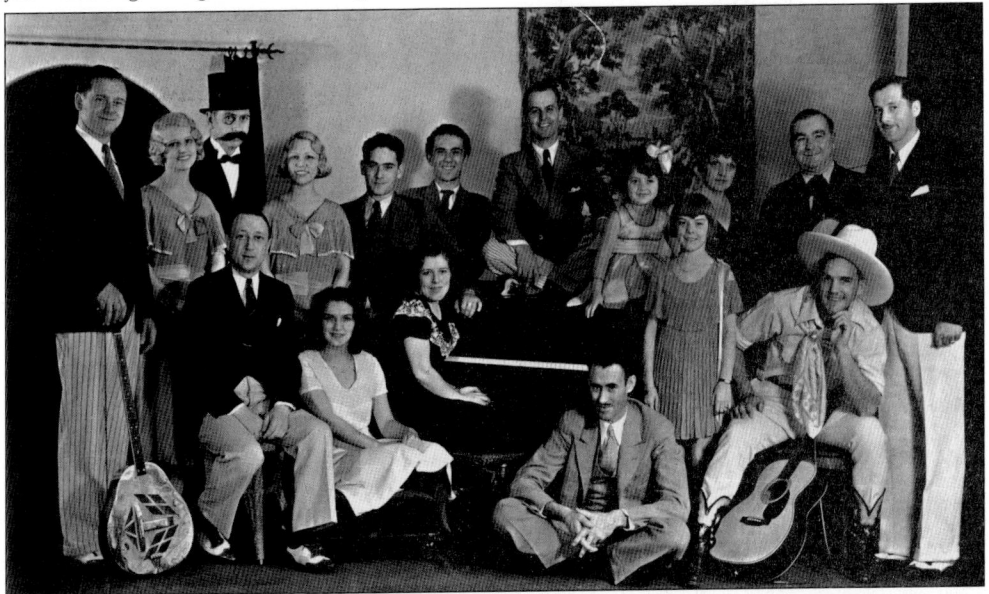

KFRC's *Happy Go Lucky Hour*, starring Al Pearce, was a spin-off from the *Blue Monday Jamboree*. It moved to NBC in 1933 and became *Al Pearce and His Gang*, a network staple until 1947. Pictured from left to right are (first row) Abe Bloom, Edna O'Keefe, Edna Fischer, Pedro Gonzales, Margie Lane Truesdale, and Cecil Wright; (back row) Al Pearce, Ruth Clark, Lord Bilgewater, Lila Clark, Tommy Harris, Charlie Carter, Norman Nielson, Jean Clairmuck, Hazel Warner, Harry McClintock, and Cal Pearce. (Author's collection.)

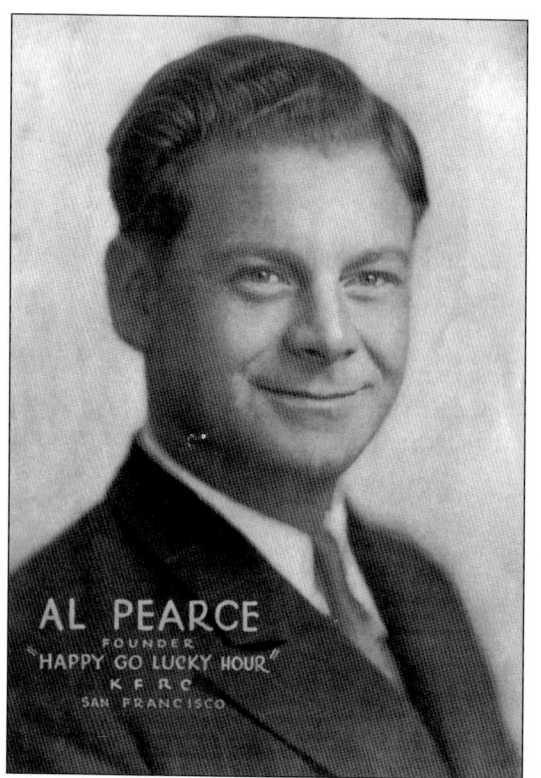

AL PEARCE
FOUNDER
"HAPPY GO LUCKY HOUR"
KFRC
SAN FRANCISCO

Al Pearce had always been a performer, but his guitar and songs had been strictly a hobby until the mid-1920s. After selling insurance and real estate door-to-door, he developed the character of Elmer Blurt, the bashful door-to-door salesman. A KFRC executive saw him performing a vaudeville sketch with his brother Cal at a real estate convention, and they were immediately launched on their radio career. (Author's collection.)

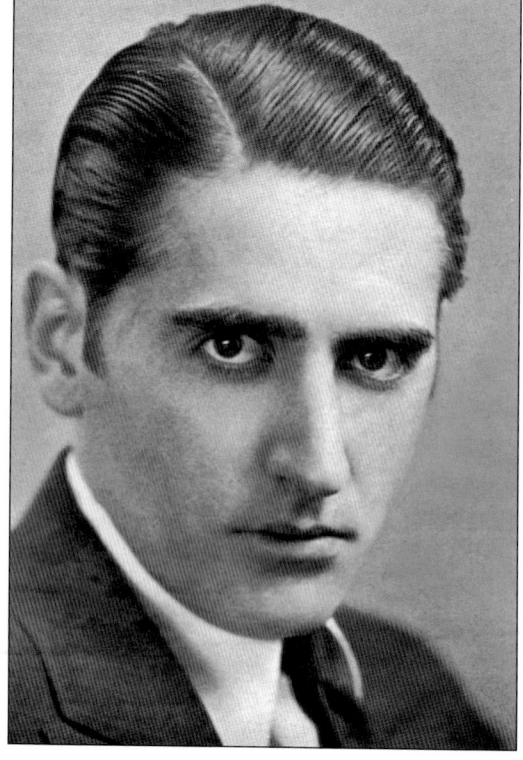

Meredith Willson, the "Music Man," was born in Mason City, Iowa, in 1902. He studied piano and flute at the Damrosch Institute, and by 19 was a soloist with the New York Philharmonic. He moved to San Francisco in the mid-1920s, and quickly gained notoriety as the music director for KFRC before becoming NBC's West Coast Music Director in 1932. (*Stars of the Radio.*)

Harris Brown (left) and Murray Bolen—the comedy team of Murray and Harris—were regulars on KFRC's *Blue Monday Jamboree*. Murray was a KFI announcer in 1928 where Brown performed as a musician. They created a comedy act and took it to KJR in Seattle. In 1929, their old friend Meredith Willson introduced them to Harrison Holliway. They joined KFRC and remained there for the next seven years. (Author's collection.)

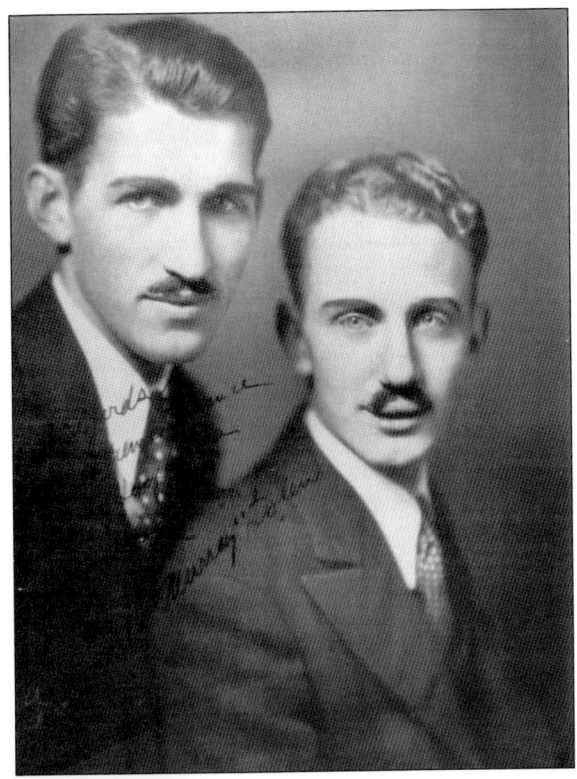

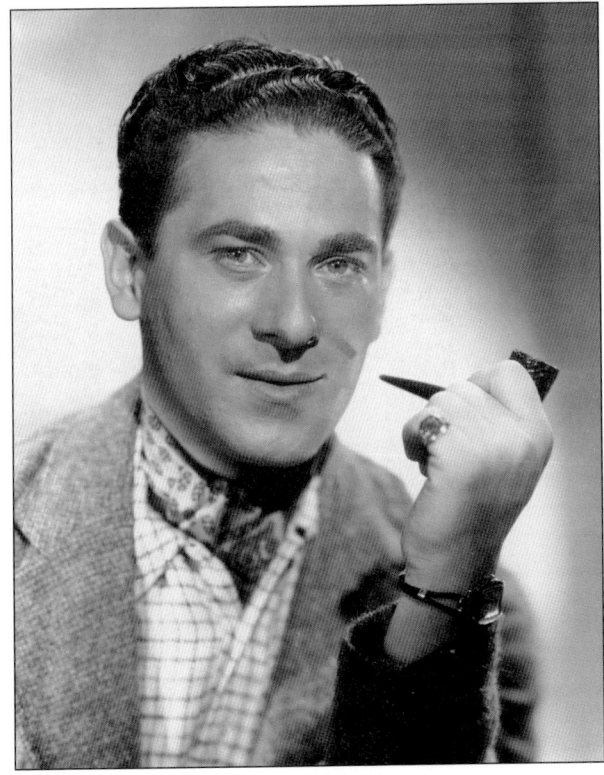

Tommy Harris, who began singing on the *Blue Monday Jamboree* at the age of 14, took the West by storm and was one of the Don Lee Network's top attractions in the 1930s. He and Joaquin Garay were regulars on *Feminine Fancies*. Tommy later opened Tommy's Joynt, a popular nightspot on Geary Avenue, which is still in business today. (Gimmy Park Li.)

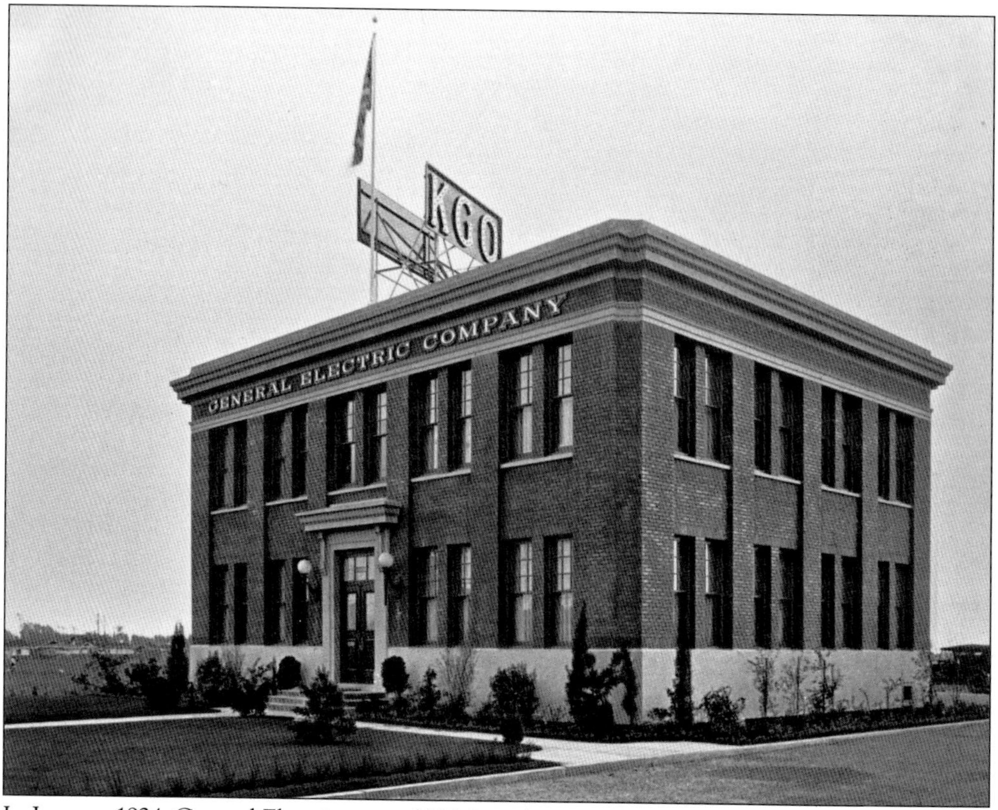

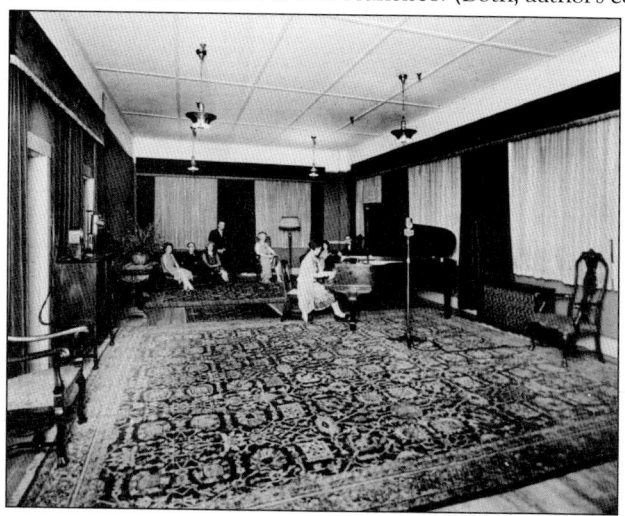

In January 1924, General Electric opened KGO as the second of its three big stations designed to cover the entire country (the others were WGY in Schenectady and KOA in Denver). It was located on the grounds of a GE transformer factory at 5441 East Fourteenth Street in Oakland. The two-story brick KGO building had offices on the first floor and studios on the second. The larger of the two studios, big enough to hold a small orchestra, is seen below. There is a condenser microphone on the pedestal in the center of the room and another one on the cabinet to the left. For the next five years, most of KGO's programs would originate from this building, until the station became part of the NBC network and the studios moved to San Francisco. (Both, author's collection.)

The KGO transmitter building and antenna were about 1,000 feet west of the studio building. The two 150-foot steel towers straddled the transmitter building so that the antenna was suspended directly over the structure. KGO was one of the few stations to have a duplicate of every piece of transmitting equipment, so the station could stay on the air in the event of any equipment failure. This was the purpose of two of its three transmitters. The third was for communicating with ships in distress, and was kept on standby at all times. The open-frame construction of these transmitters was typical of early GE designs, but it was soon abandoned for safety reasons. KGO started with 1,000 watts, but this was soon raised to 7,500 watts. KGO remained in this location until 1947. (Author's collection.)

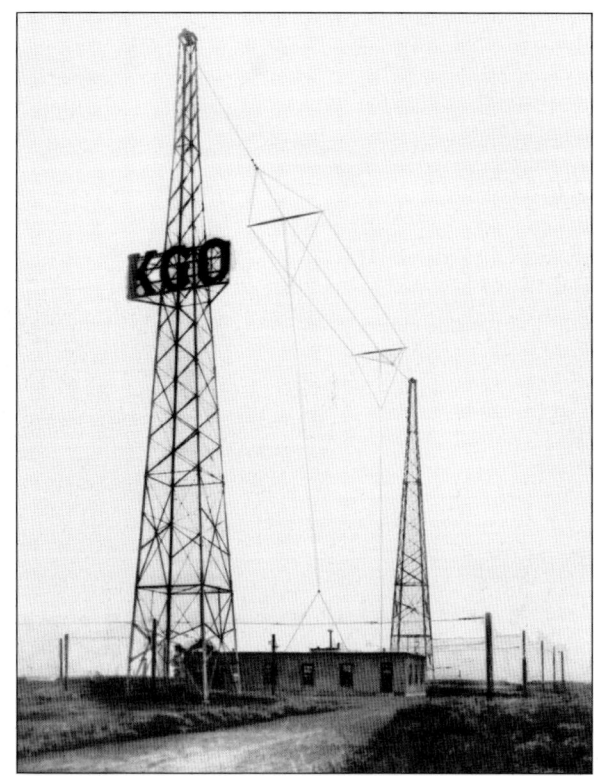

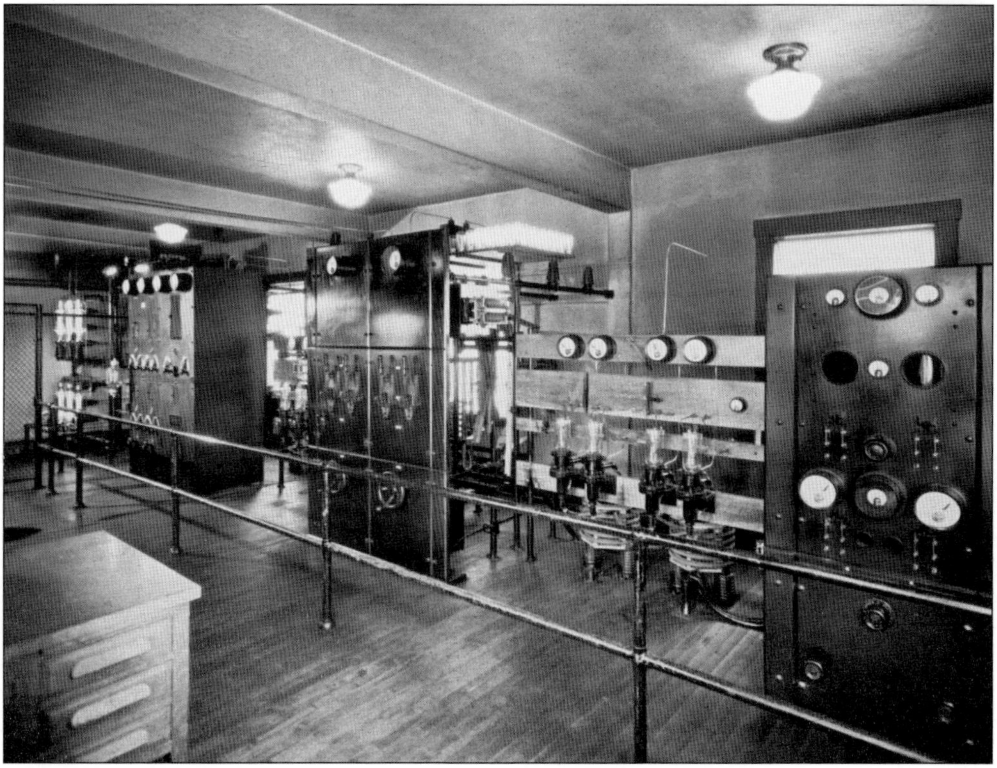

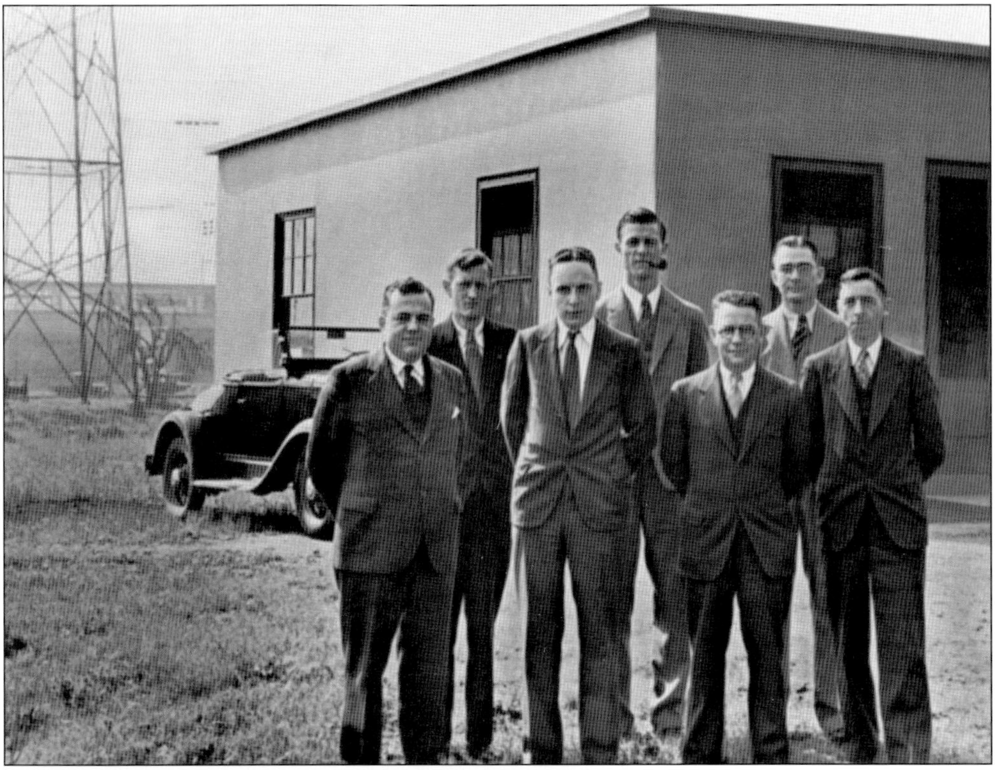

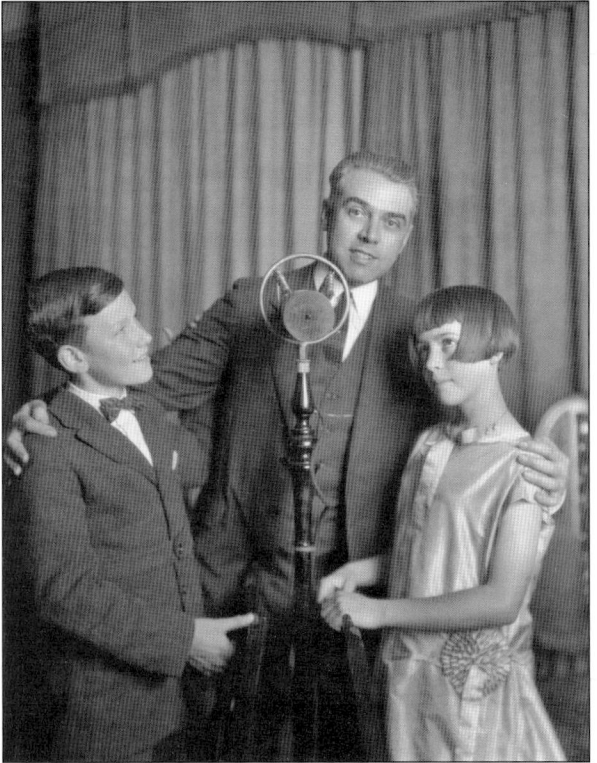

This photograph shows the transmitter staff of KGO outside the transmitter building in Oakland sometime during the 1930s. One of the two towers is visible in the background. Pictured from left to right are M.O. Smith, H.C. Dunton, J.I. Ball, D.H. Atkins, A.E. Evans (station chief engineer), A.E. Fisher, and A.E. Eldredge. (Author's collection.)

Howard Milholland was KGO's studio manager in the 1920s. KGO and the other GE stations were pioneers in the art of radio drama. Here he is in 1925 posing with Richard Shadburn and Marion Cramer, two young radio actors who performed in the radio play *The Volga River*. (Author's collection.)

Rose Brown was the leading lady of the *KGO Players*. Quoting an article from *Radio Broadcast* magazine from December 1924, "That lovely voice of hers prompted a rush request to station KGO for Miss Brown's picture, for we felt sure that anyone with such speaking tones would be good to look upon." (Author's collection.)

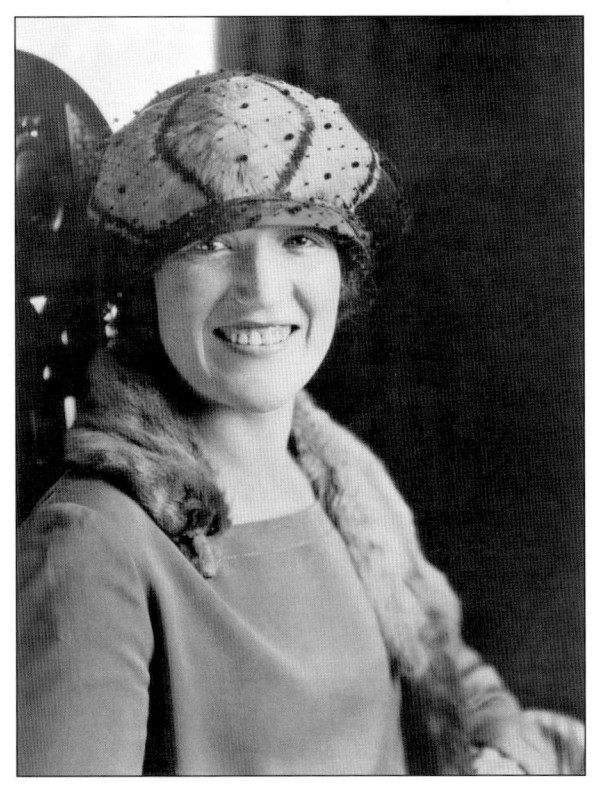

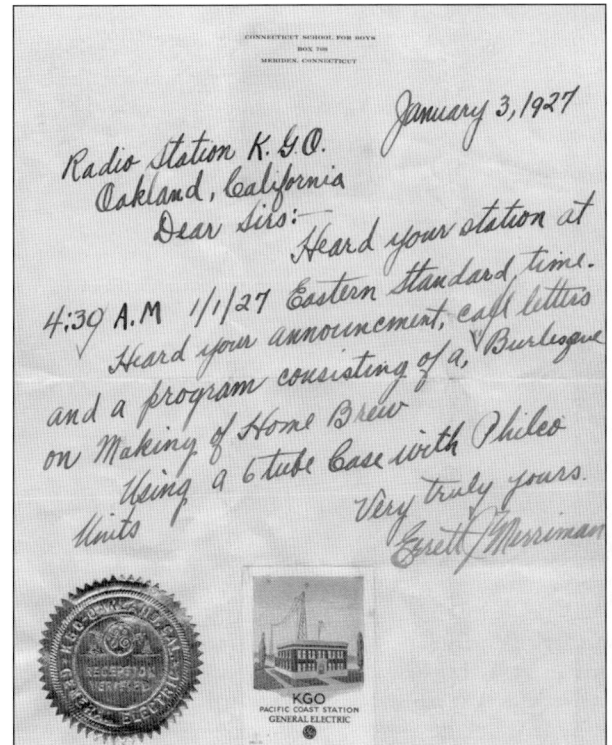

This letter of verification was sent by Erritt G. Merriman to KGO in 1927. It was returned to the writer with KGO verification stamps affixed to the letter. Years later, in 1976, Jim Eviston bought an old TRF radio receiver at Merriman's farm auction in Indiana. He found this letter inside the radio. (Jim Eviston.)

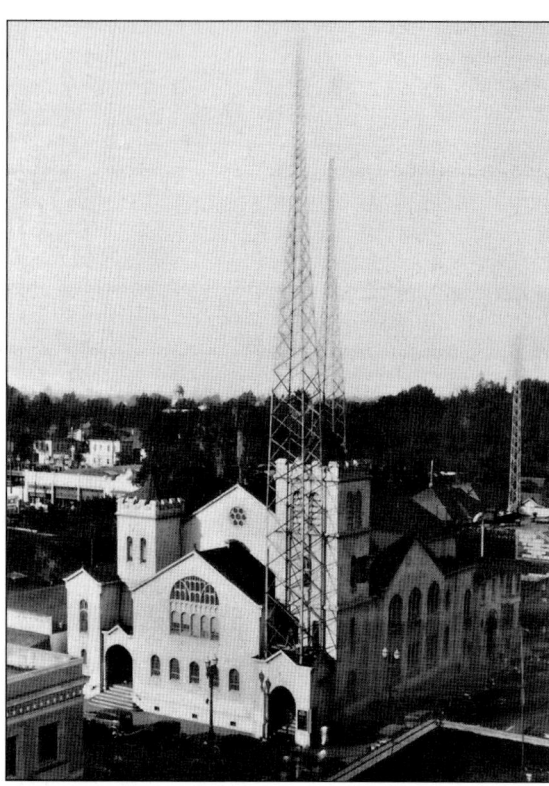

In 1925, Doc Herrold turned over the operation of his station KQW to the First Baptist Church of San Jose. The church applied the slogan "King's Quickening Word" to the station and installed new equipment in the church building. The photograph shows the towers built on the church property to hold the KQW antenna. (KCBS brochure.)

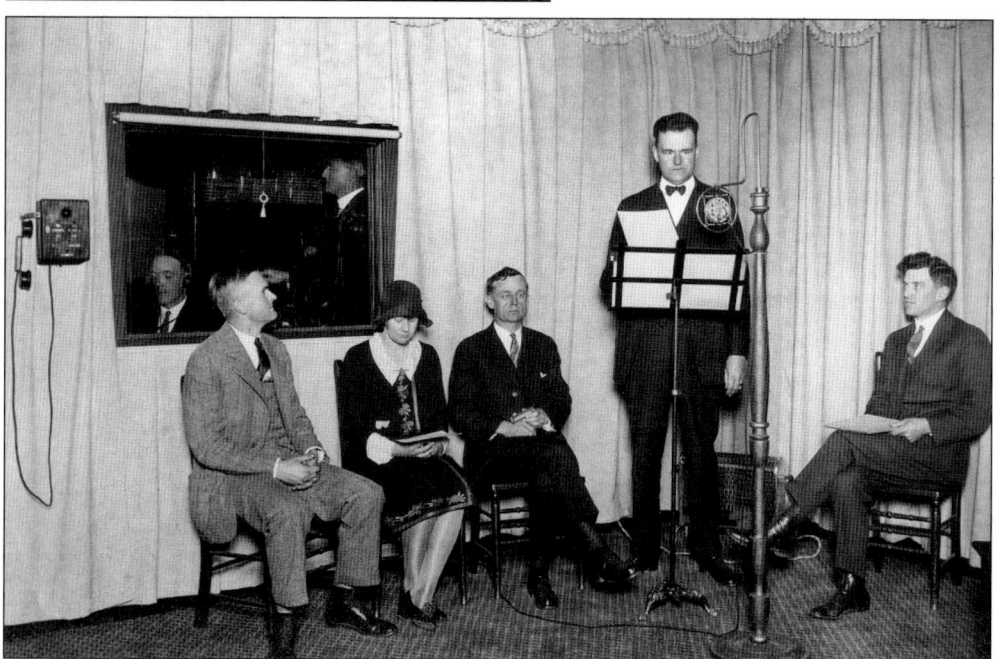

Here is an early KQW live studio broadcast taking place at the First Baptist Church. The standing performer seems to eye the microphone suspiciously while the other participants look on. Meanwhile, the technicians in the control room are oblivious to the drama going on in the studio. (San Jose State University Special Collections.)

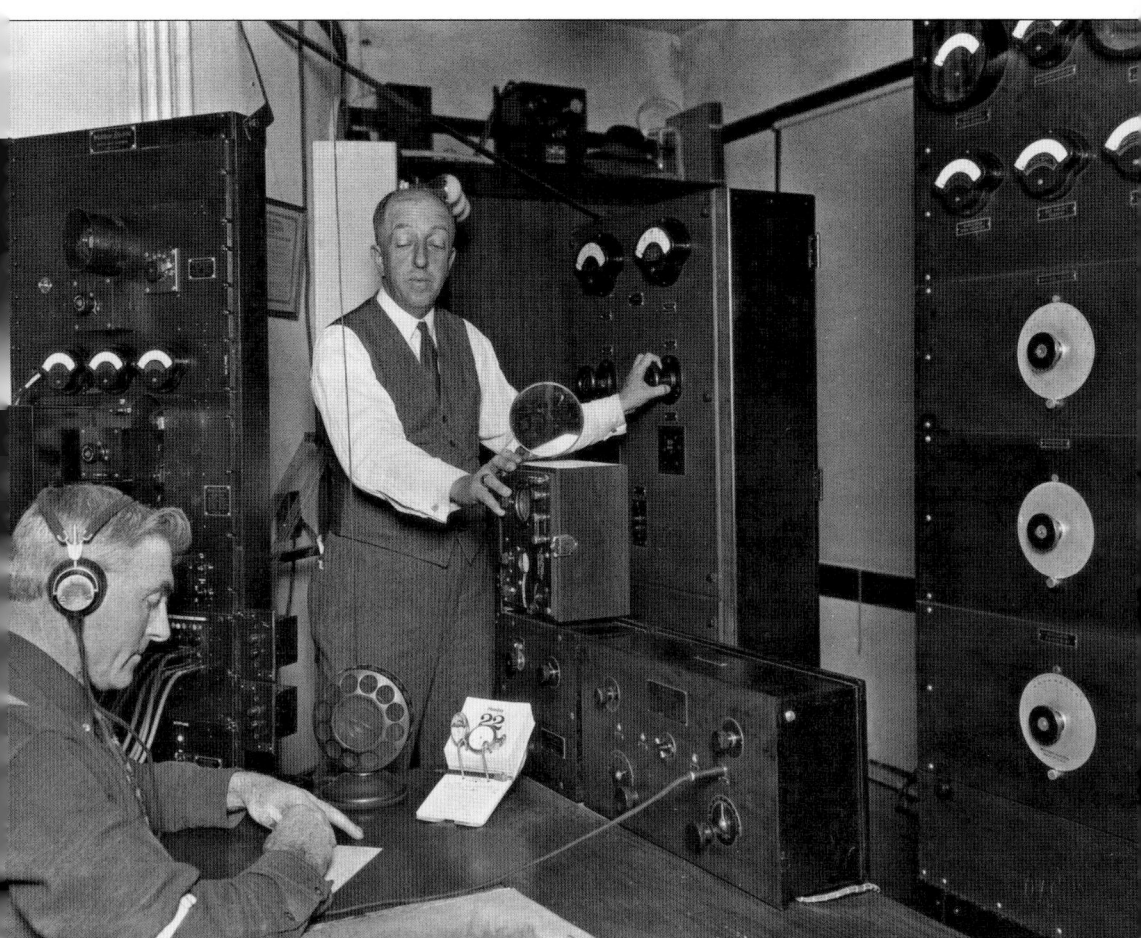

Doc Herrold is seen adjusting KQW's new 500-watt Western Electric transmitter in 1925. The three panels in the room are (from left to right) the audio control panel, power control panel, and the transmitter. The operator at the desk is copying a Morse code message from the tabletop radio receiver. To the left of the receiver is an early Western Electric carbon microphone. On top of the receiver is a wave meter, which was used to adjust the transmitter's frequency. Herrold used a magnifying glass to carefully read and adjust the meters on the transmitter. After he transferred control of KQW to the First Baptist Church, Herrold continued as a station employee for a short time, but the station founder was soon fired by the church in a move to cut operating costs. (San Jose State University Special Collections.)

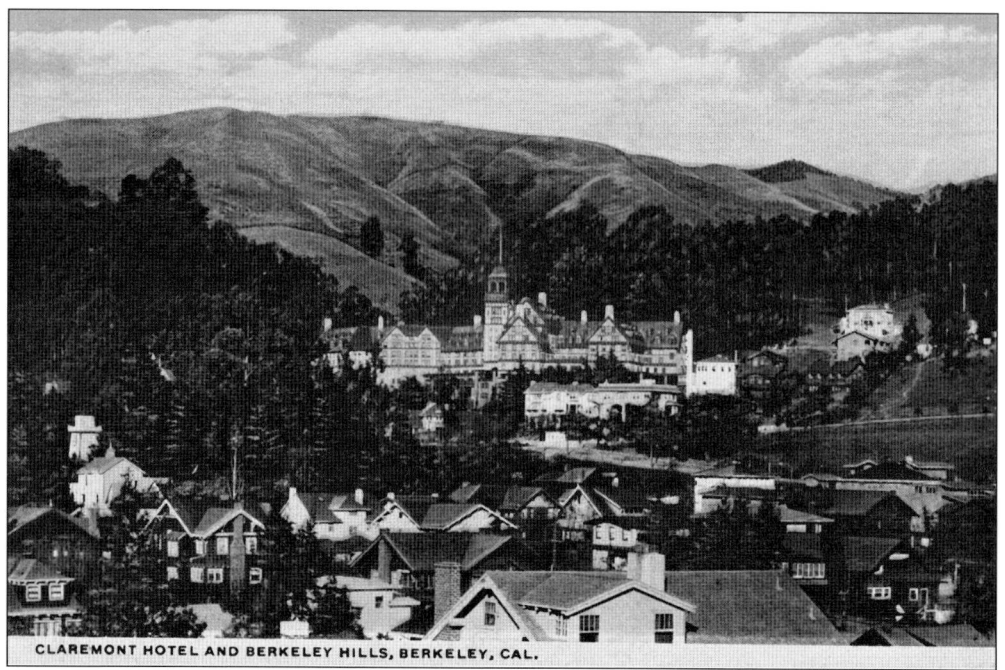

CLAREMONT HOTEL AND BERKELEY HILLS, BERKELEY, CAL.

The Maxwell Electric Company, a small radio store on Adeline Street in Berkeley, opened station KRE in 1922. The job of constructing and operating the station fell to employee Thomas A. Fite. A small transmitter was constructed and installed at the scenic Claremont Resort Hotel in the Berkeley Hills, and a studio was assembled on the second floor. KRE's first broadcast took place on March 11, 1922. Above is a 1920s postcard view of the Claremont Hotel, KRE's first home, and below is a view of the first KRE studio in the hotel. A piano was loaned to KRE by Benjamin's Music Store, and the wicker phonograph came from White's. (Both, author's collection.)

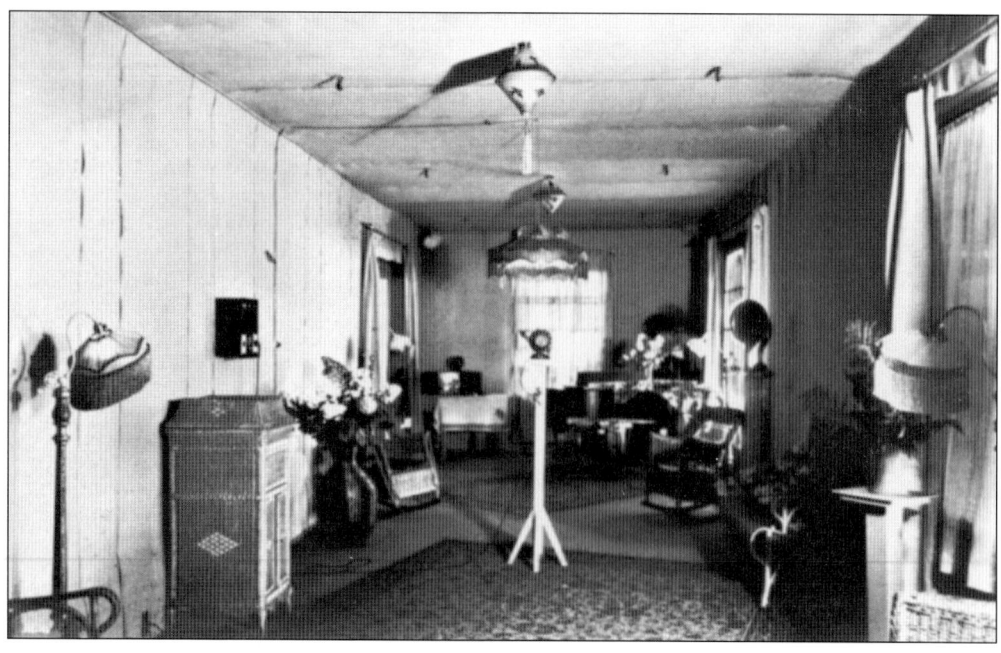

Maxwell Electric Company built this 50-watt transmitter for KRE in 1922, which it nicknamed "Big Mike." The transmitter itself is the large pipe-frame cabinet seen behind the operator's desk. The antenna for KRE was a vertical wire suspended from the cupola on the roof of the Claremont Hotel. (Author's collection.)

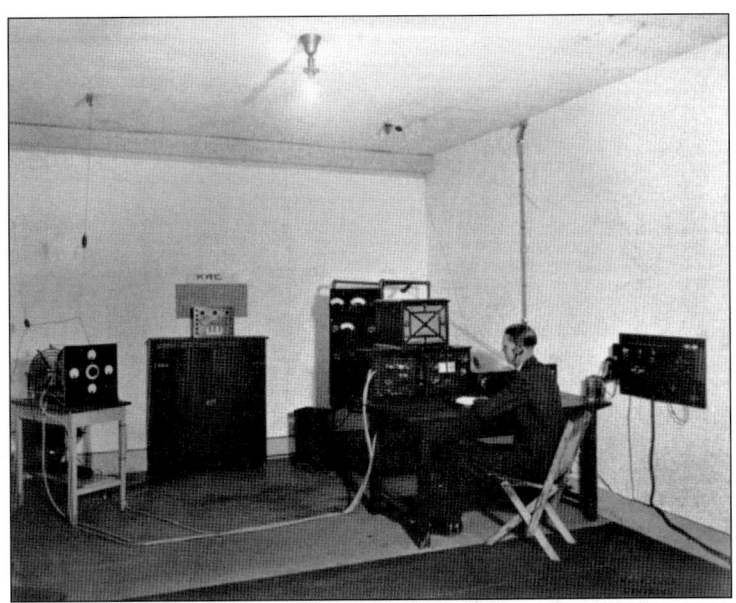

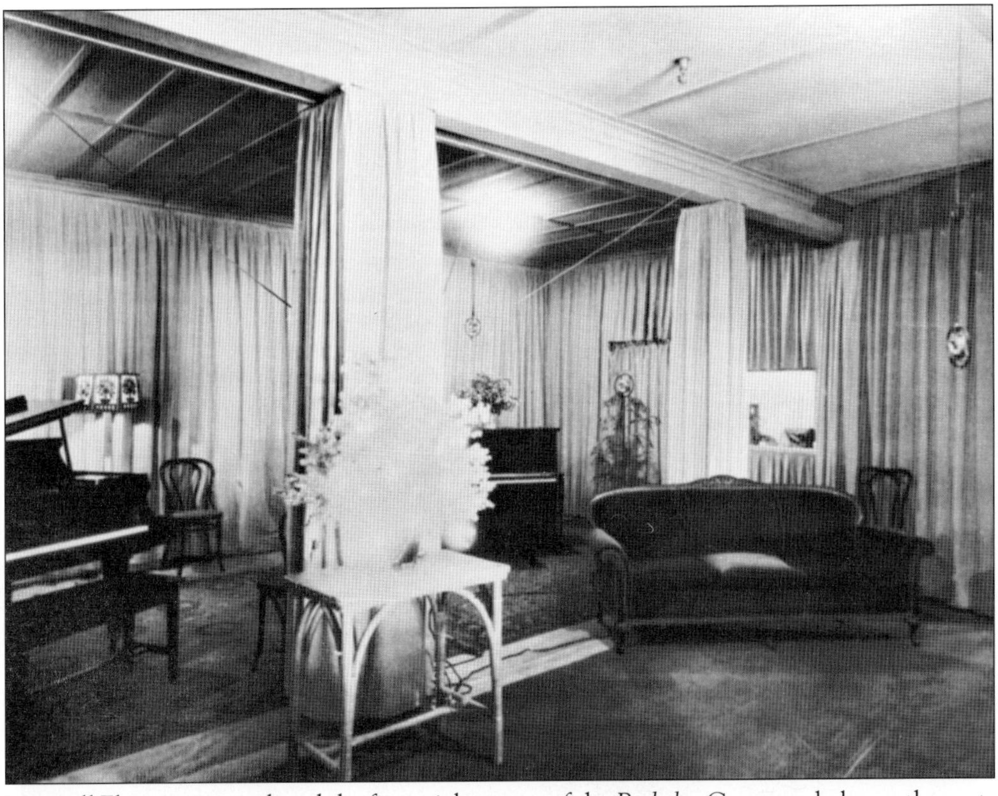

Maxwell Electric soon enlisted the financial support of the *Berkeley Gazette* to help pay the costs of operating KRE. With improved funding, the studio was rebuilt and hung with draperies to improve the acoustics. Initially the station operated for just two hours every Sunday night, but Wednesday night was added to the schedule in 1923. (Author's collection.)

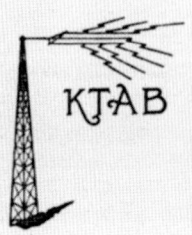

You are cordially invited to be the guest of Tenth Avenue Baptist Church, Oakland, August first, nineteen twenty-five at 8 P.M. on the occasion of the Official Opening of their new Thousand-watt Radio Station

THE STAFF

KTAB

From San Francisco ▸ Take Key Route Ferry, 12th Street Train, transferring at the Shredded Wheat Station to waiting 'K' Car which passes door of Radio KTAB, 10th Ave. and East 14th Street

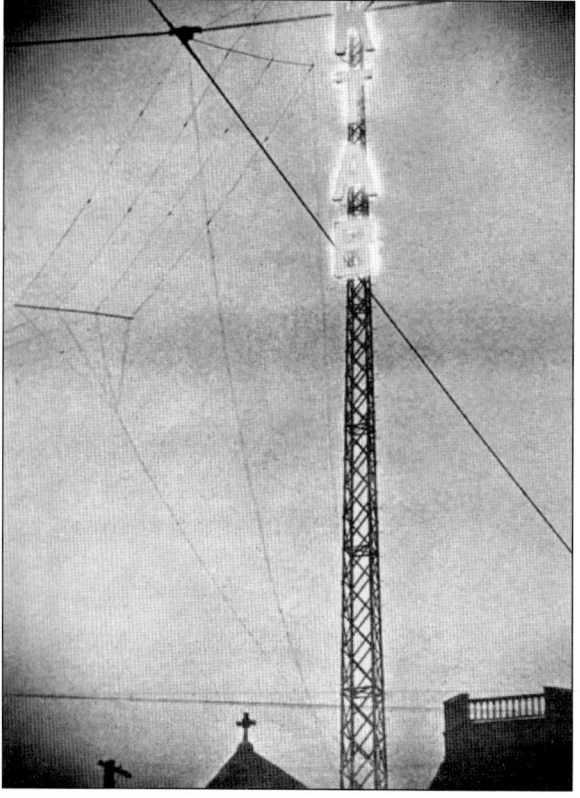

In 1925, the Tenth Avenue Baptist Church in Oakland started broadcasting a program called *The Hour of Prayer* over KGO. The church received hundreds of letters in response to the program, but then KGO suddenly cancelled the program. Convinced of the value of radio to the church, Pastor George W. Phillips proposed to his congregation that they construct their own church station. By the end of the night, his parishioners had pledged $35,000 to underwrite the project. The church building was raised a story and studios were built in the basement. A neighbor deeded space on his property for one of the new 155-foot towers. Before long, the new station was ready, and the engraved invitation above was sent to dignitaries and other important persons for the inaugural broadcast of KTAB in 1926. (Above, author's collection; left, Phil Lasky.)

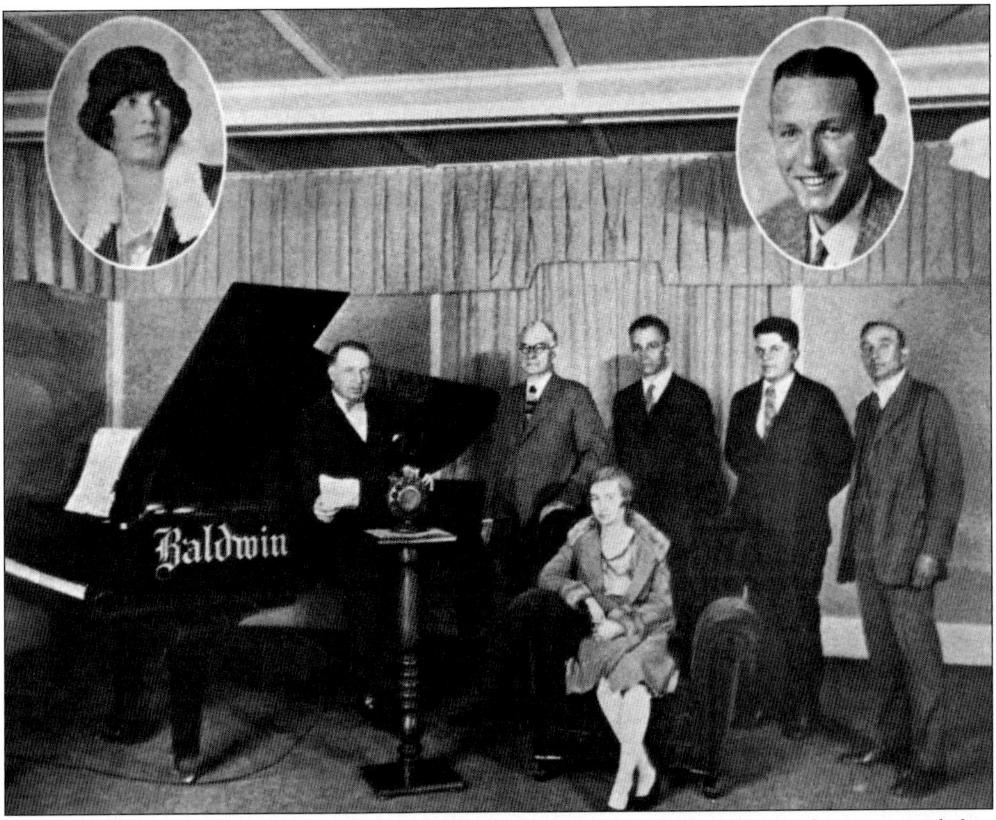

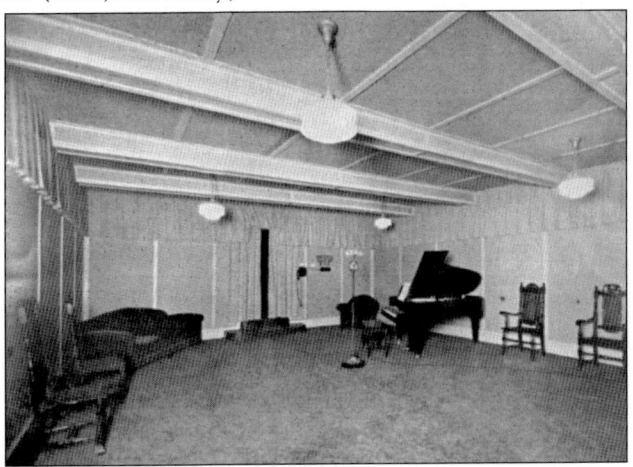

Above, the entire KTAB staff is shown seated in the station's main studio. In the cutout at left is program director Ada Morgan O'Brien, and announcer E. Harold Dana is at right. Standing, from left to right, are Rod Hendrickson, treasurer and announcer; Wilbur S. Tupper, business manager; E.L. Spaulding, announcer; Erroll Peck, assistant engineer, and R.M. Bitzer, chief engineer. Seated is Elsie Bishop, secretary. Radio announcers in the 1920s were known on the air only by their initials. Hendrickson was "R.H.," Dana was "H.D.," and Spaulding was "L.S." Below, this was the larger of two KTAB studios located on the first floor of the Tenth Avenue Baptist Church. All of the weekday evening broadcasts took place in this studio. These images are from KTAB's anniversary booklet. (Both, Phil Lasky.)

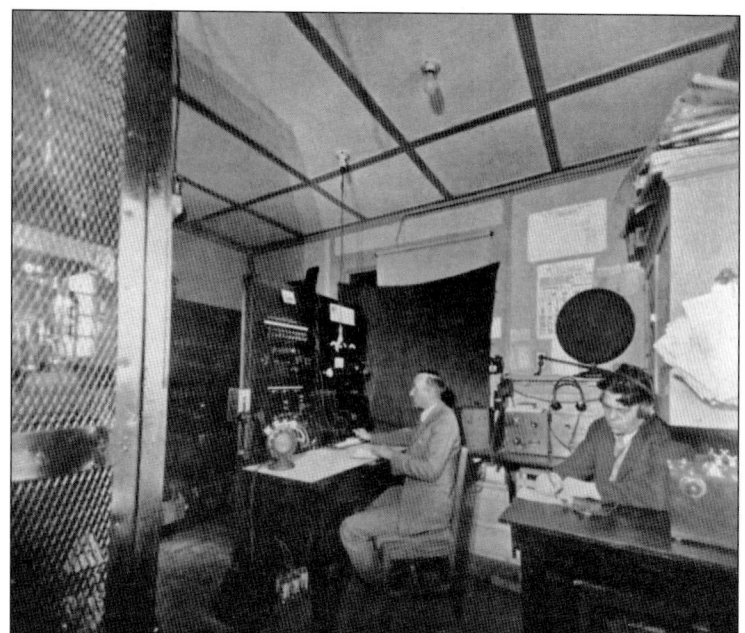

The KTAB transmitter was installed in the steeple tower, on the fourth floor of the Tenth Avenue Baptist Church. Chief engineer R.M. Bitzer is seated at the audio control panel, while his assistant Erroll Peck monitors a receiver, listening for distress calls. The Western Electric 1,000-watt transmitter is visible at the far left. This image is from KTAB's anniversary booklet. (Phil Lasky.)

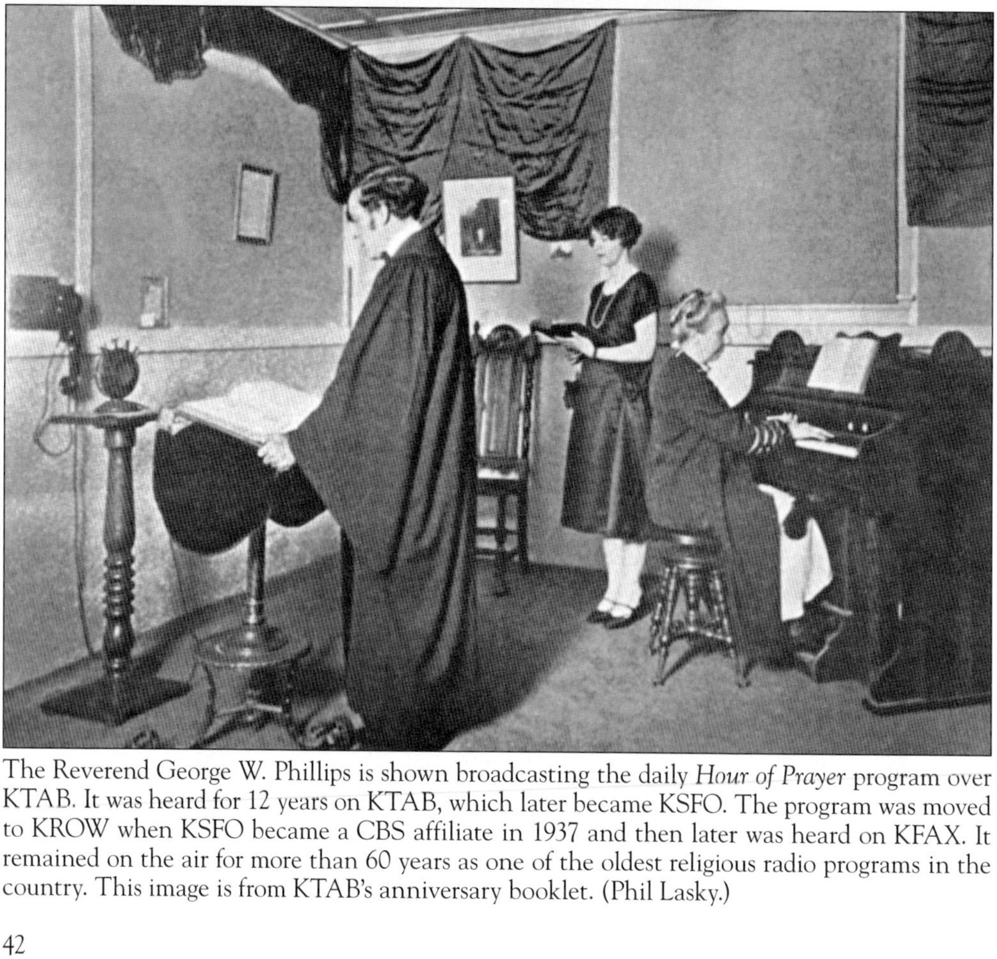

The Reverend George W. Phillips is shown broadcasting the daily *Hour of Prayer* program over KTAB. It was heard for 12 years on KTAB, which later became KSFO. The program was moved to KROW when KSFO became a CBS affiliate in 1937 and then later was heard on KFAX. It remained on the air for more than 60 years as one of the oldest religious radio programs in the country. This image is from KTAB's anniversary booklet. (Phil Lasky.)

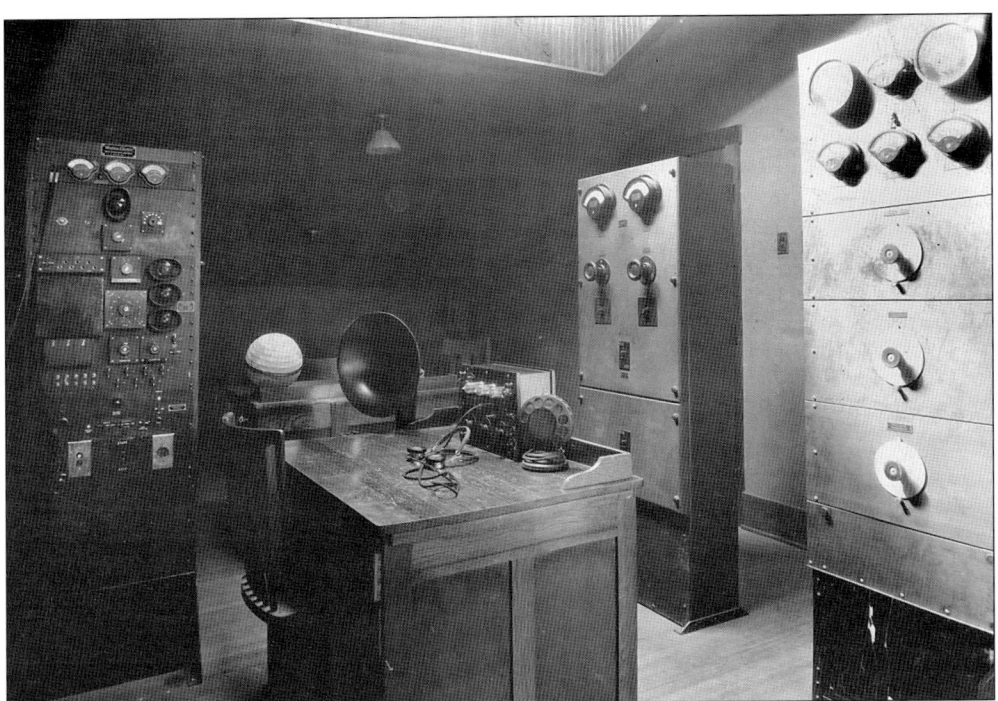

The *Oakland Tribune* opened KLX in July 1922, an outgrowth of KZM, an earlier station located at the Hotel Oakland. KZM's owner, Preston D. Allen, became the KLX manager. The transmitter and studio were located behind the big clock on the top floor of the Tribune Tower in downtown Oakland, and the antenna stretched from the tower to a building across the street. The view above shows the new Western Electric 1B transmitter, the same as the one seen on page 21 at KPO. Below is the studio, adjacent to the transmitter room. Most studios in the 1920s were draped with "monk's cloth" to dampen the acoustics, resulting in a very "dead" air sound. Later broadcasters would use a combination of absorbing and reflective surfaces to create a controlled live sound in the studio. (Both, Perham Collection, History San Jose.)

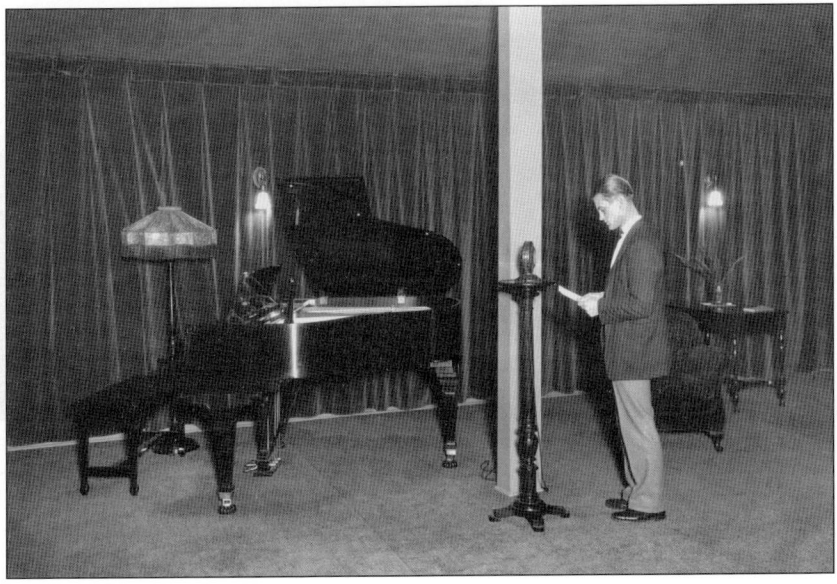

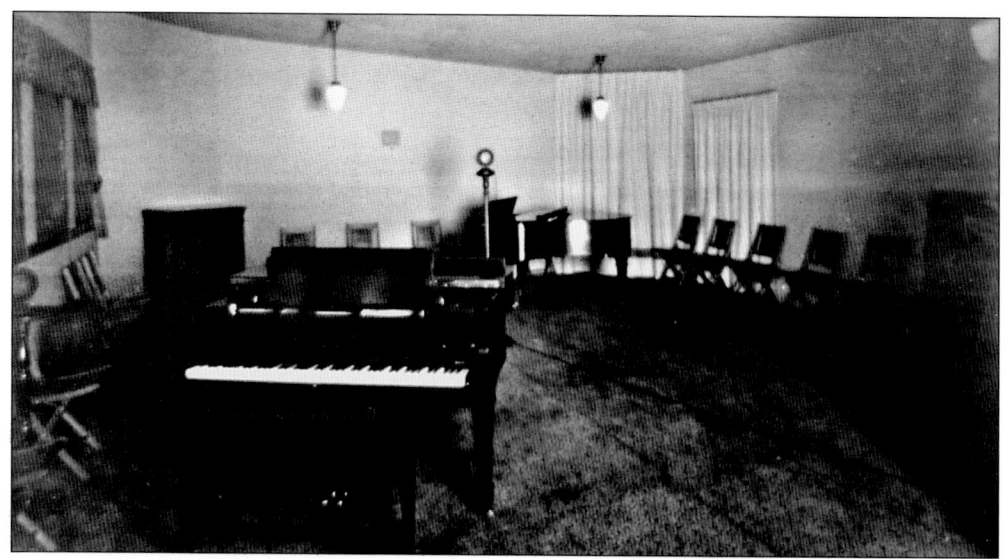

KYA signed on December 18, 1926, from this studio on the fifth floor of the Clift Hotel. It was operated by Vincent Kraft's Pacific Broadcasting Company. Kraft also owned KJR in Seattle. Over the next three years, Kraft built several other stations on the West Coast, and even started a nascent network, the American Broadcasting Company. However, everything collapsed suddenly in 1929 when one of the investors, a Seattle banker, was caught embezzling bank funds to keep the stations afloat. KYA and the remains of the ABC network were acquired in receivership by NBC in 1930, which installed this 1,000-watt RCA transmitter on the 16th floor of the Clift Hotel. It operated from there until 1937 when KYA built its present site on Candlestick Hill. NBC sold KYA to the *San Francisco Examiner* in 1934. (Above, author's collection; below, Kevin Mostyn.)

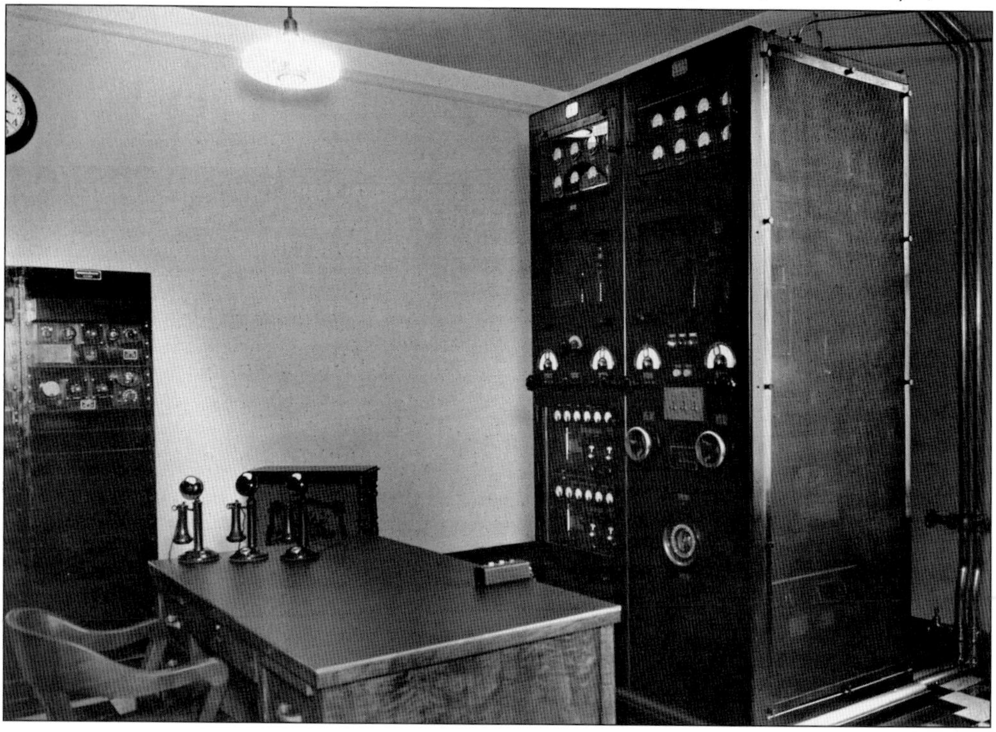

Three

NETWORK CENTER
OF THE 1930S
1926–1942

The National Broadcasting Company, the nation's first true radio network, debuted in New York in 1926. Programs originating from WEAF were heard on the "Red Network," and programs from WJZ went out on the "Blue Network." But these networks were "nationwide" in name only because AT&T's broadcast quality phone lines did not yet cross the Rocky Mountains.

NBC's solution was to establish another studio in San Francisco to generate programs for the Pacific Coast. Full studios were built at 111 Sutter Street and a complete staff of actors, announcers, and musicians duplicated the programs being heard on the East Coast. The scripts and musical scores were shipped from New York, to be performed a week later. Inaugurated on April 5, 1927, this "Orange Network" served seven stations from San Diego to Seattle, with KPO as the key station. Soon NBC also acquired KGO and opened a second NBC "Brown Network."

For 14 years, NBC in San Francisco would be the biggest radio operation on the Pacific Coast. Program duplication ended when the transcontinental line was completed in 1930. But instead of dissolving its San Francisco operation, NBC expanded it, feeding new programs eastward to the rest of the country. Soon, there was a staff of 250 people, including a full orchestra, a dramatic stock company, and even five pipe organists. National programs originating in San Francisco included *Hawthorne House, Death Valley Days, Carefree Carnival,* and *One Man's Family.*

Outgrowing its original space, NBC planned to build an elaborate new "Radio City" building, but forces were conspiring to end San Francisco's radio reign. AT&T completed a new broadcast line to Los Angeles just as the big movie moguls ended their prohibition against radio appearances by movie stars. Suddenly, the radio center needed to be in Hollywood. New York executives sent orders to stop the new building, but it was too late. An NBC executive reportedly attended the ground-breaking with a "Stop Work" telegram in his pocket.

Radio City opened in 1942 but never saw the full use it was designed for. Within a few years, it was empty except for a few local shows.

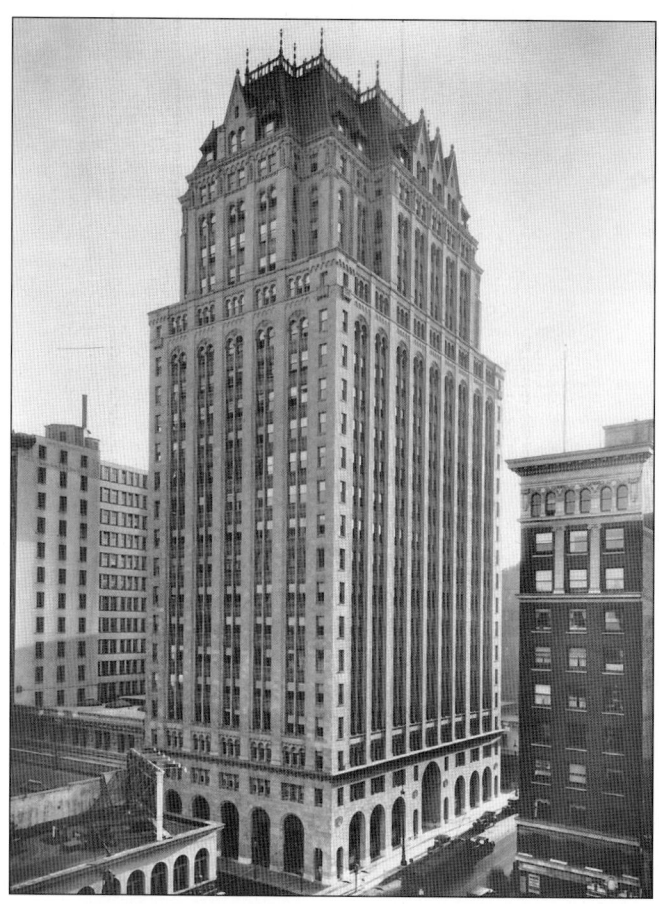

For its West Coast radio center, the National Broadcasting Company leased the entire top (22nd) floor and half of the 21st floor of the Hunter-Dulin Building at 111 Sutter Street in San Francisco. The structure at the corner of Sutter and Montgomery Streets—completed and opened for occupancy in 1926—would serve as the West Coast NBC headquarters for the next 15 years. The reception lobby, executive and business offices, and production departments were on the second and third floors, while three broadcasting studios, each with its own control room and monitor booth, were on the 21st and 22nd floors. Also on these floors were the master control room and the music library, the largest of its kind west of New York. The reception lobby is shown below. (Both, Bill Newbrough.)

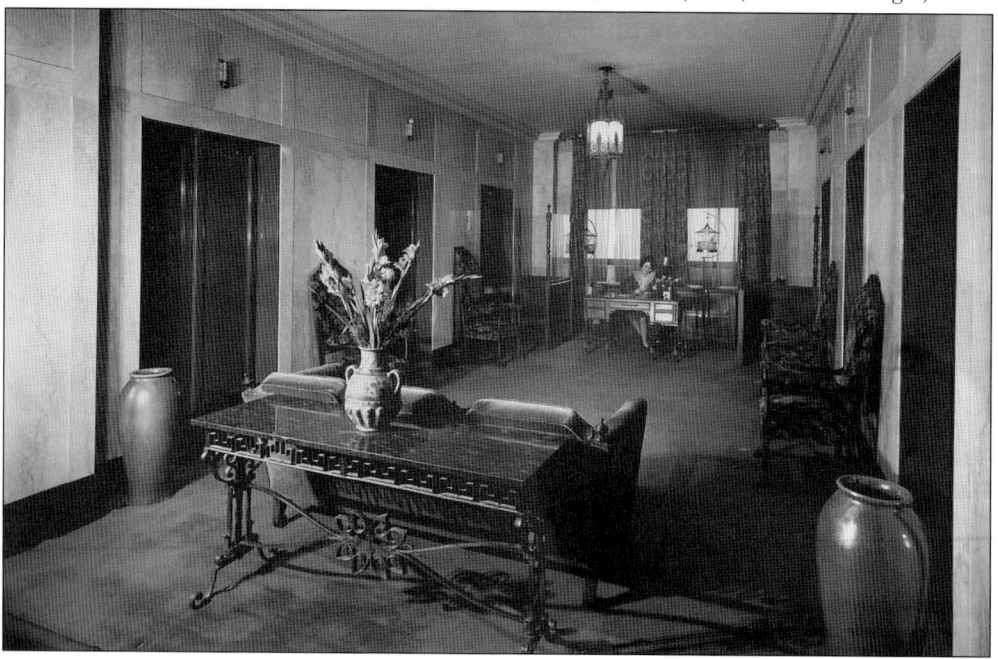

The door at left is the entrance to NBC's main studio A at 111 Sutter Street (see cover). The colonial Spanish motif of the NBC facility is visible here, with its tapestry and wrought-iron fixtures. The stairway leads up to a glass-enclosed mezzanine viewing room, decorated to resemble a Spanish patio. Program sponsors were its most frequent users, sparking the establishment of sponsors' booths in studios across the country. (Bill Newbrough.)

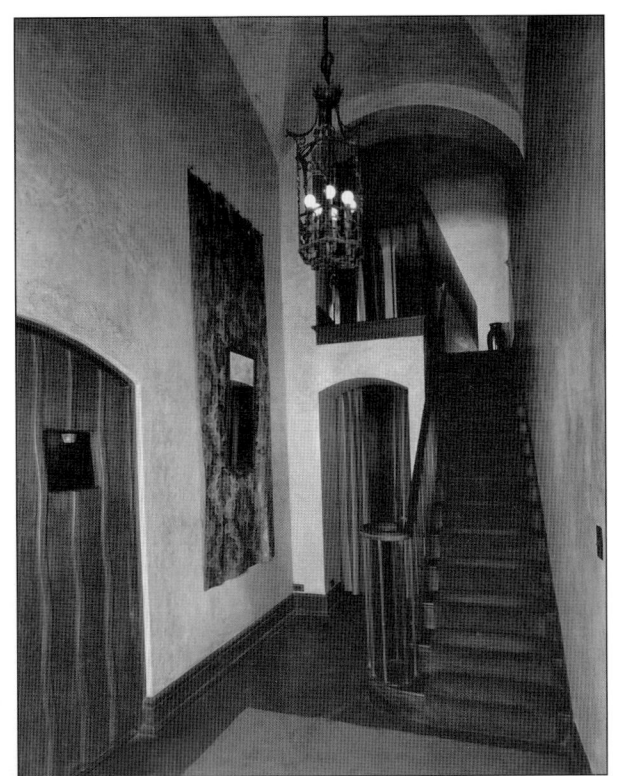

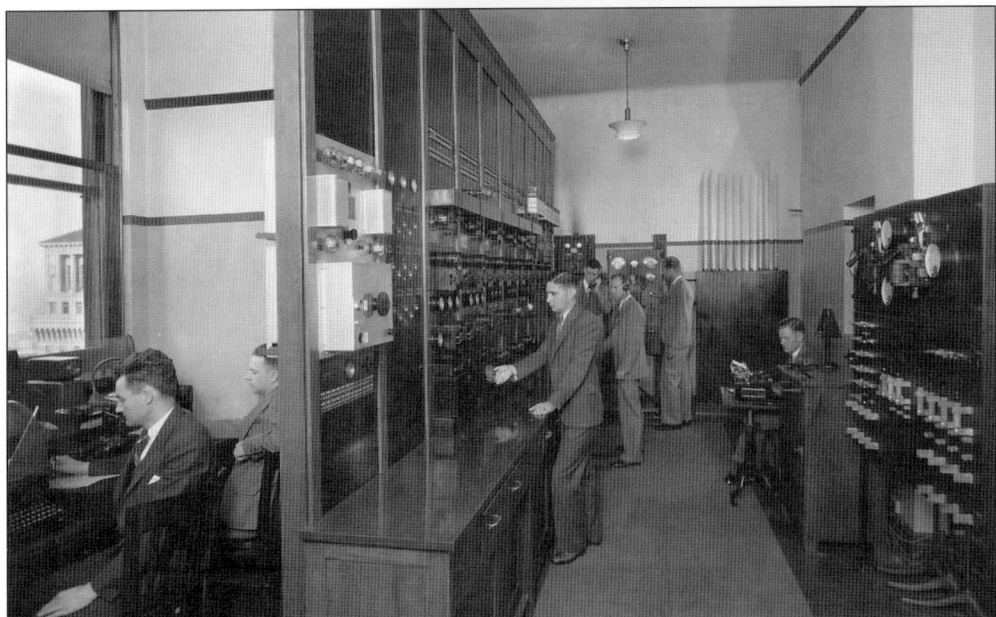

This main control room at 111 Sutter Street was used from 1927 to 1942. All program feeds to network stations originated here. At the left, Morse wires connect to New York, Chicago, and other cities. In the center are line amplifiers, bridging equipment, power and test equipment, and incoming lines. On the back wall are the generator controls, and at the right is the supervisor's desk. The DC switchboard is at the far right. (Bill Newbrough.)

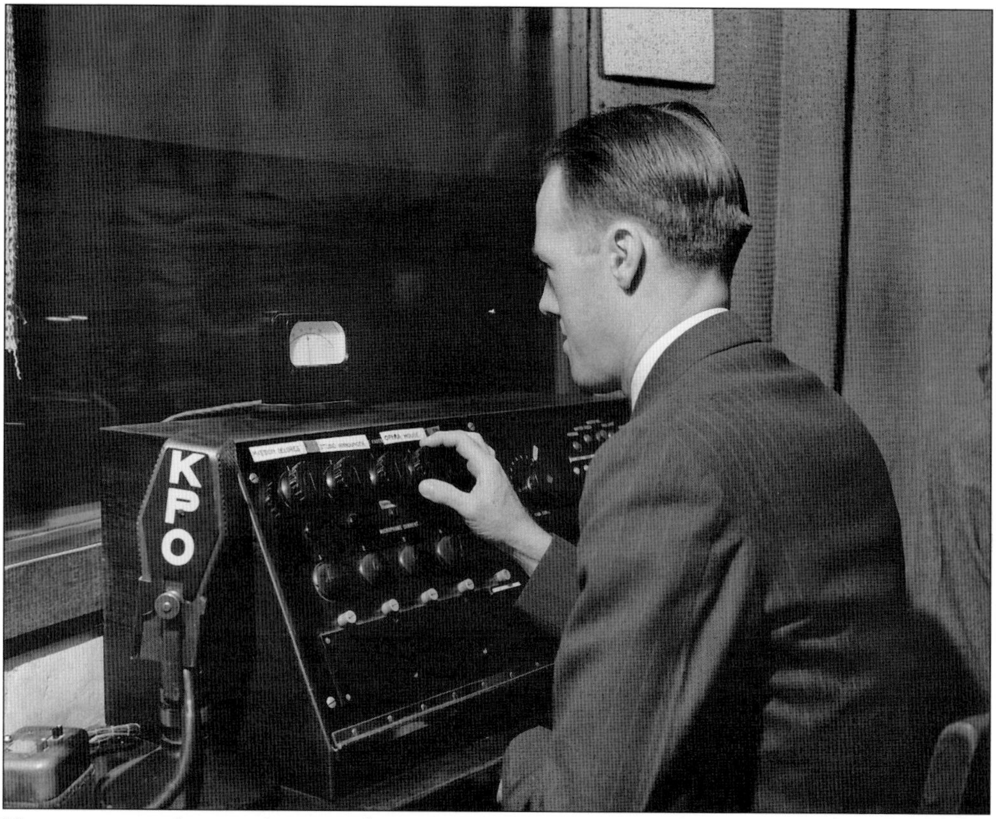

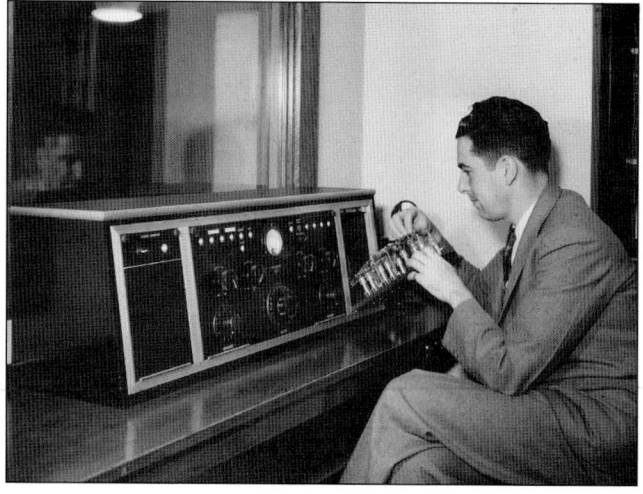

Here are views of two studio control rooms at 111 Sutter Street. Above, Frank Fullaway runs the control board for a remote broadcast of the program *Mine to Cherish* in the middle to late 1930s. A "VU" meter has been added to the microphone mixer, indicating that the mixer dates from an earlier era. Also, there are knobs labeled "microphone current," verifying that the mixer was made for use with early carbon microphones instead of the later ribbon microphone, at left. The labels over the mixer knobs read "Mission Dolores," "Studio Announcer," and "Opera House." Below, NBC engineer George Greaves performs maintenance on a later-vintage audio mixing console. The three knobs at the bottom are labeled "announce," "program," and "master." (Both, Bill Newbrough.)

Every San Francisco NBC announcer had stories to tell about his own encounters with the Announcer's Delight console. Network announcers, not technicians, were responsible for pushing the correct series of buttons that directed the programs to the proper stations. Sometimes the wrong show or an inappropriate announcement went out over the airwaves. Once an errant voice interrupted a speech by the Pope to announce, "This nonsense was brought to you by the National Broadcasting Company." At right is an early version of the infamous contraption, while engineer Oscar Berg and Alice Tyler inspect a later incarnation below. (Right, author's collection; below, Bill Newbrough.)

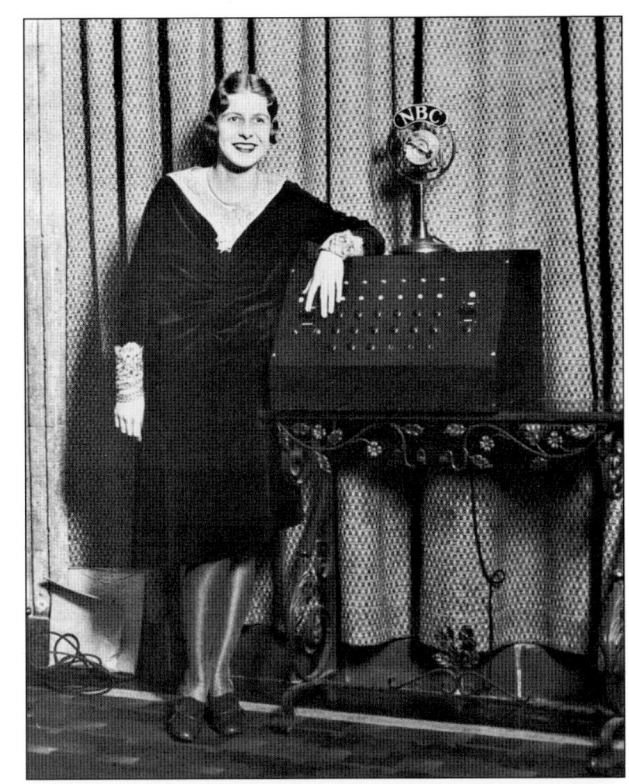

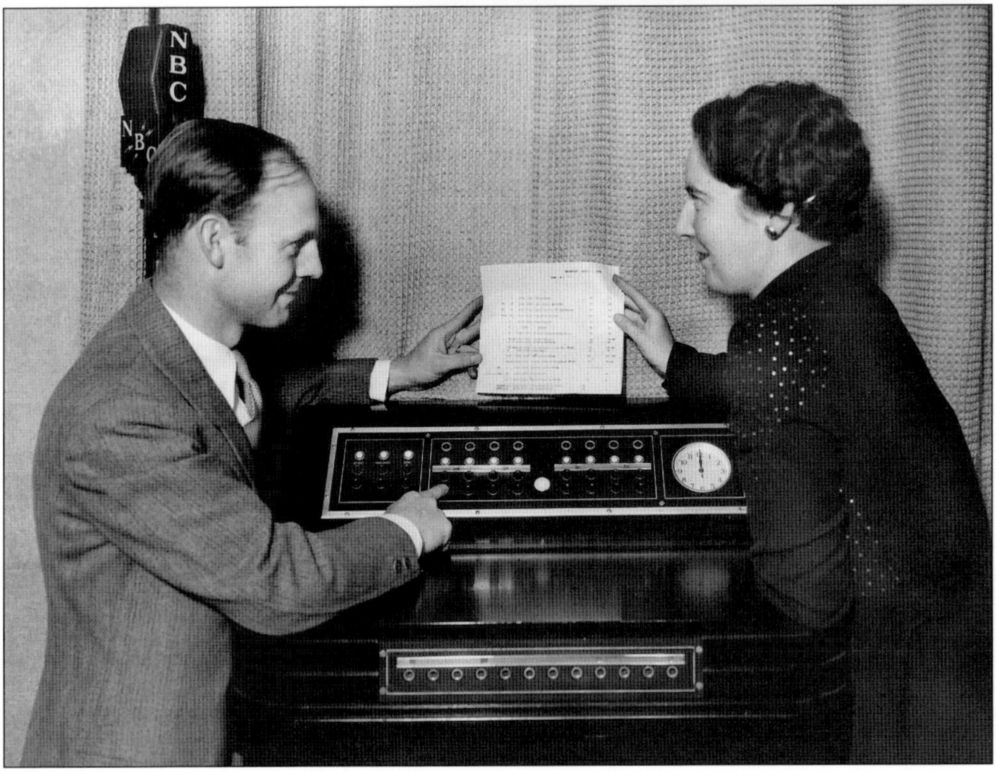

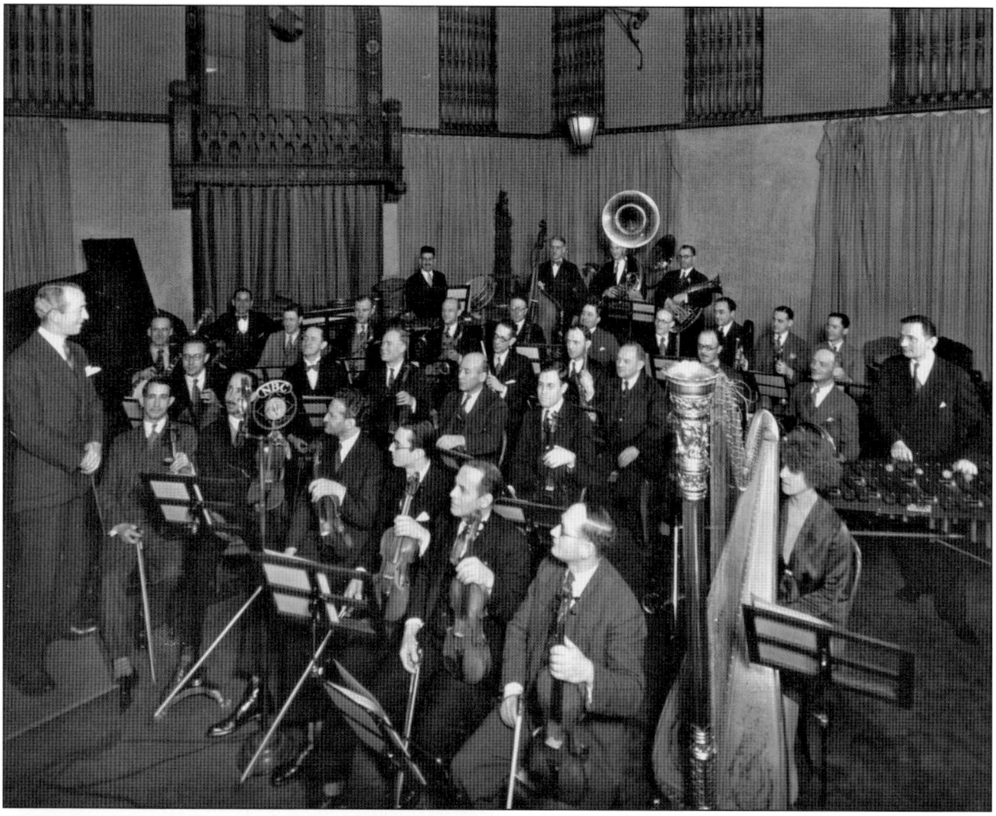

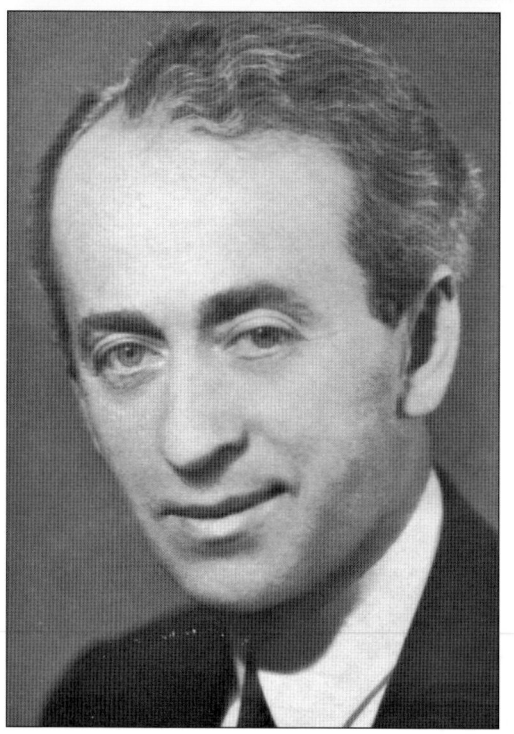

Max Dolin was NBC's first Pacific Coast music director. Dolin, a Russian immigrant, was a violinist and orchestra leader, one of the first to introduce jazz to Cuba. His orchestra performed regularly at New York's Biltmore Hotel in 1920, and he made a number of Latin recordings for Victor Records. He relocated to San Francisco about 1923, then in 1926, NBC hired him to be the music director for the new network it was forming on the West Coast. In addition to conducting the NBC Orchestra and Opera Company, his violin was heard on West Coast programs such as the *Shell Happy Time Program* and *Don Amaizo, the Golden Violinist.* Above, Dolin conducts the NBC Orchestra in studio A at 111 Sutter Street in San Francisco. (Above, author's collection; left, *Stars of the Radio*, 1932.)

Don E. Gilman (left) was the Western Division manager of NBC in San Francisco in the 1930s. Gilman was recruited from a local advertising agency to head the operation in 1927. He was one of the best-known advertising men in the West and had been president of the Pacific Advertising Clubs Association. He is seen here with O.D. Fisher, the owner of NBC's Seattle affiliate KOMO. (Author's collection.)

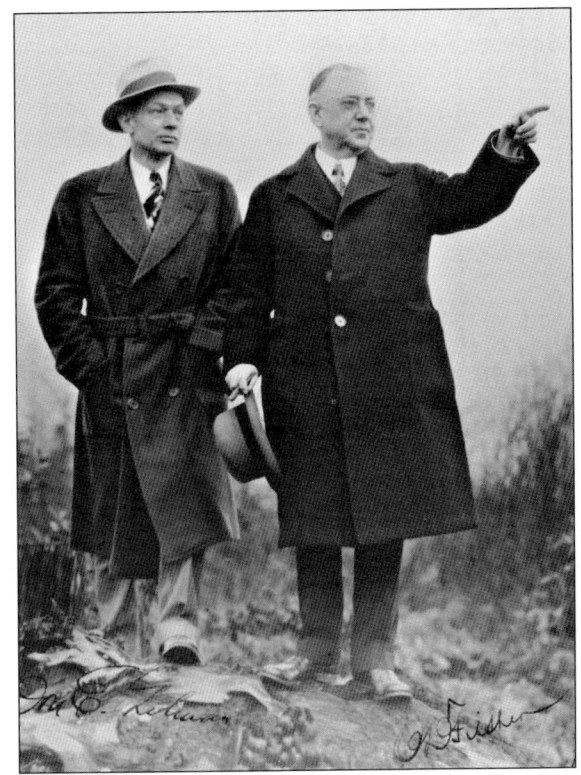

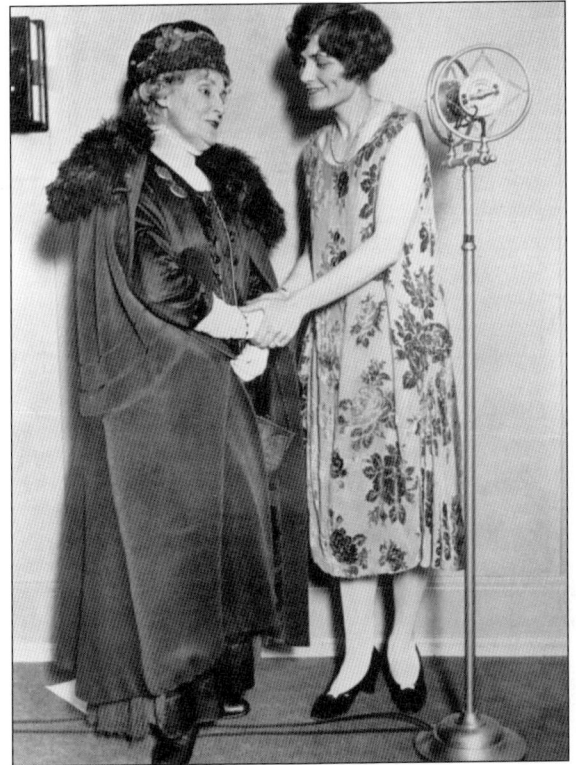

Wilda Wilson Church (left) was a pioneer radio drama producer. An English teacher and dramatic instructor at a private girls' high school in Berkeley, she was recruited by KRE to produce radio drama in 1922. She honed her talents at KRE and KGO before joining NBC as a dramatic program producer. She produced more radio dramatic programs than anyone else on the West Coast up to that time. (Author's collection.)

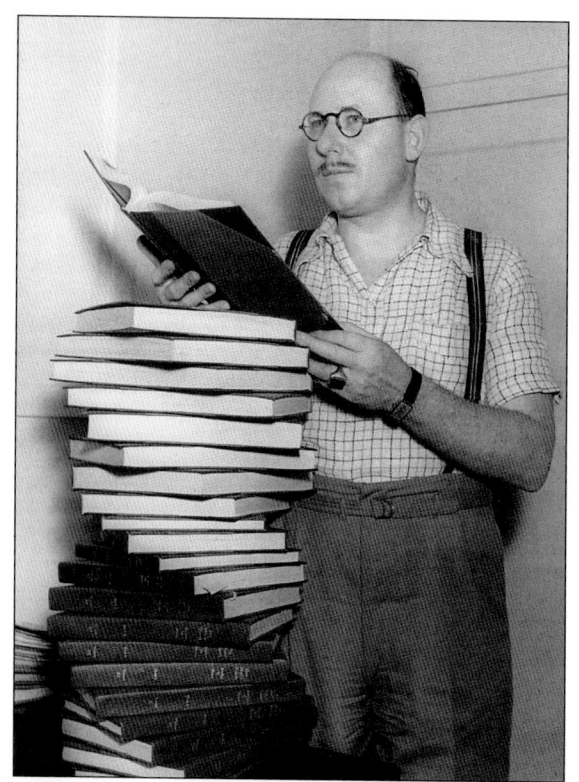

Carleton E. Morse (left) was the creator and author of *One Man's Family*, the most popular program ever to originate from San Francisco. Morse joined NBC in 1929, writing radio drama and action shows. He created *One Man's Family* as counterpoint to the high drama of his other programs. It debuted on April 29, 1932, on KPO and the Pacific Coast Network and remained on the air for 27 years. Morse also created the popular series *I Love a Mystery*. Below, *One Man's Family* is broadcast from studio C in San Francisco in 1934. Shown, from left to right, are Kathleen Wilson ("Claudia"), Barton Yarbrough ("Clifford"), Bill Andrews (announcer), Ed Ludes (sound effects), Bernice Berwin ("Hazel"), Mike Raffetto ("Paul Barbour"), Minetta Ellen ("Mother Barbour"), Page Gilman ("Jack"), and J. Anthony Smythe ("Father Barbour"). (Left, Carleton Morse; below, author's collection.)

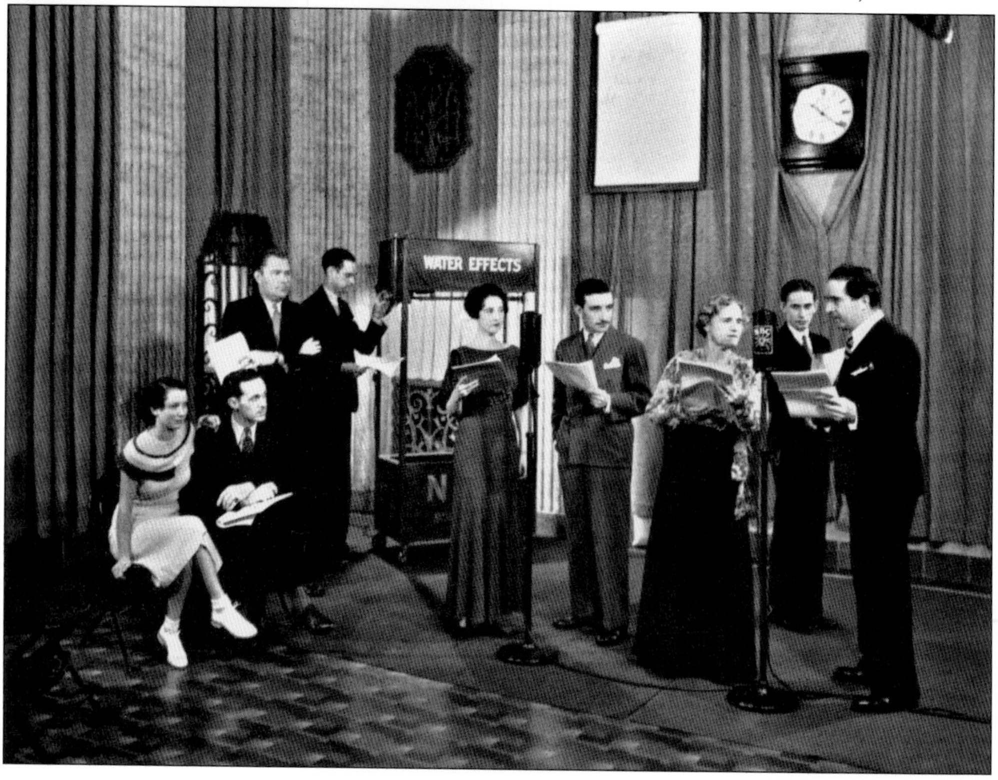

Radio actor Mike Raffetto played the role of Paul Barbour on *One Man's Family*. In later years, Raffetto also served as a substitute writer and director when Carleton Morse was away. Raffetto also played the role of Jack Packard on Morse's other big radio hit, *I Love a Mystery*. (Author's collection.)

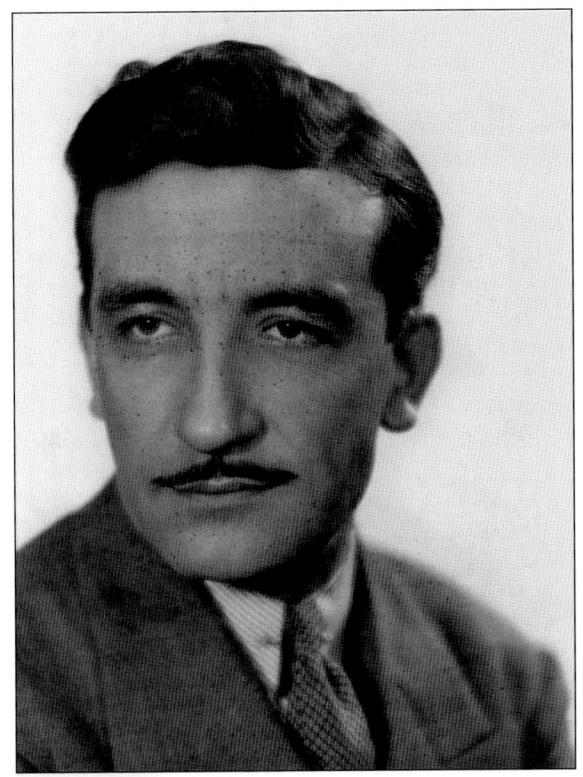

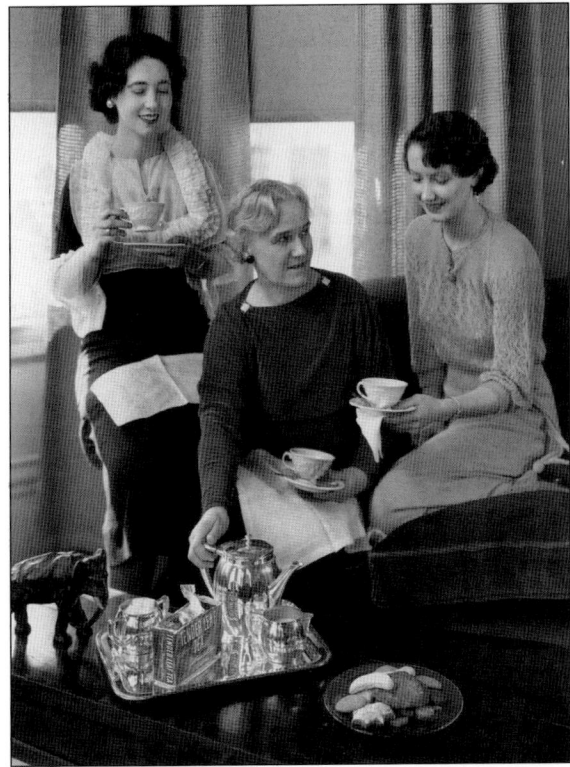

The women of the *One Man's Family* cast are pictured. From left to right are Bernice Berwin ("Hazel"), Minetta Ellen ("Mother Barbour"), and Kathleen Wilson ("Claudia"). Berwin was introduced to the theater while attending the University of California, Berkeley, and then she was an early participant in the *KGO Players* drama company. She joined NBC in 1928 and played a variety of roles before being tapped by Morse for the role of Hazel. (Gimmy Park Li.)

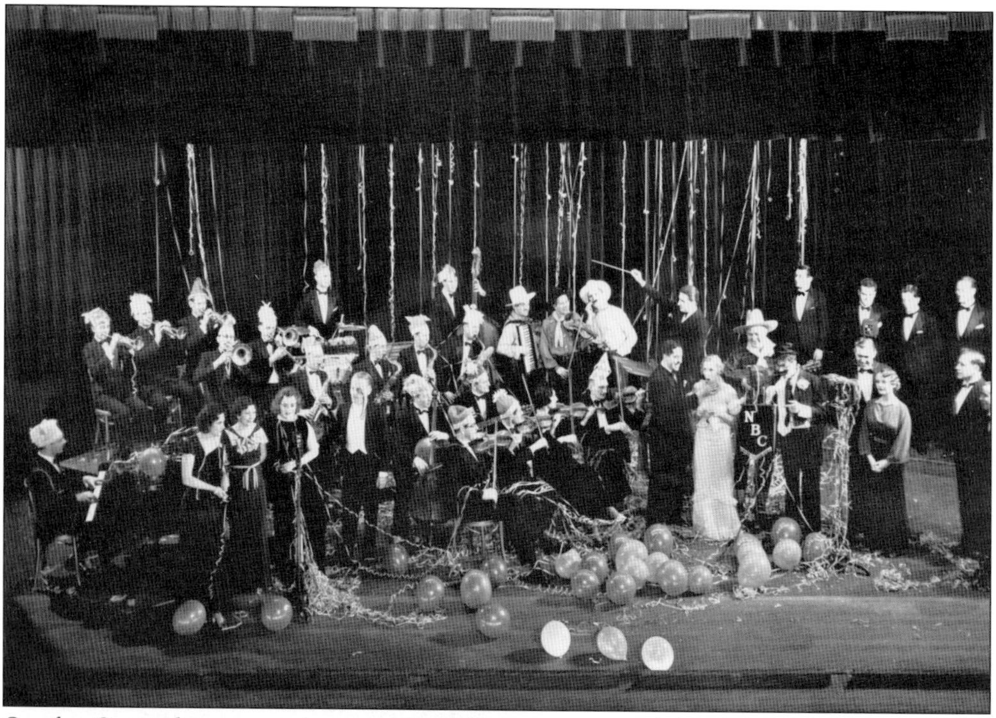

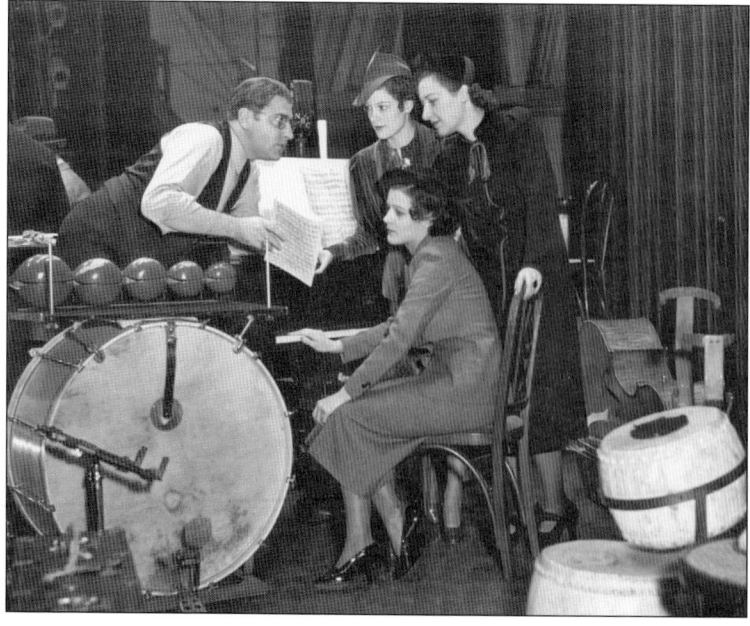

Carefree Carnival was a popular program of Western music and skits heard nationwide starting in 1934. It was performed in front of a live audience at the Marines' Memorial Theatre, hosted by Western singer Charlie Marshall. In the 1936 photograph above, Marshall is behind the microphone in his Western hat while Meredith Willson conducts the orchestra. Willson, who left KFRC to be NBC's second Pacific Coast music director in 1932, is seen below during a rehearsal with the Williams Sisters. On the left and standing is Laura Williams, on the right is Alice Sizer, and sitting is Ethelyn Williams. (Above, author's collection; below, David Alexander.)

Elmore Vincent started at KJR in Seattle in 1929 as part of the *Mardi Gras Gang*, singing lumberjack songs with yodel arrangements. At KJR, he developed a comedy routine for the word-mangling "Senator Frankenstein Fishface," a friend of "the Pee-Pul." NBC loved the act and persuaded Vincent to move to San Francisco to join the cast of *Carefree Carnival*, where his routine became a nationwide hit. (Author's collection.)

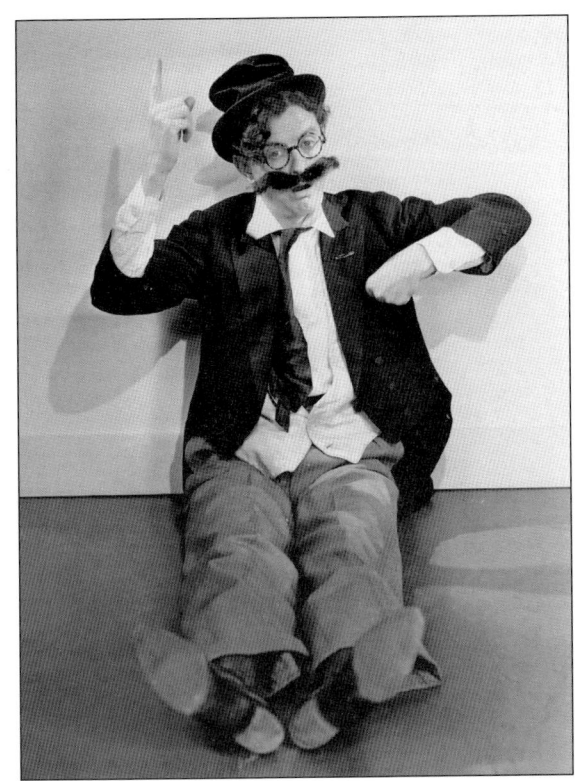

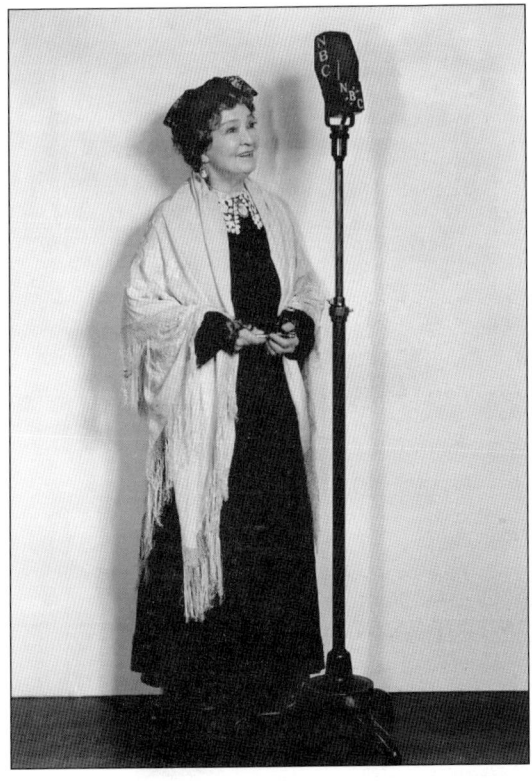

Olive West, a veteran stage and radio actress, played the role of Grandma Liston on the NBC serial *Hawthorne House*, written by San Francisco's premier radio writer, Sam Dickson. The program was heard on the West Coast over NBC from 1935 until the mid-1940s, sponsored by Wesson Oil and Snowdrift. West's little old lady character had a pungent philosophy that won an intimate place in the hearts of *Hawthorne House* listeners. (Author's collection.)

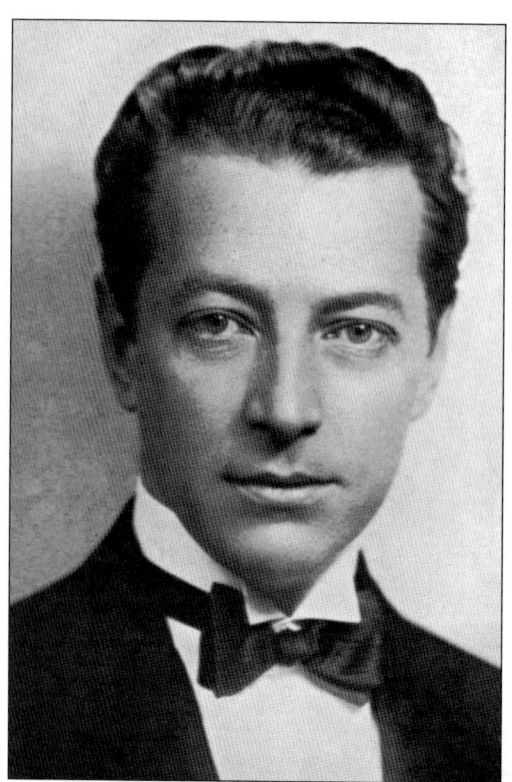

Paul Carson was the creator of the popular Pacific Coast program *Bridge to Dreamland*. It featured Carson playing organ music and reading his wife's poetry. He was also the organist on a variety of other early network programs, including Carleton E. Morse's two epic shows, *I Love a Mystery* and *One Man's Family*. He composed the latter show's theme song, *Waltz Patricia*. (*Stars of the Radio*, 1932.)

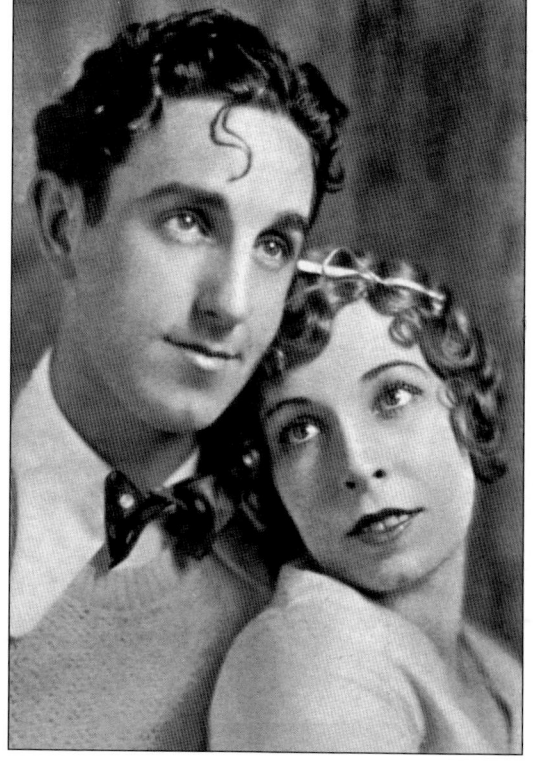

"Cecil" and "Sally" were the air names of Johnny Patrick and Helen Troy, who developed a comedy routine while working at KYA. The serial *Cecil and Sally* debuted on Seattle's short-lived ABC network before moving to NBC in 1929. It was also syndicated nationally via disk recordings. Troy's character endeared herself to listeners with her girlish lisp, referring to her partner as "Theethil." (*Stars of the Radio*, 1932.)

George Mardikian (1903–1977) was an Armenian-born restaurateur, chef, author and philanthropist who opened the well-known Omar Khayyam's restaurant in San Francisco in 1938. He broadcast the 15-minute dining show *Dinner at Omar Khayyam's* on KPO every day at noon during the 1940s. Mardikian became friends with NBC's George Snell and Floyd Farr, which later led them to become life-long business partners when they opened KEEN in San Jose. Below, announcer Budd Heyde dines on the air with George Mardikian during a live broadcast of *Dinner at Omar Khayyam's*. Heyde is third from the left; Mardikian is in the chef's hat at right. (Right, courtesy Eyria Amirian; below, Caryl Heyde Saunders.)

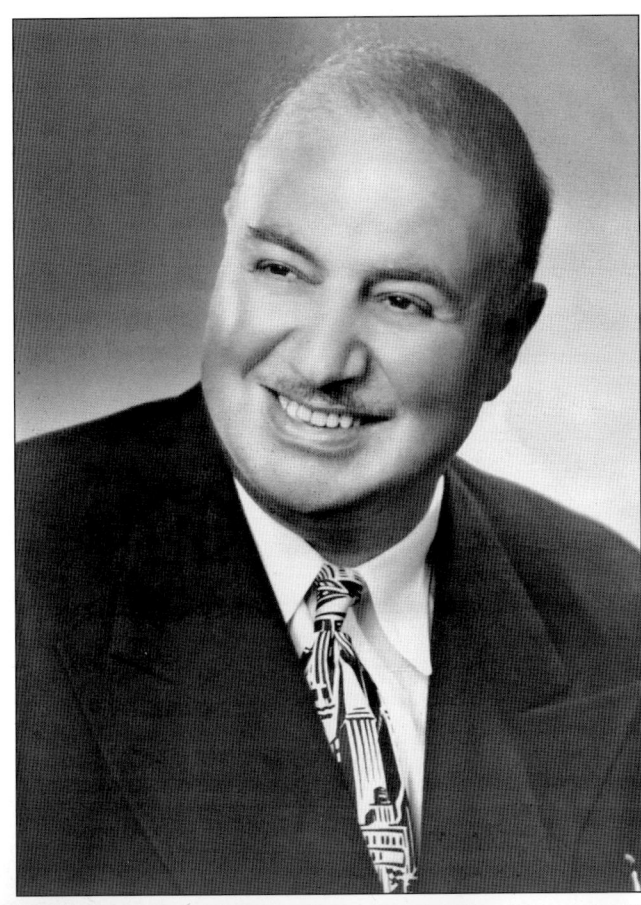

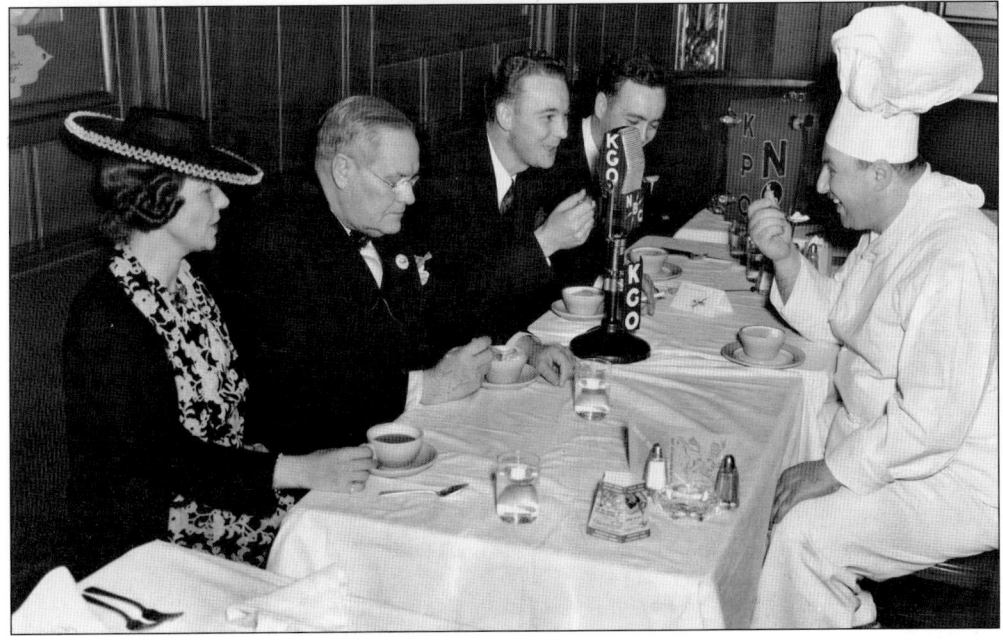

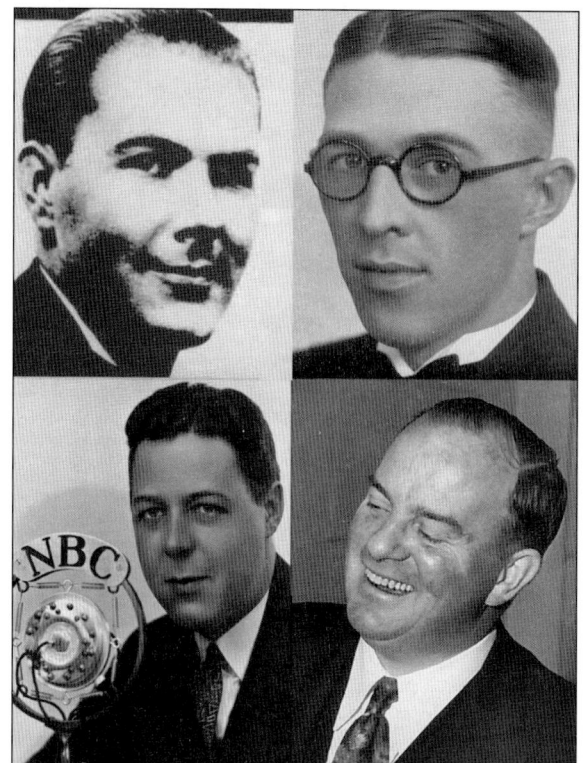

Pictured here are some early NBC Pacific Coast network announcers. Starting clockwise from the top left is Bill Andrews, NBC-Pacific's first announcer, who was hired away from KLX in 1926; Cecil Underwood, from KHQ in Spokane, hosted the *Associated Spotlight*; Bennie Walker was host of the KPO morning show *Women's Magazine of the Air* which moved to the Pacific Coast Network in the 1930s; and Jack Keough was a KPO announcer and children's program host before joining NBC as an announcer and sportscaster. (Andrews and Walker, author's collection; Underwood, Stars of Radio; Keough, Gimmy Park Li.)

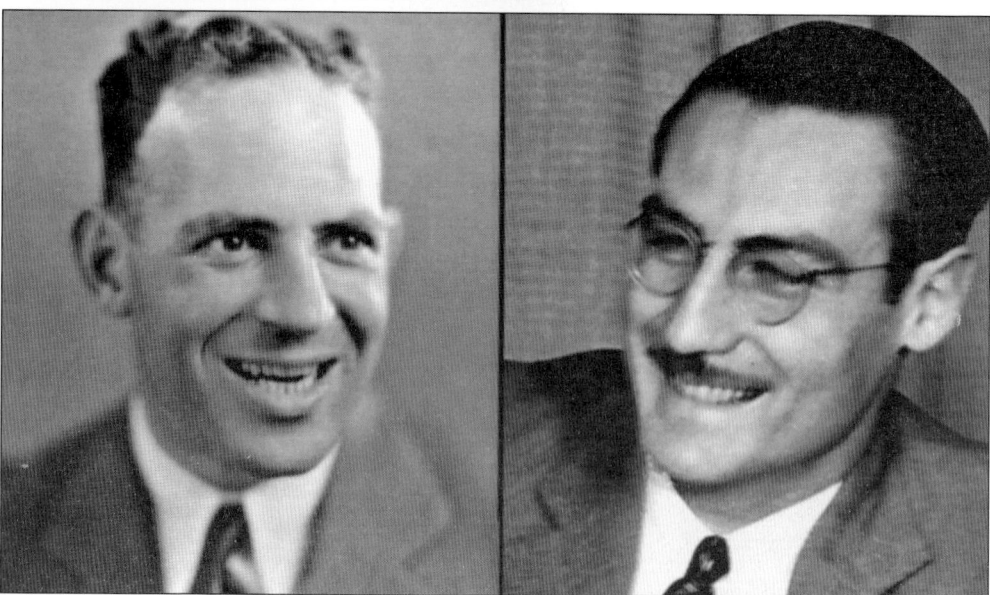

Examiner sports writer Ernie Smith (left) joined KYA in 1926, where he was heard on the short-lived ABC network and then on NBC. His enthusiastic, detailed descriptions of San Francisco Seals baseball games and other events won him a loyal following. At right, panic struck during a 1928 football broadcast when the regular sportscaster failed to show up, spotter Don Thompson stepped in and gave a great performance, leading to a lifetime career at NBC. (Left, author's collection; right, Bill Newbrough.)

Floyd Farr announces a coast-to-coast network feed from NBC's San Francisco studios in the late 1930s. Farr started at KLO in Ogden and then joined KDYL in Salt Lake City. NBC executives heard Farr on KDYL and offered him a job in 1935. Within months, he was appointed chief announcer. Farr left NBC in 1947 to become a partner and general manager at KEEN in San Jose. (Keith Farr.)

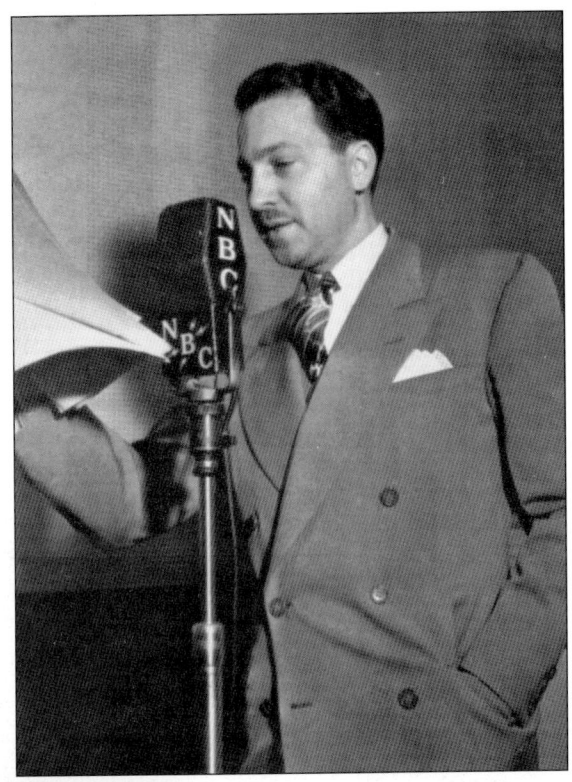

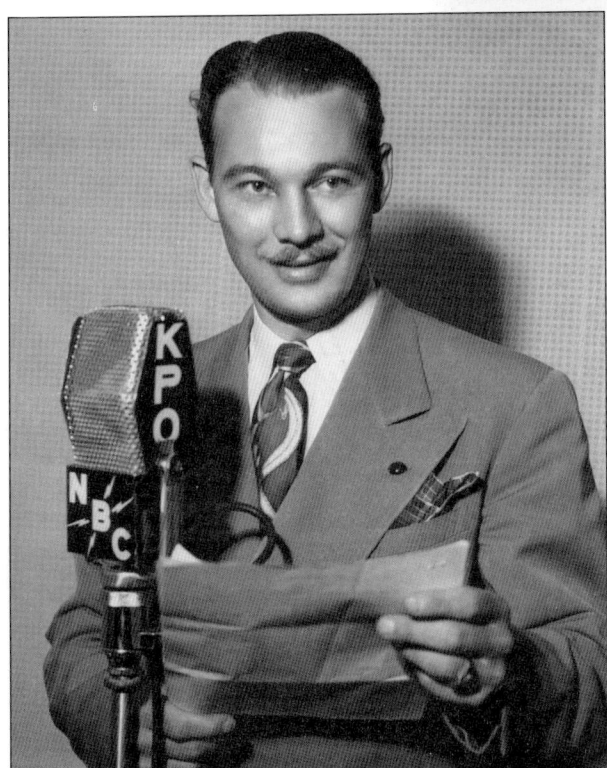

Announcer Budd Heyde was a music major who planned to make a career as a theater organist. But when he graduated from college, talking pictures had replaced most theater organists, so Heyde instead became a radio announcer. Versatile and talented, Heyde hosted a variety of programs from children's shows to historical dramas. His career with KPO, KNBC, and KNBR spanned three decades. (Caryl Heyde Saunders.)

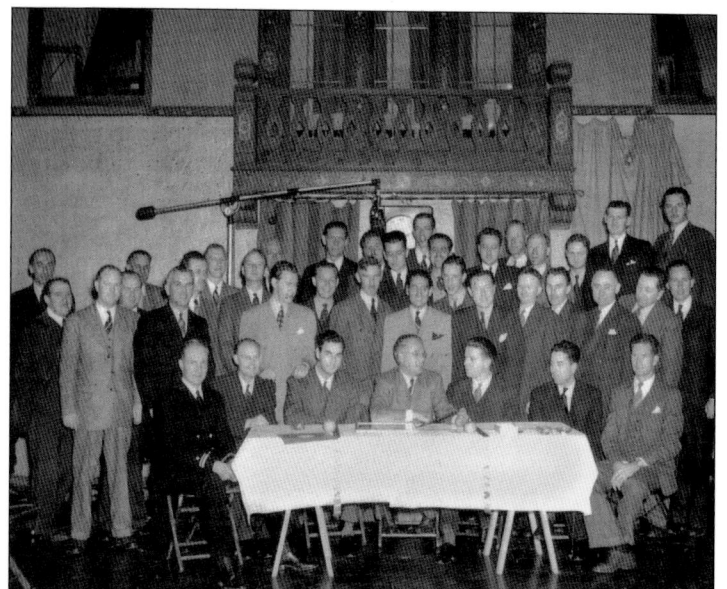

Announcers, engineers, and other staff of NBC San Francisco assemble in studio A at 111 Sutter Street in 1941. The occasion was announcer Bill Wood's last day before entering active service as Lt. J.G. Bill Wood. Several men from NBC New York are in the photograph, perhaps because of the concurrent construction of the NBC Radio City building. (Broadcast Legends.)

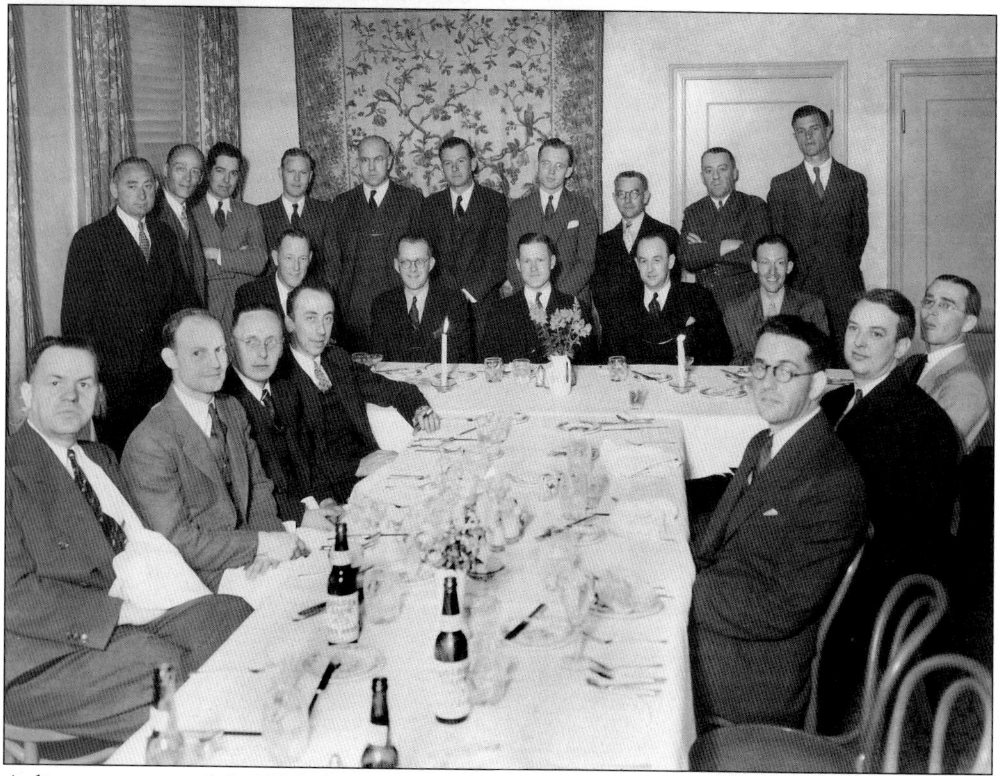

A dinner meeting of the NBC Association of Technical Employees at the Lake Merritt Hotel on May 8, 1936, includes the following, from left to right: (seated) Tom Watson, Oscar Berg, James Ball, George McElwain, Joseph Baker, Albert Saxton, E.C. Callahan, Lester Cully, Ray Ferguson, Aubrey Fisher, Orin Brown, and Walter Kellogg; (standing) Guy Cassidy, Edgar Parkhurst, George Greaves, Warren Andresen, Edward Poage, William McAulay, George Maher Jr., Albert Evans, Edward Manning, and David Atkins. (Bill Newbrough.)

Donald DeWolf of the NBC Plant Department prepares to leave 111 Sutter Street with the equipment for another remote broadcast. Here, he says goodbye to NBC actress Helen Musselman. Of interest in this photograph is the large parabolic reflector, which was probably used for the directional microphone pickup of a sporting event. (Bill Newbrough.)

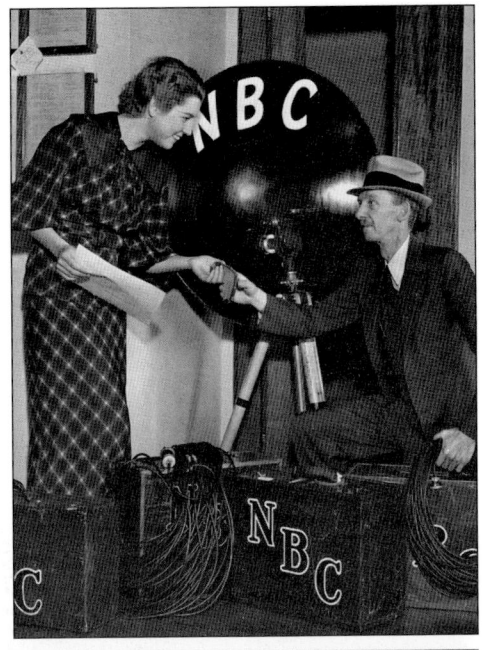

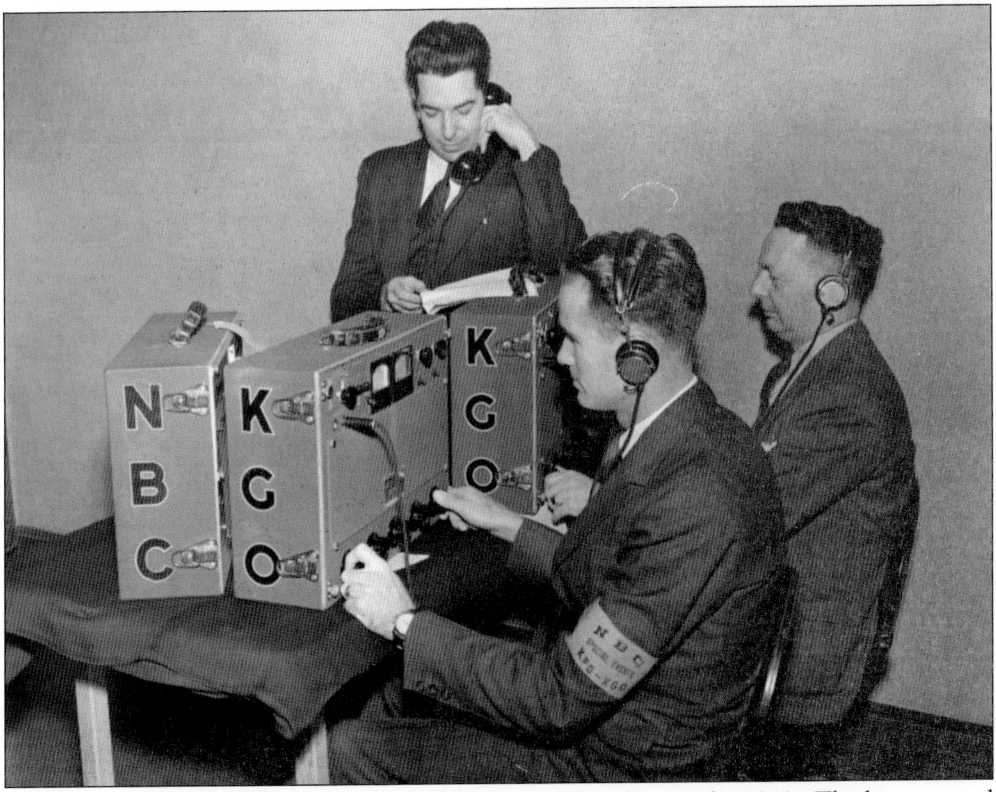

Here is another view of an NBC remote broadcast taking place in the 1940s. The location and event are unknown. The engineer operating the "portable" microphone mixer at left is Ernie Jefferson, and the engineer on the right is G.B. Dewing. The man on the telephone is George Greaves. (Bill Newbrough.)

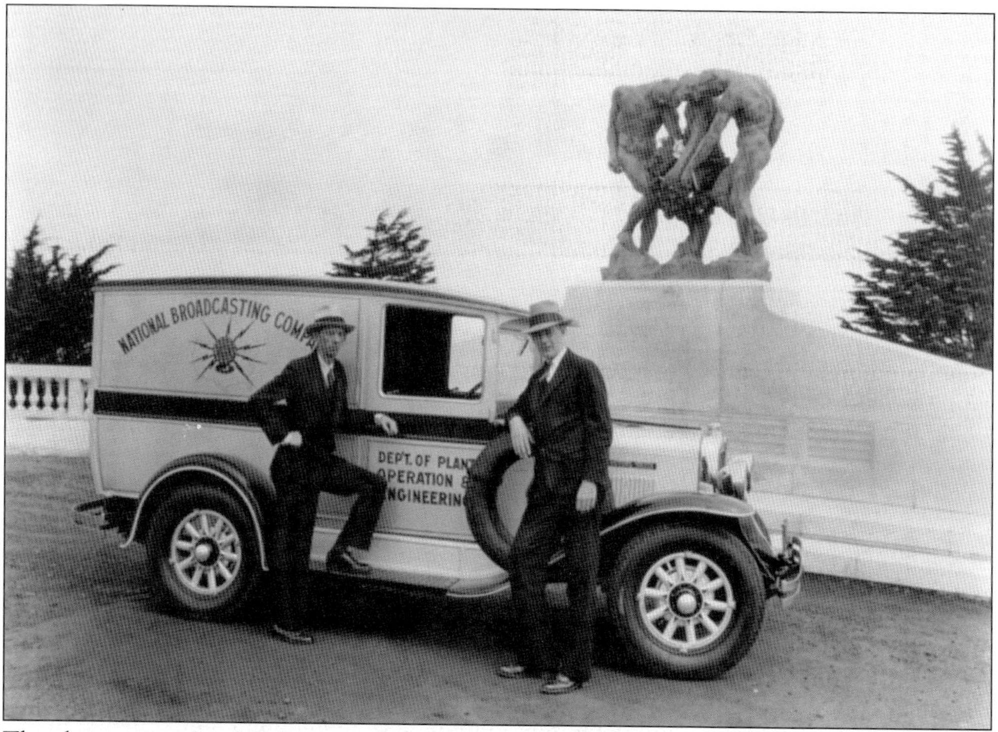

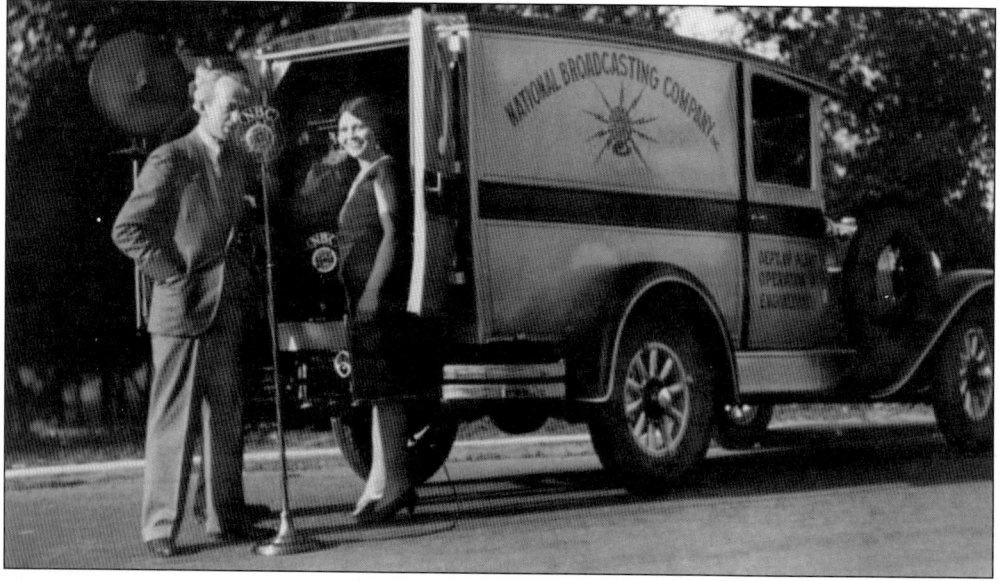

The above view of an NBC remote broadcast truck was taken outside the California Palace of the Legion of Honor, San Francisco, in the early 1930s. These big General Motors trucks were NBC standard issue at all of their broadcast centers. Technicians Donald DeWolf and Alfred H. Saxton pose with the vehicle before the start of the broadcast. Below, NBC's West Coast music director Max Dolin announces the Palace of the Legion of Honor program. The microphones are all early-issue carbon mikes. The large remote amplifier seen in the back of the vehicle would have been connected to telephone lines feeding the program back to the Sutter Street studios. (Both, Bill Newbrough.)

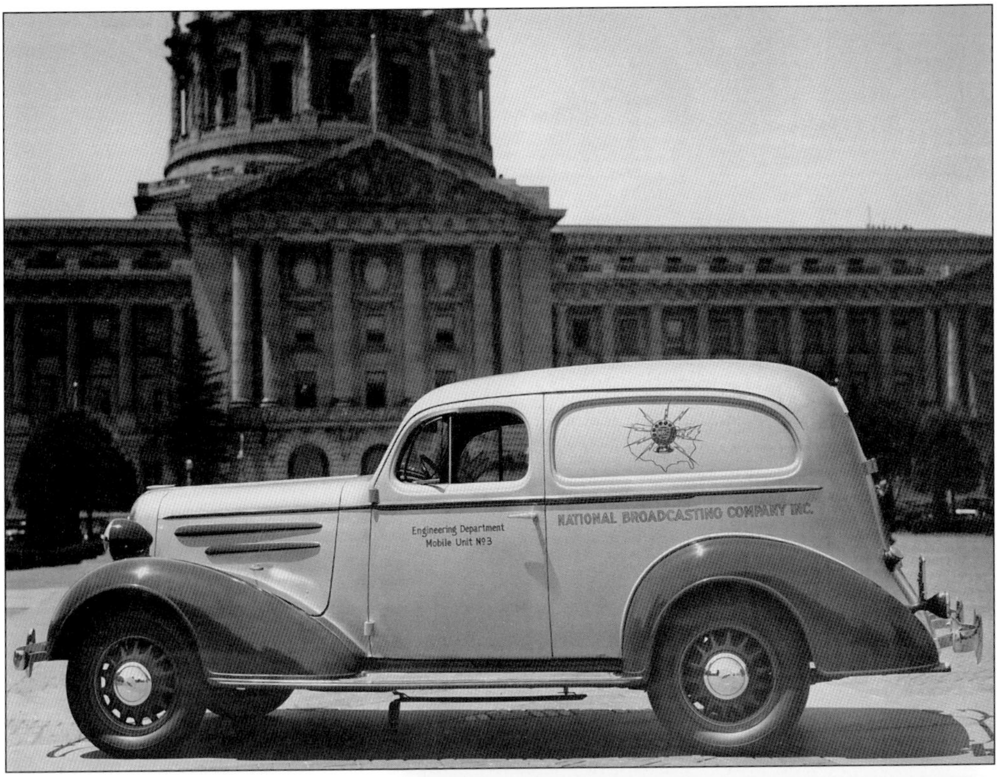

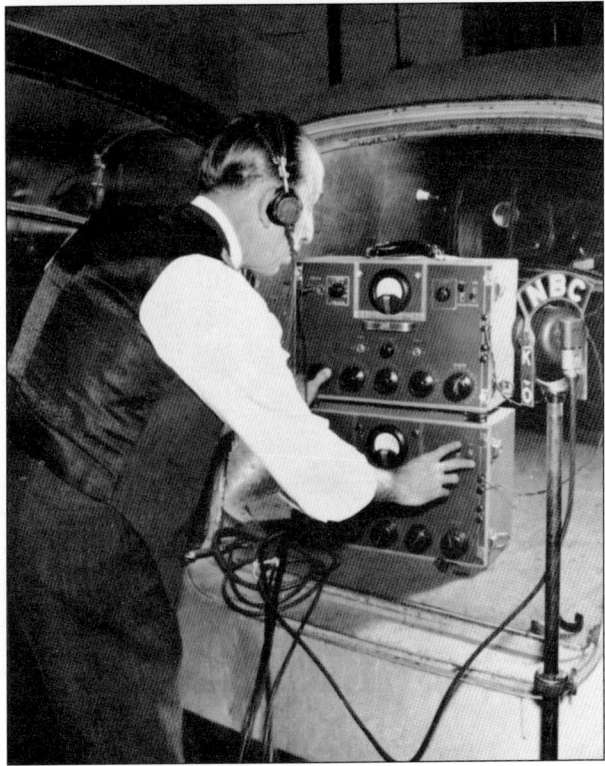

The above image of a later remote broadcast vehicle in front of San Francisco City Hall, dated August 17, 1936, shows the technical progress that was made in just a few short years. The new, smaller vehicle, referred to as Mobile Unit No. 3, was said to be a mobile studio on wheels—able to go anywhere an automobile could. At right, remote broadcast technician George McElwain runs the controls of a more compact broadcast mixer in the rear of Mobile Unit No. 3. The microphone shown is a newer RCA dynamic mike, whose greater ruggedness was important for field use. The vehicle was also equipped with a shortwave transmitter to enable wireless remote broadcasts. (Both, Bill Newbrough.)

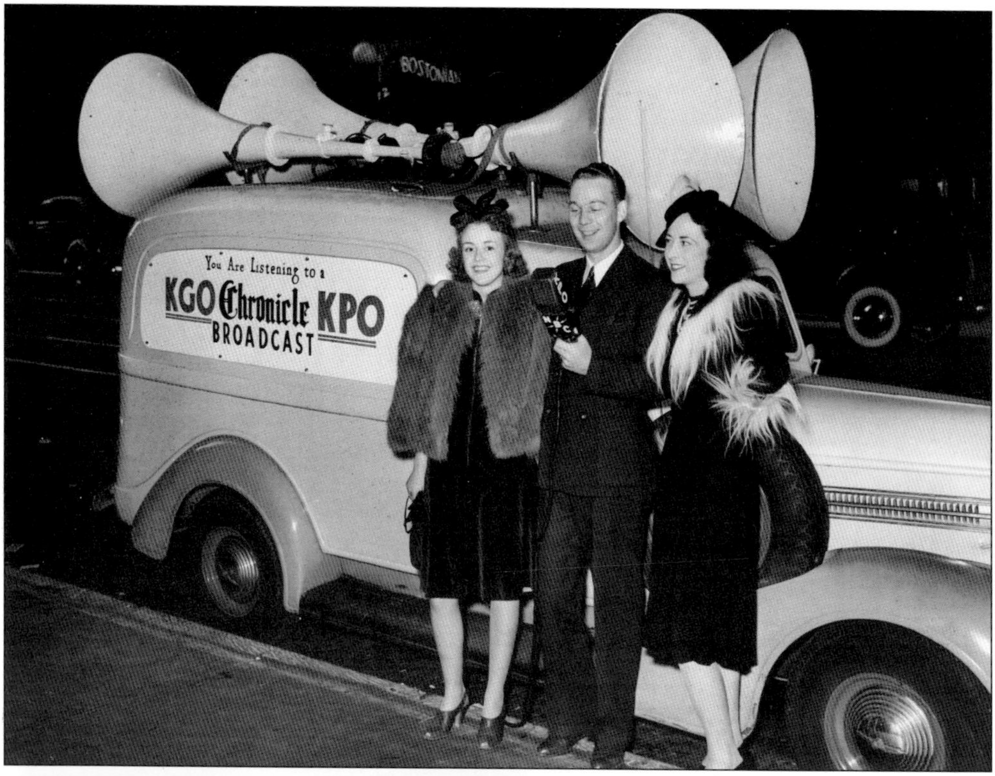

NBC announcer Budd Heyde stands in front of an NBC-*Chronicle* sound truck with radio actress Ruth "Susie Que" Sprague (left) and singer Helen Morgan. The photograph was taken in front of the NBC studios at 111 Sutter Street before an election night broadcast. The four large horn speakers on the roof of the vehicle allowed passers-by to listen to the live broadcast of the election results. (Caryl Heyde Saunders.)

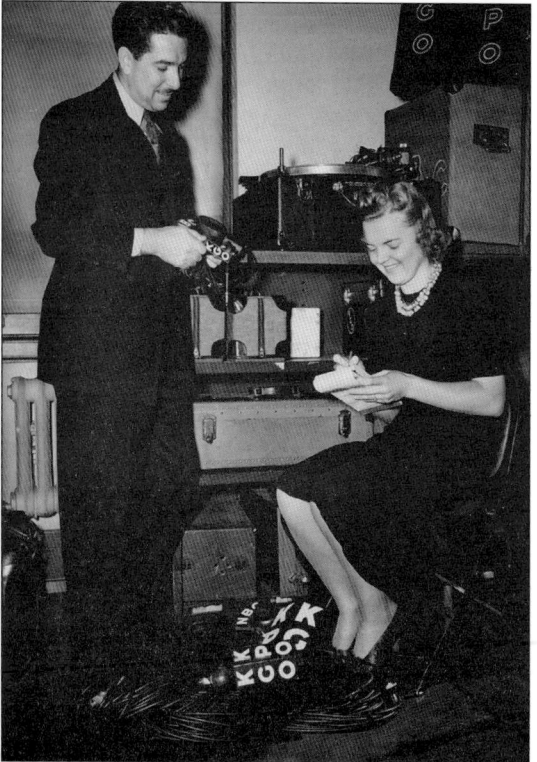

Remote broadcasts were a continuous fact of life for NBC's engineers and announcers. Here is chief studio engineer George Greaves and Marion Hanson taking inventory of NBC's remote broadcasting equipment at 111 Sutter Street. A number of microphones, cables, remote amplifiers, and even a portable recording disk lathe are visible. (Bill Newbrough.)

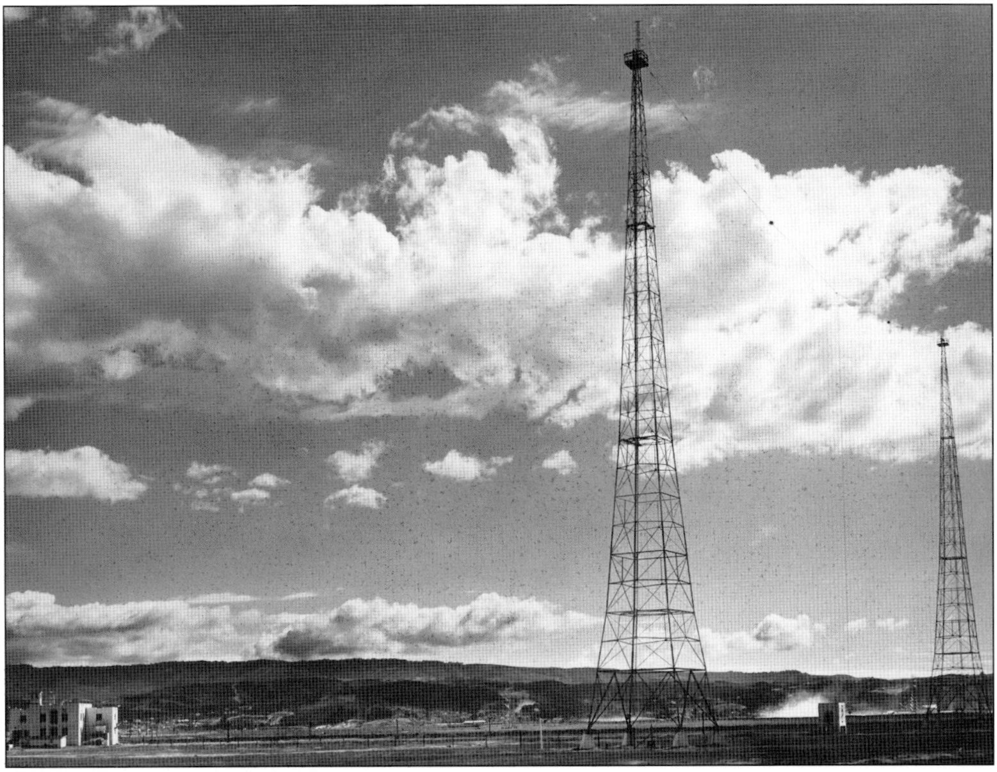

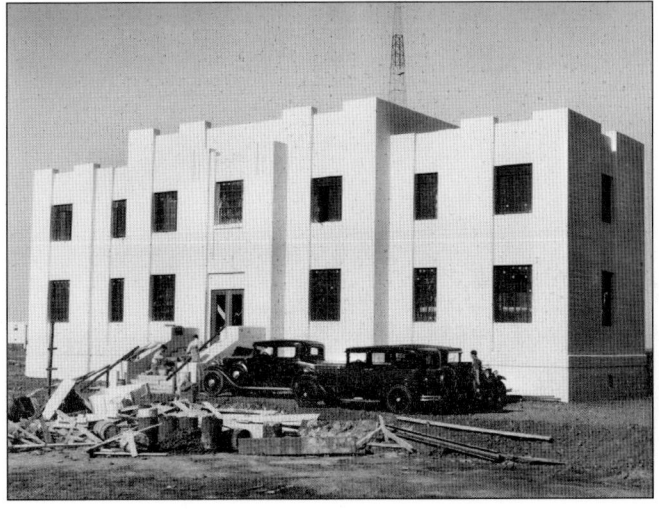

In 1932, KPO became just the second station on the Pacific Coast to be granted the power of 50,000 watts. NBC contracted with General Electric to build a brand-new site on the San Francisco Bay salt flats near Belmont. A view of the site (above) shows the T-style wire antenna supported between two self-supporting towers. The antenna was oriented east to west, giving KPO a strong signal up and down the coast. A two-story concrete building was built to house the big transmitter (below), which was on the second floor, along with an audio control room, shop, and living quarters. The first floor contained motor generators, batteries, transformers, water-cooling equipment, parts storage, a kitchen, and a garage. An outdoor water spray pond provided cooling for the water-cooled tubes. The building is still used today by KNBR. (Both, Bill Newbrough.)

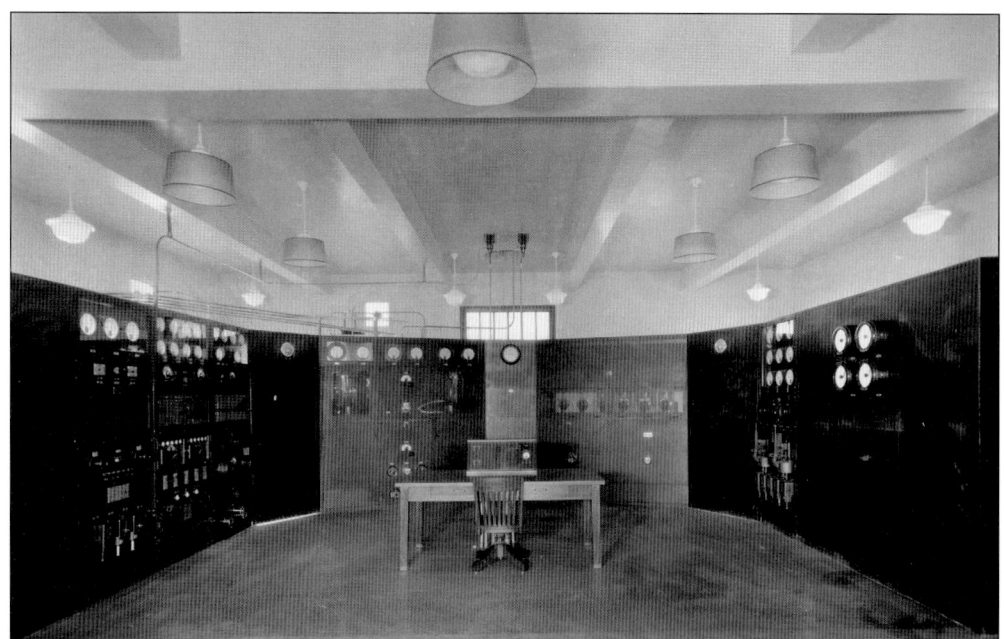

The above photograph shows the 50,000-watt KPO transmitter as originally installed by General Electric and is dated March 1933. The transmitter cabinets are arranged in a U-shape around a central control desk. On the left is a 5,000-watt transmitter, which served as the driver for the 50 kW power amplifier at left center. At center right are the mercury vapor rectifier tubes for the amplifier. The far right cabinets contain controls for the motor generators and water-cooling system pumps. Below is a view of the same transmitter in 1949, with chief transmitter engineer Joe Baker at the controls. NBC had instituted a policy that all of its stations must use only RCA equipment, but there was no desire to replace the big old transmitter. So, the station engineers just painted the transmitter and rebranded it as an RCA product! (Both, Bill Newbrough.)

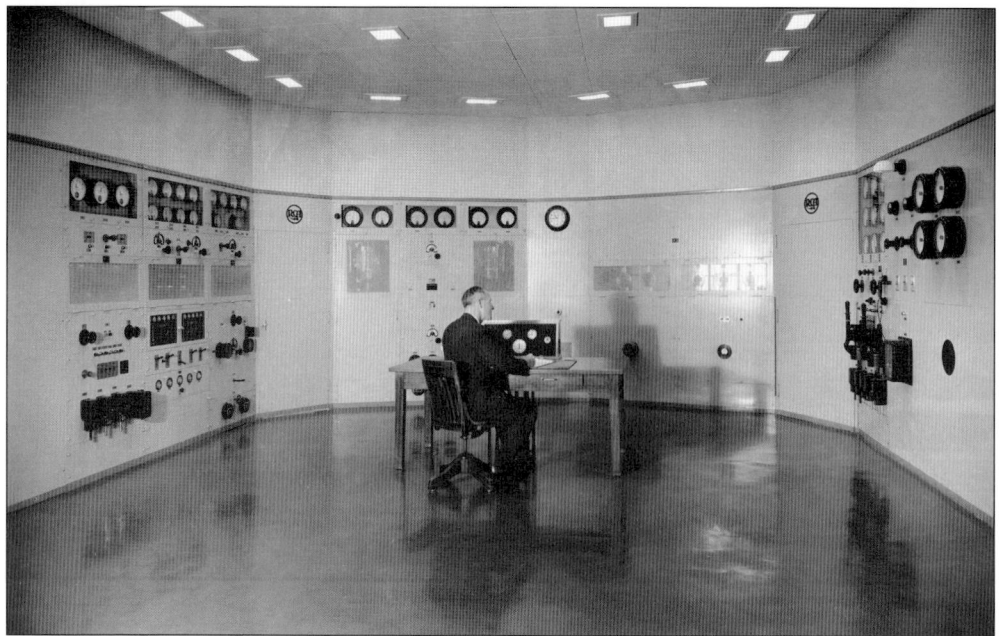

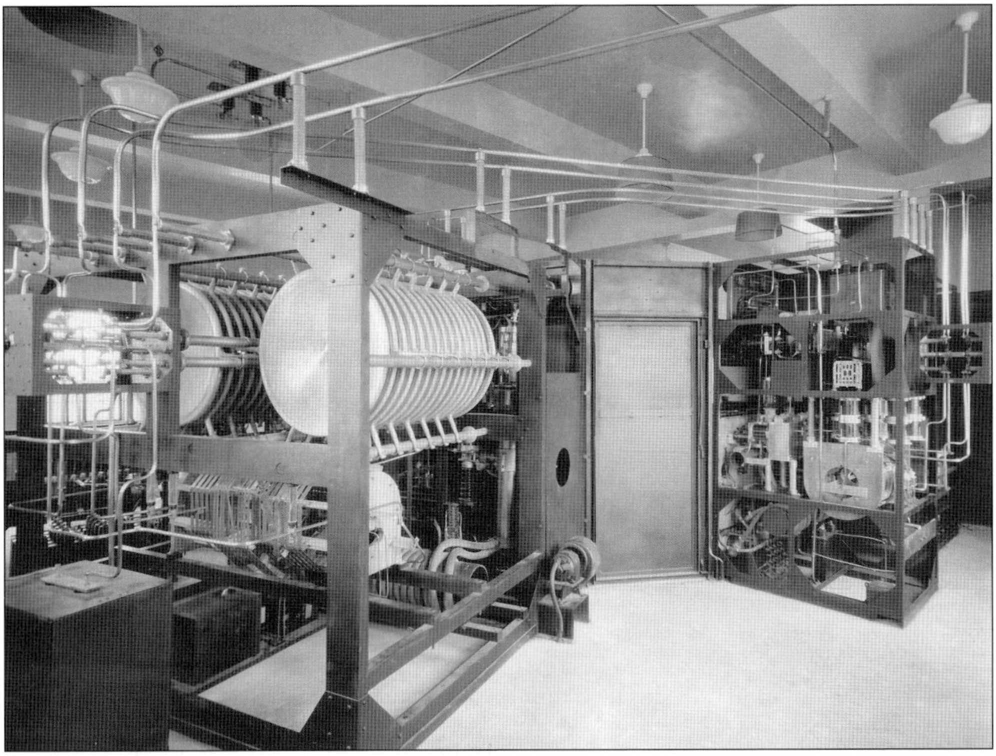

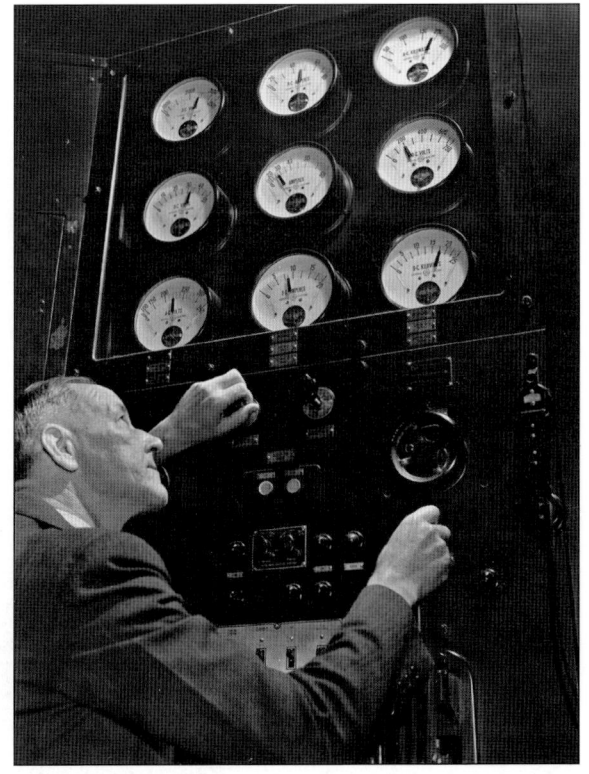

The monstrous GE transmitter was not exactly self-contained. The open-frame cabinets were placed in a semicircle inside the room. If one were to open a door on either end of the row of cabinets, he or she would be standing inside the transmitter. (Interlock switches would shut down the transmitter for protection.) This inside view shows the tank circuit tuning equipment, harmonic eliminator, antenna transfer switches (left), and the 5,000-watt driver (right). (Bill Newbrough.)

Chief engineer Joe Baker adjusts the power controls on KPO's 50 kW transmitter. The system consumed huge amounts of electrical power, especially by today's standards. The linear amplifiers were very inefficient. The tube filaments ran on DC voltage, which came from a duplicate set of motor generators on the first floor. All electrical power for the transmitter was controlled from this panel. (Bill Newbrough.)

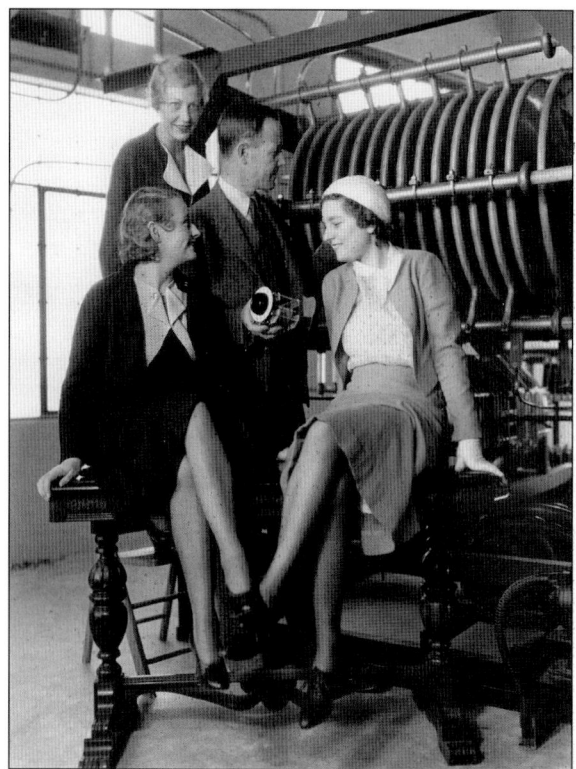

Joe Baker and NBC actresses Rita Lane, Anne Chase, and Helen Musselman pose inside the new transmitter in 1933. Baker is comparing the small capacitor in his hand to the big capacitor plates on the new transmitter. The silver-plated tubing over his head carries the 50,000-watt signal to the antenna. (Bill Newbrough.)

NBC division engineer Alfred H. Saxton shows actress and singer Helen Musselman one of the two large final amplifier tubes used in the KPO transmitter. She holds a small tube in her hands for comparison. The giant water-cooled tubes cost about $2,000 each in 1933 and had a life span of about five years. A small crane was required to remove the tubes from their sockets. (Bill Newbrough.)

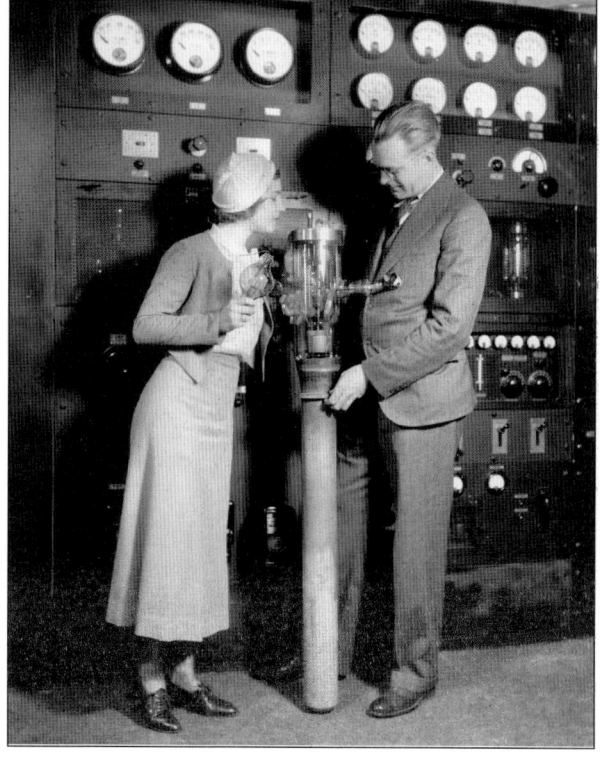

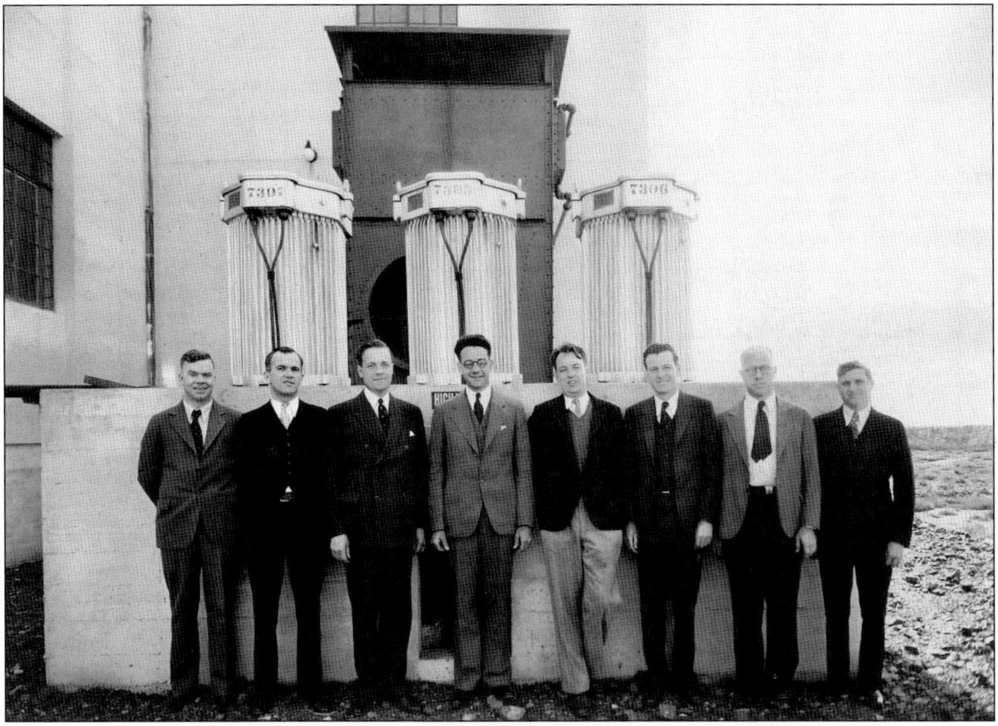

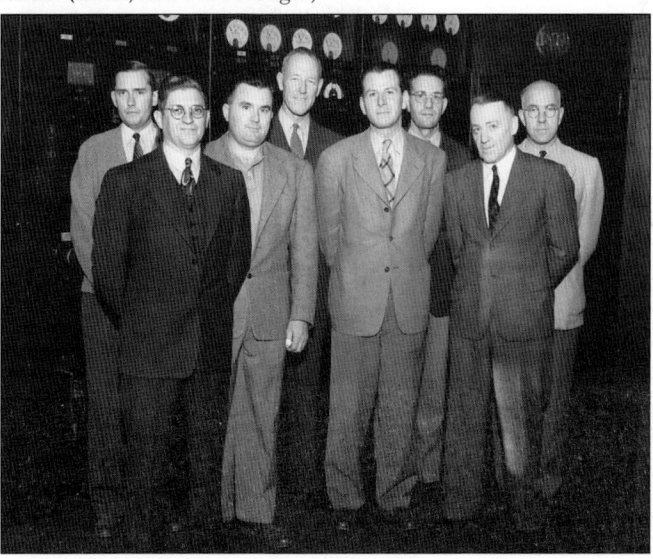

Here are two views of the technical staff that kept the Belmont transmitter plant humming. In the 1937 view above, they are standing in front of the big AC transformers that provided electrical service to the building, in front of the transmitter's giant heat exchanger. The indoor view below is dated 1941. Two operators were on duty at all times, 24 hours a day. Their tasks included operating the transmitter, adjusting the audio level, maintaining a typewritten log of all programs that were broadcast and maintaining all the equipment in the huge facility. Operators worked three eight-hour shifts, which rotated weekly. An operator would work five days on the 8 a.m. shift, then after two days off he would work on the 4 p.m. shift and then the following week on the midnight shift. (Both, Bill Newbrough.)

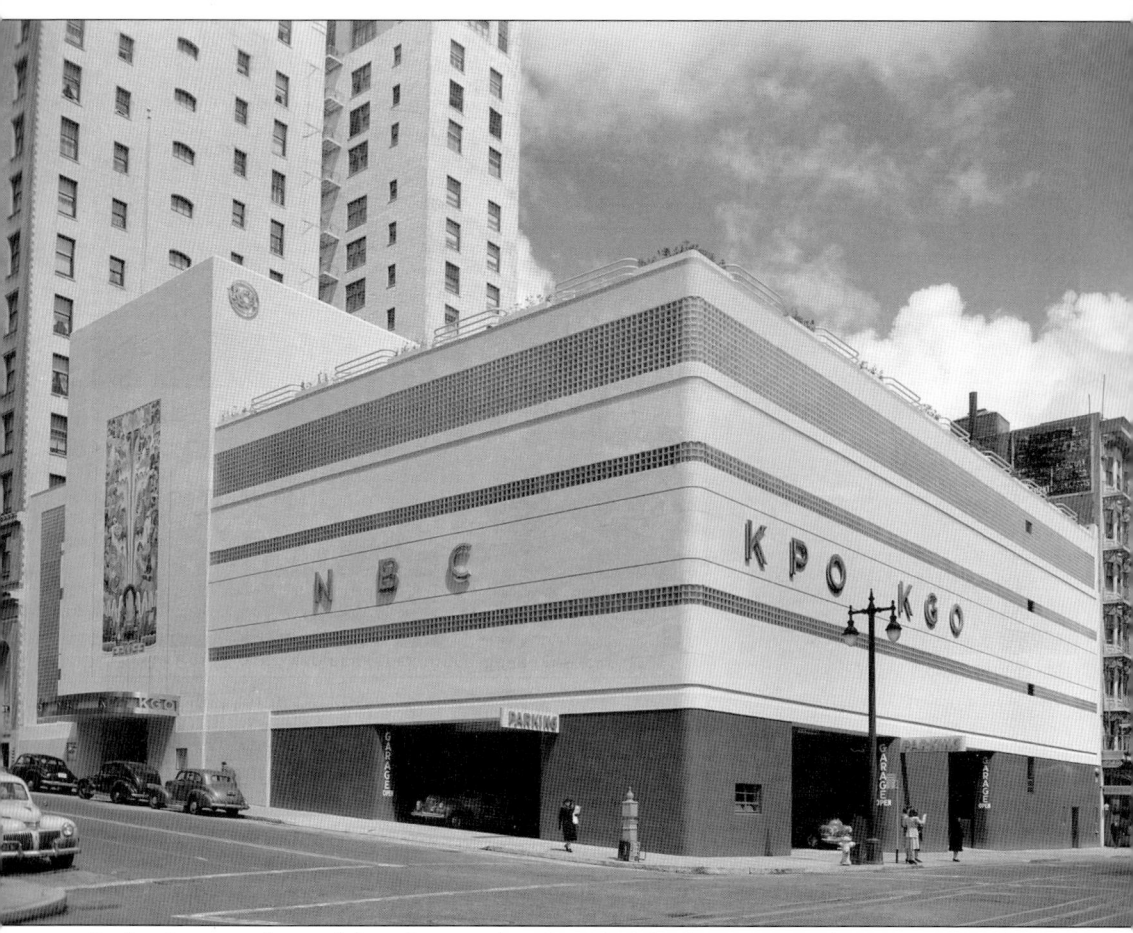

Radio City was the model studio complex that NBC built in 1942 at the corner of Taylor and O'Farrell Streets in San Francisco. While impressive in its architecture and state of the art, the building was a white elephant the day it opened its doors. New AT&T program lines to Southern California were making live broadcasts from Hollywood practical for the first time. Also, the big movie studios finally dropped their restrictions against their stars appearing on the radio. This started an exodus that saw virtually all West Coast network programming move to Hollywood within three years. By mid-decade, the big studios sat mostly empty, with the building being used just for disc jockey shows and an occasional live local program. KGO moved out in 1954 and KNBR (formerly KPO) left when NBC's 25-year lease expired in 1967. Radio City enjoyed a second life as the studios of KBHK television. Finally, after sitting unused for a few years, it received a major makeover and today is the headquarters of the ABM Corporation. (Author's collection.)

This ceramic mural, measuring 16 by 40 feet, towered over the entrance to the Radio City building above the main entrance marquee. Artist C.J. Fitzgerald designed the mosaic to represent the radio industry, using 126 different colors of tiles. NBC said it "symbolizes the vast extent of radio and the unlimited service it gives to all the lands and all the peoples of the earth." The mural was covered over with a large sign when KHBK-TV used the building as its studios during the 1970s and 1980s, but it was uncovered again in the early 1990s and can be enjoyed again today at the corner of Taylor and O'Farrell Streets. (Right, Bill Newbrough; below, author's collection.)

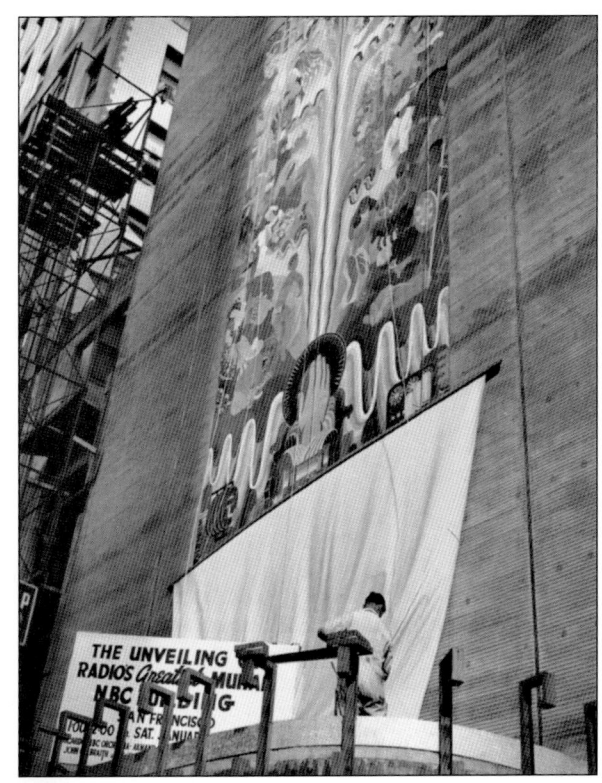

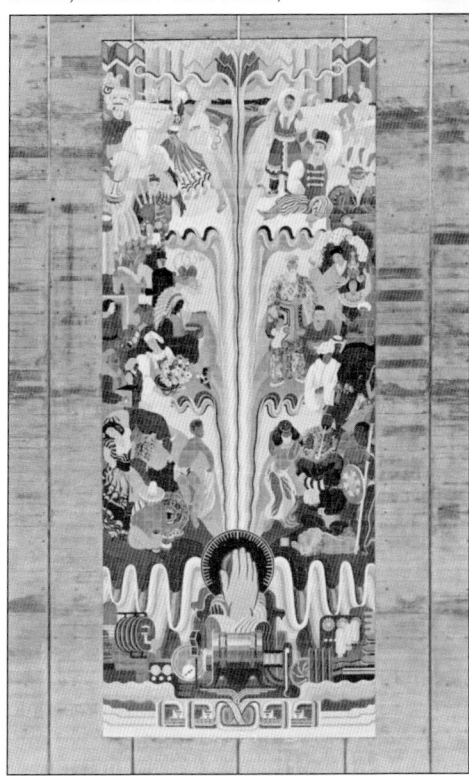

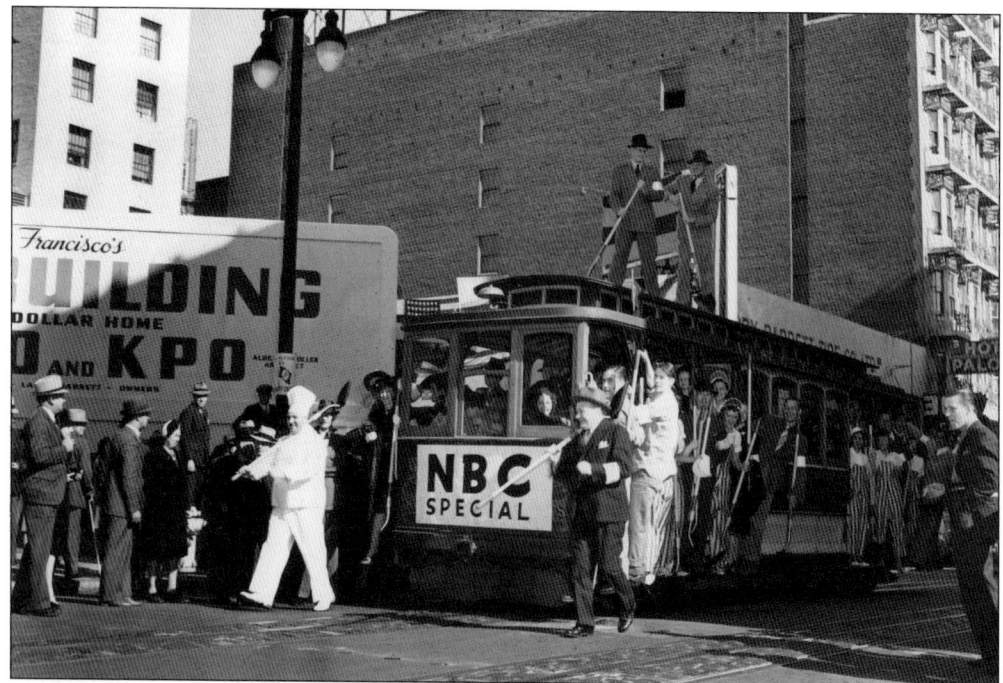

NBC turned Radio City's official 1941 ground-breaking into a big San Francisco event. Above, a cable car full of local NBC stars and Barnum and Bailey circus performers arrive at the new studio site. George Mardikian leads the way in his white chef's uniform. Below, Al Nelson, NBC's general manager in San Francisco, addresses the microphone during the live broadcast of the Radio City ground-breaking ceremony. NBC's vice president and chief engineer O.B. Hanson, from New York, is sixth from the left, and Budd Heyde (far left) and George Mardikian (wearing white) are on his right. The heads of the construction company and other officials also look on. (Caryl Heyde Saunders.)

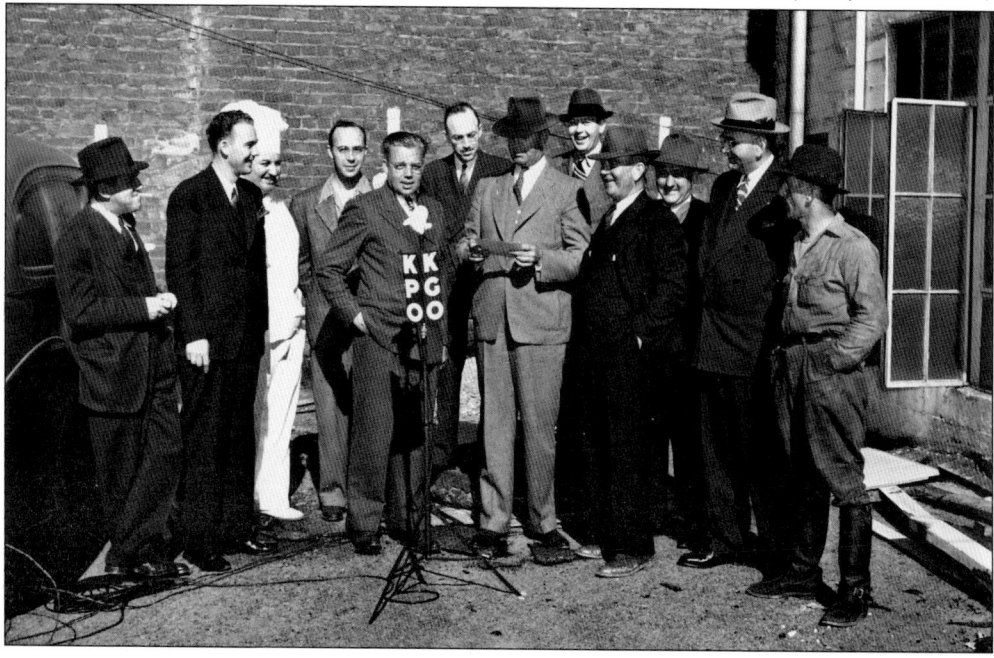

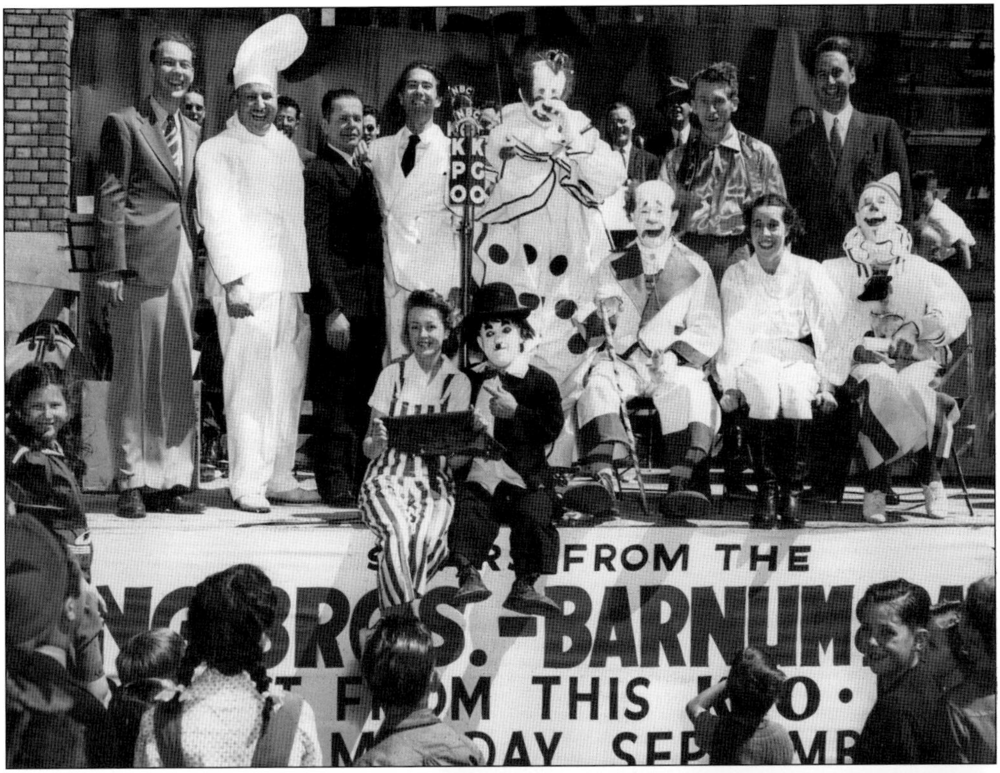

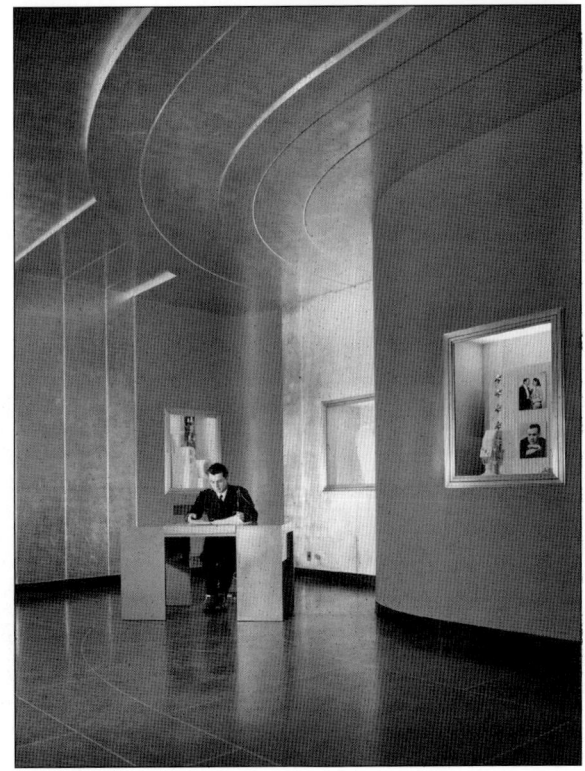

The Ringling Bros. and Barnum & Bailey Circus played in San Francisco September 8–10, 1941, and NBC took advantage of its presence to promote the studio's ground-breaking. Here, NBC stars and executives share the microphone with several circus performers for the live broadcast. The famous clown Felix Adler is at the center, and Budd Heyde and George Mardikian are at the far left. (Caryl Heyde Saunders.)

The spacious main lobby entrance to Radio City was decorated in gold, silver and Chinese red. Two elevators with Art Deco–engraved doors opened into the lobby. Beyond the elevators, a grand curved stairway flanked by illuminated curved glass block walls led up to the second floor studios. A receptionist sat at a desk near the entrance doors. (Bill Newbrough.)

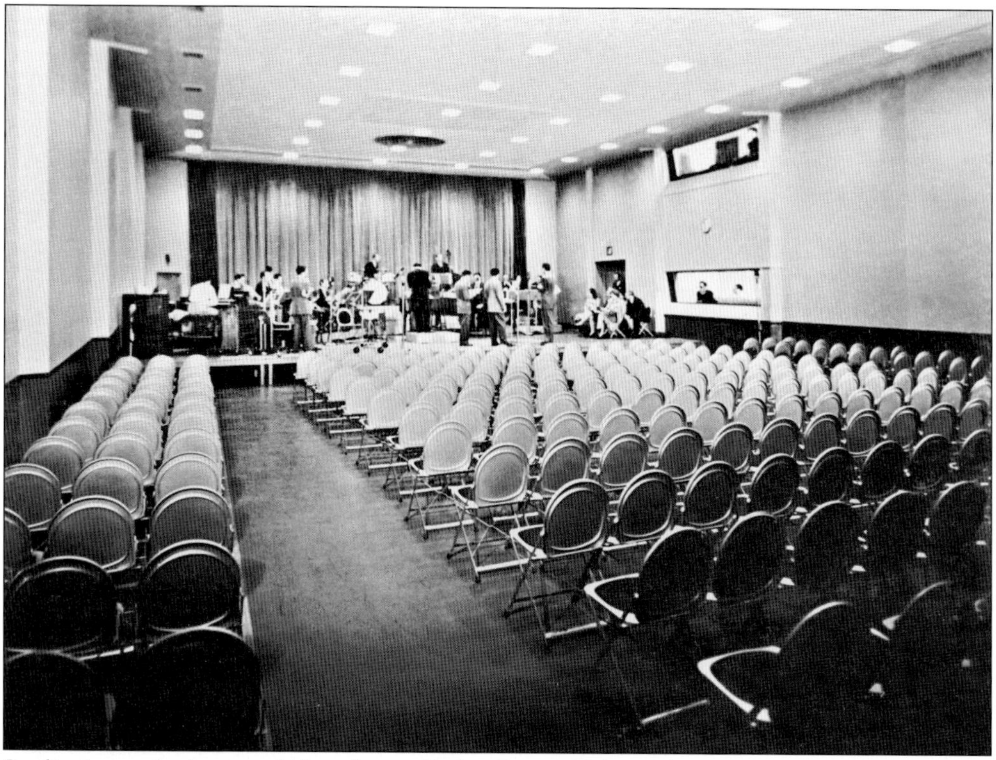

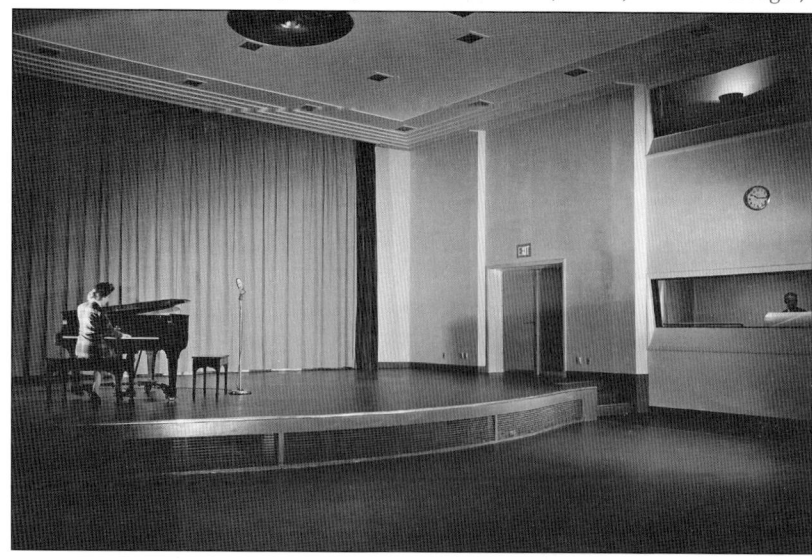

Studio A was the largest of 10 studios in Radio City at 73 by 41 feet, seating an audience of 425. The studio floors, interior walls, and ceilings were isolated from the building by springs. A program rehearsal is seen in progress in the view above. The room behind glass on the lower right is the control room, with the sponsors' booth located above it. Below is a close-up view of the stage, which was large enough to hold about 30 musicians. For a full orchestra, used during programs such as the *Standard School*, the musicians would sit in the audience area. This studio received very little use during the years NBC used the building. In later years, after KBHK-TV took over the facility, it became the main television studio. (Above, author's collection; below, Bill Newbrough.)

This was the control room operator's position for studio A. The producer sat at the operator's right. Each studio had its own control room, and the audio from these mixers was then routed to the master control room for assignment either to the network or the local KGO or KPO transmitters. (Bill Newbrough.)

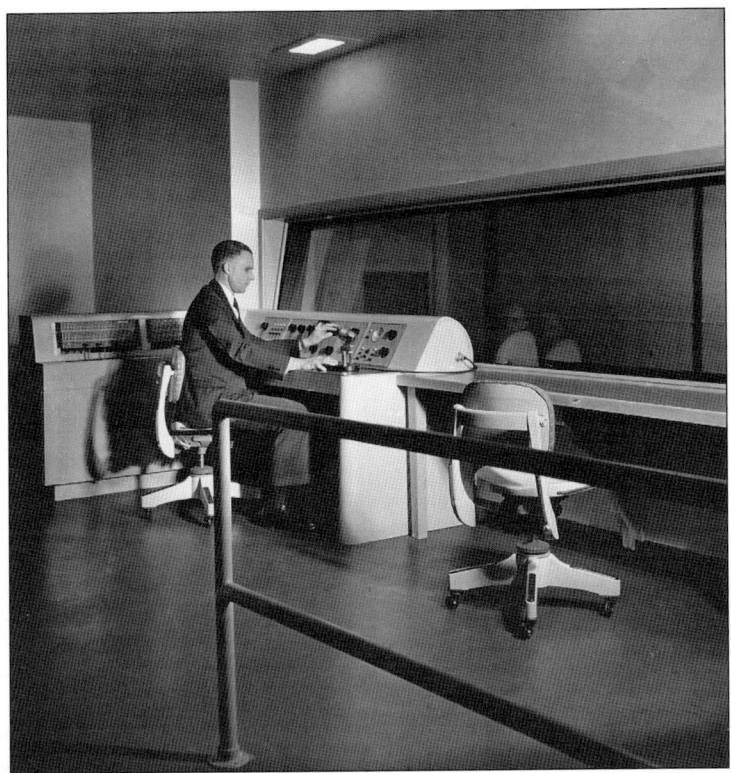

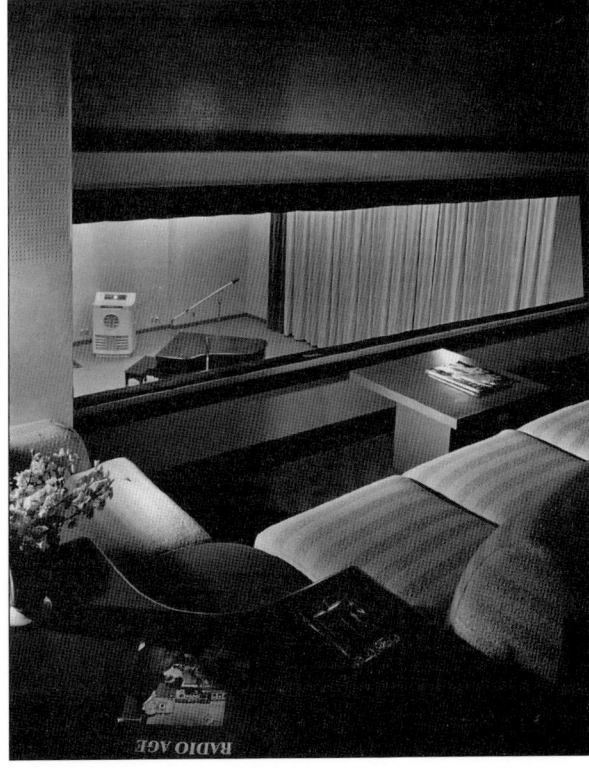

Studios A, B, and C each had sponsors' booths on the mezzanine level looking down into the studios. These were private booths where program sponsors or other VIP's could watch the live broadcasts. A boom microphone, grand piano, and massive monitor speaker can be seen in the studio below. (Bill Newbrough.)

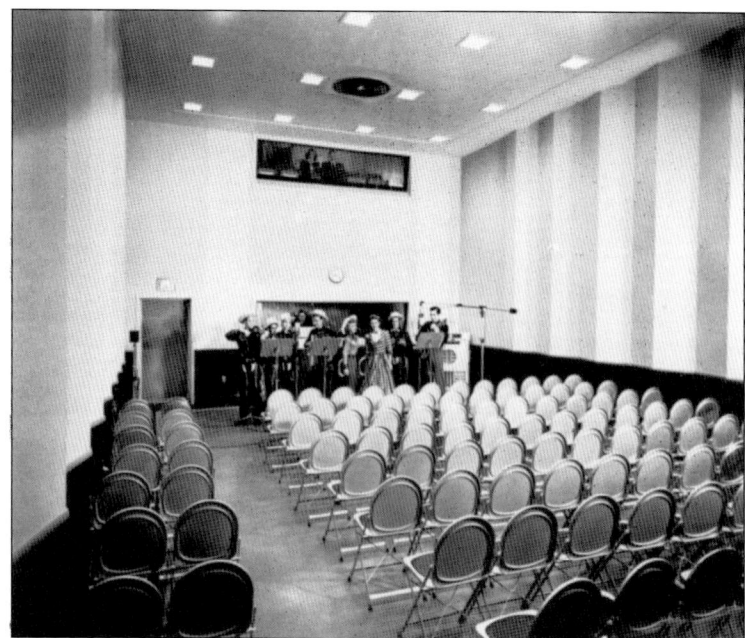

Radio City's identical studios B and C were 24 by 44 feet and seated an audience of 120 people. Like studio A, the ceilings were 16 to 18 feet high. Studio B also had a Wurlitzer theater pipe organ with an adjoining sound chamber. In 1949, studio C became the first studio for KGO-TV. (Author's collection.)

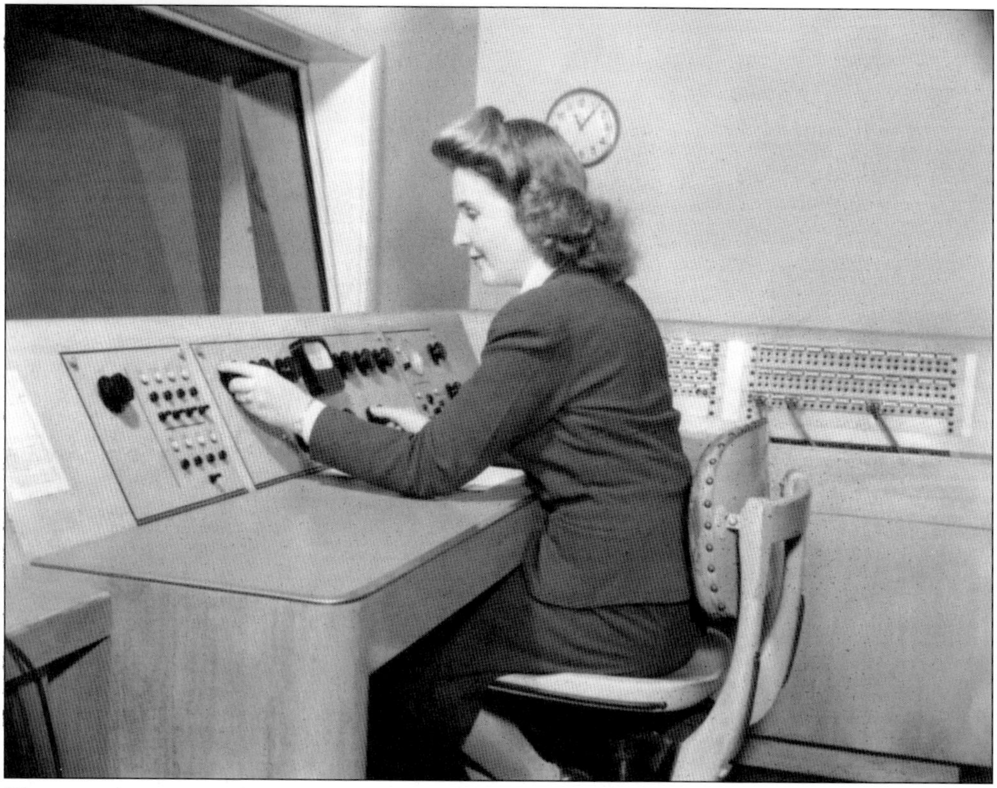

This was the operator's position in a control room for one of the medium-sized studios. All studios featured custom-made audio consoles, which were in reality just passive mixers. The audio amplifiers for all studios were located in the master control area, requiring about a million feet of wire to connect everything. (Bill Newbrough.)

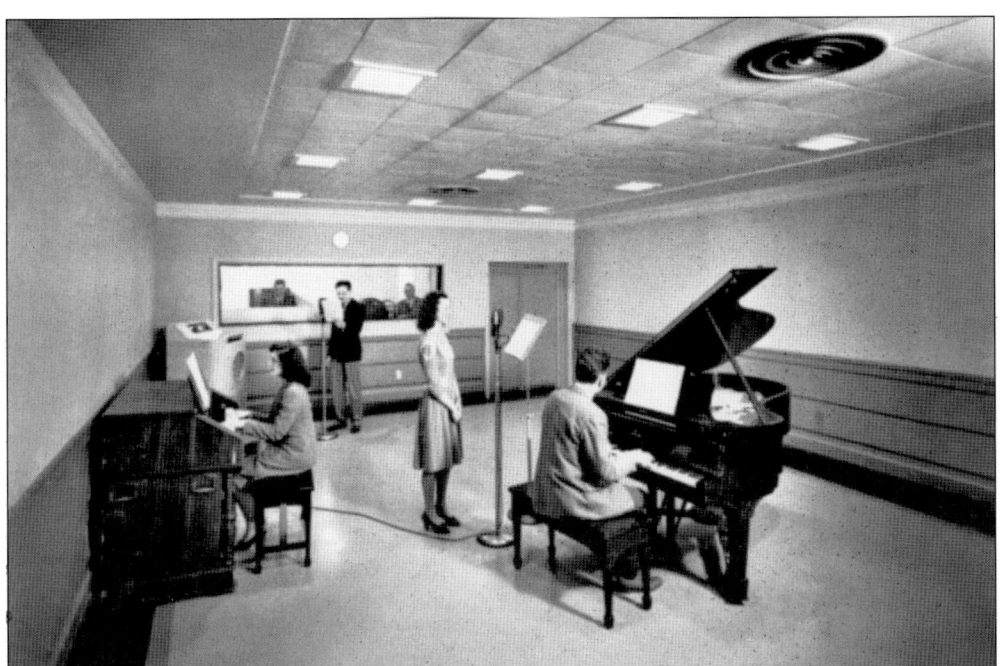

Radio City's studios D, E, and F were suitable for small studio programs with just a few performers. Each room measured 20 by 30 feet, did not have sponsors' booths, and could not accommodate a live audience. Farther down the hall was studio G, which was used for interview programs. It was small and intimate, decorated to look like a home living room to reduce a guest's "mike fright." (Author's collection.)

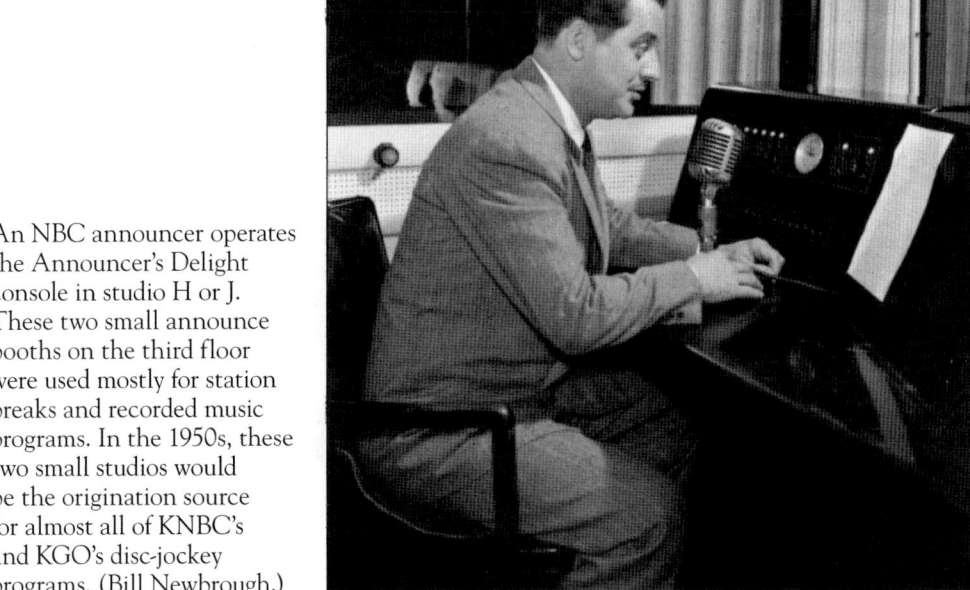

An NBC announcer operates the Announcer's Delight console in studio H or J. These two small announce booths on the third floor were used mostly for station breaks and recorded music programs. In the 1950s, these two small studios would be the origination source for almost all of KNBC's and KGO's disc-jockey programs. (Bill Newbrough.)

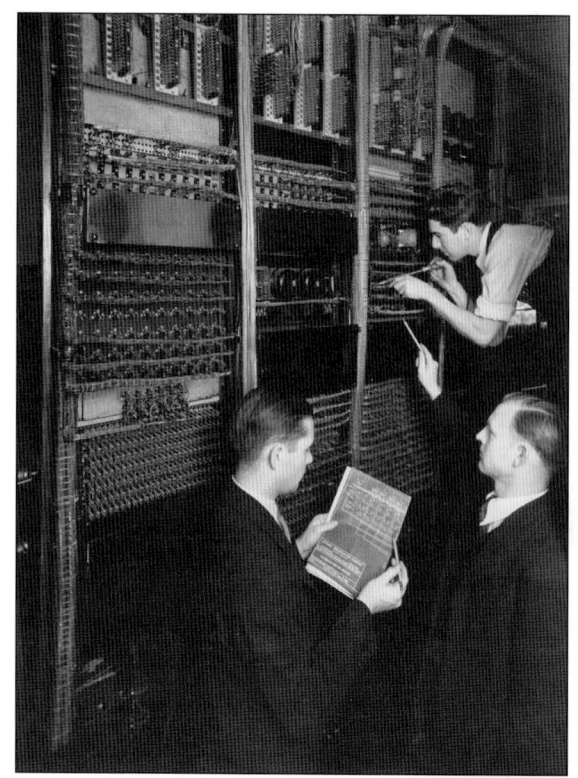

At left, technicians are seen finalizing the elaborate wiring at the rear of dozens of program amplifiers just before opening day at Radio City. All amplifiers for the entire facility were located in this room behind the master control console on the third floor. A complete duplicate set of amplifiers was kept on standby at all times, ready to be switched on line at a moment's notice. All the amplifiers were made, of course, by RCA. The DC power for all amplifiers came from a bank of power supplies with battery backup. Below, an engineer is using a test meter to check the operating conditions of the amplifiers. (Both, Bill Newbrough.)

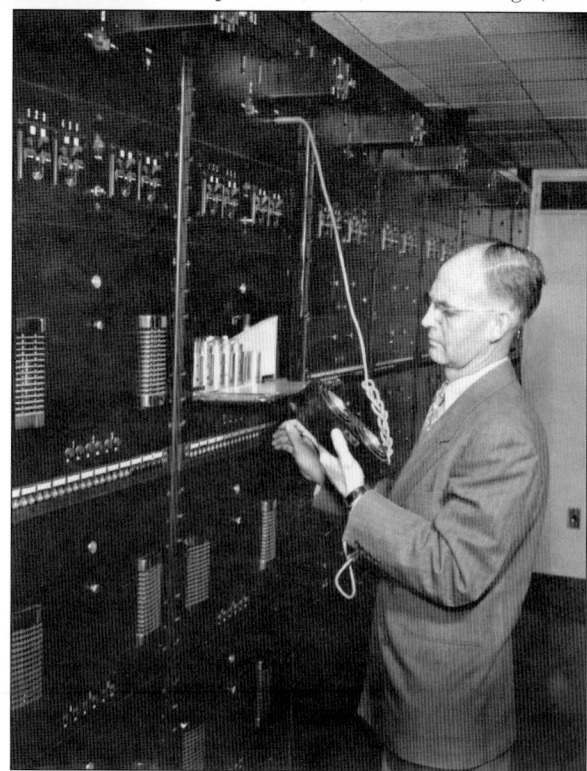

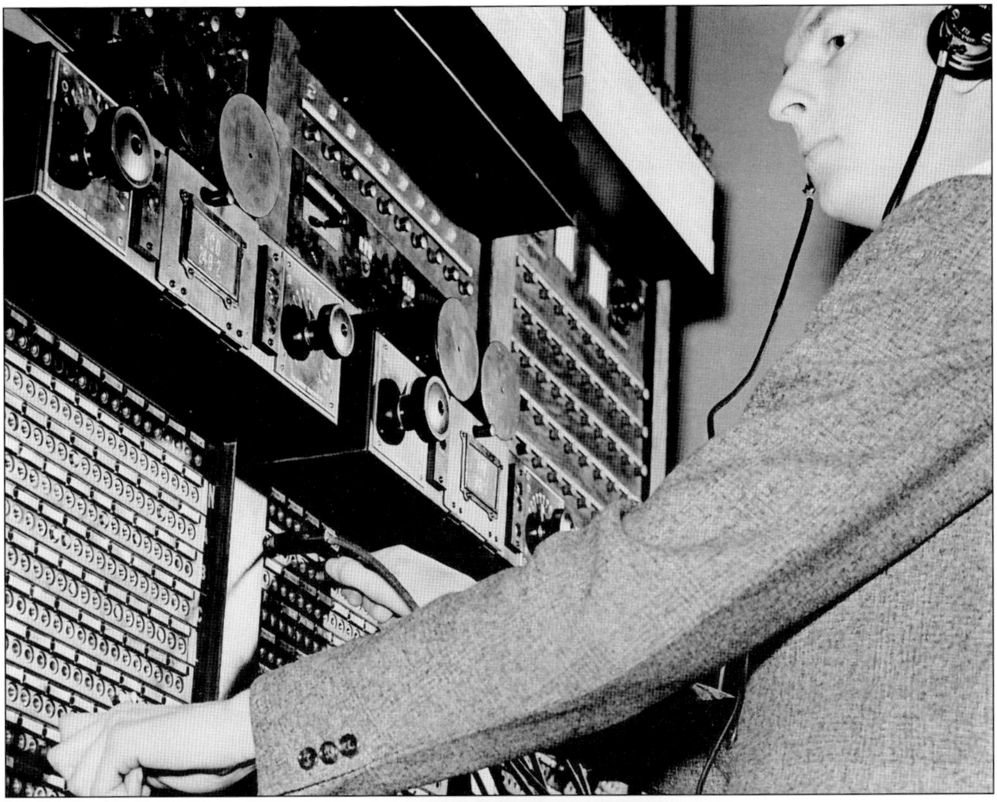

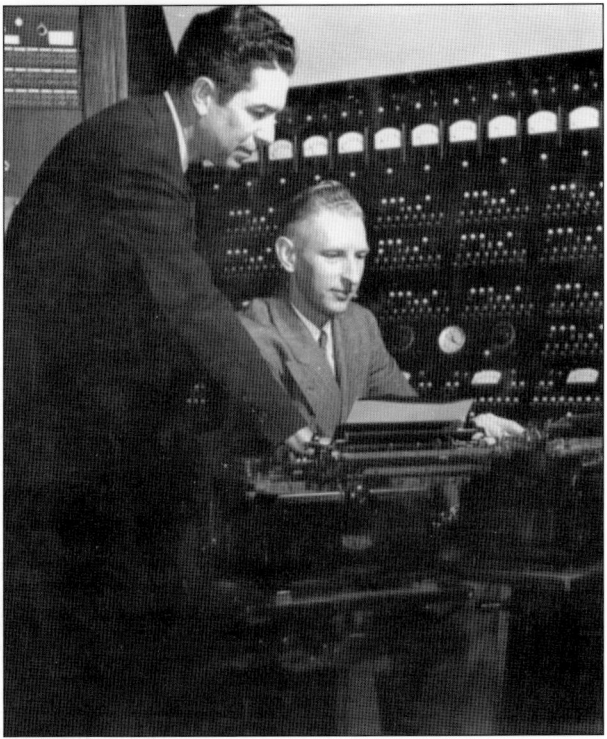

In the old master control room at 111 Sutter Street, the operator stood in front of rows of amplifiers that sent NBC programs out to the affiliated stations. Each amplifier had its own controls. Above, Lee Kolm stands at the old operating position. Compare this to the new Radio City control room, at right. Here, studio chief engineer George Greaves trains Kolm on the master control console. All programs fed to KPO, KGO, and the two Pacific Coast networks went through this equipment. Each module on the panel was for a different station on the network, and the lights and buttons on each module represented the studios. The operator could thus assign any program to any station on the network. The telegraph sounder on the desk was for communication with the KPO transmitter in Belmont. (Above, Bill Newbrough; right, Rich Kolm.)

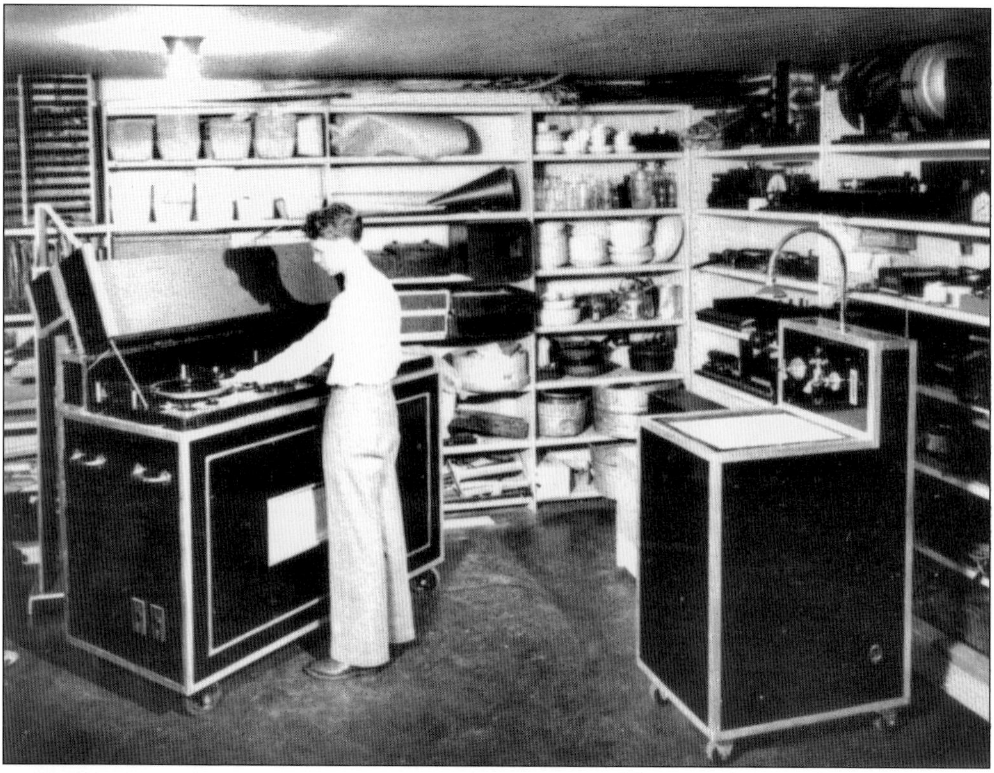

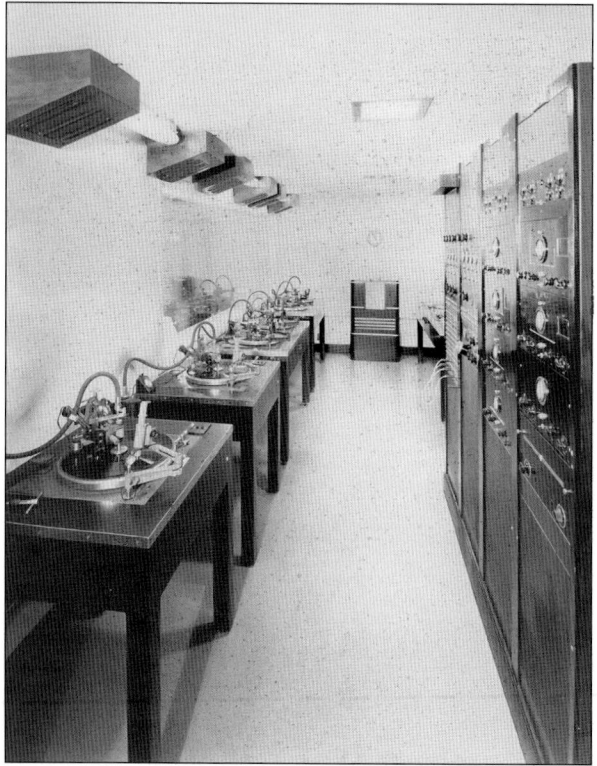

This was the sound effects room at Radio City. In addition to the library of disc recordings at the upper left, there was a wide variety of props used to create different sounds. The cart at right with the sprinkler was used for water and rain sounds. The operator is cueing a sound effects recording on a turntable dolly, which could be wheeled into any studio. (Author's collection.)

This room in the Radio City building was the center for all recordings. Six transcription lathes were used to record programs onto 16-inch 33-1/3 RPM acetate disks, 15 minutes to a side. The four turntables at the right rear of the room were for playback purposes only, used to audition recordings. The cabinets at right contained the recording amplifiers and audio switching equipment. (Bill Newbrough.)

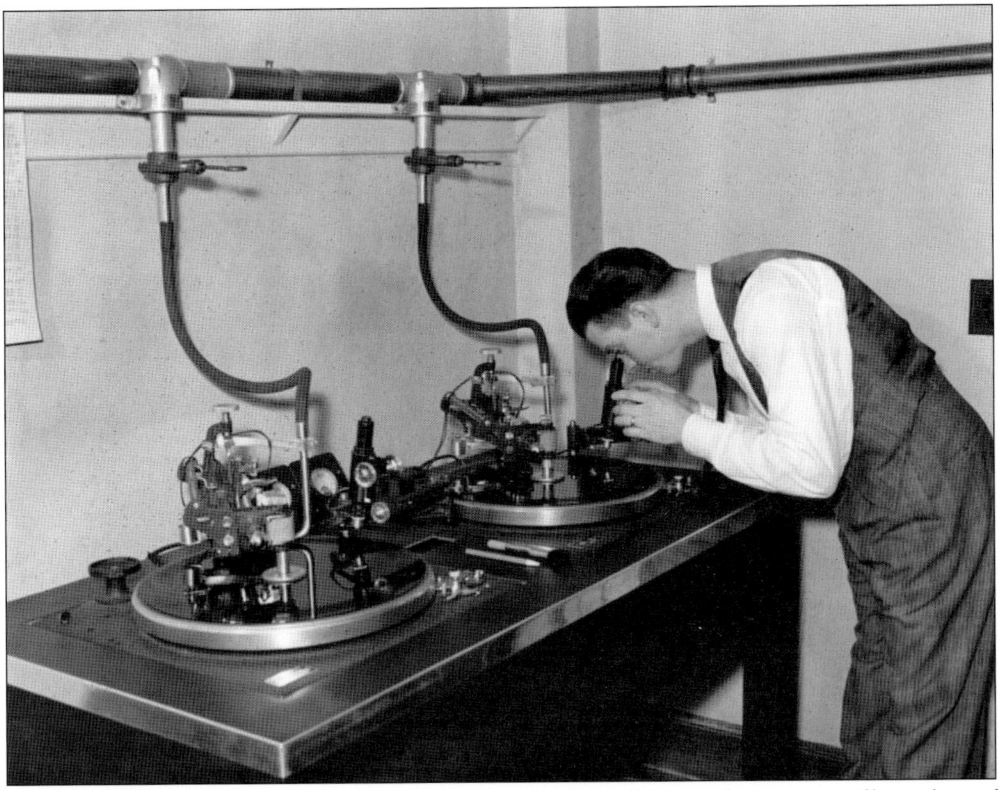

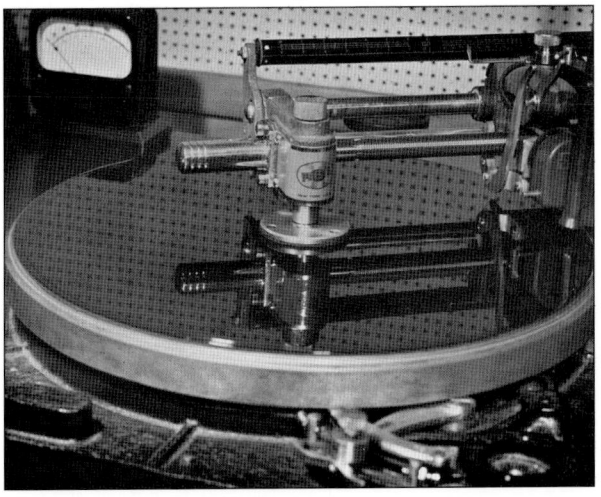

While NBC maintained a strict "No Recordings" policy, the recording room still saw lots of activity. Some programs originating in New York or Chicago were recorded to "time shift" them to a more convenient hour for the West Coast. Above, engineer Alan O'Neal inspects the cutting depth by viewing the grooves through a microscope. A vacuum hose at the center of the turntable extracted the highly flammable shavings as they were cut from the disk. Below is one of the six Presto lathes. Recordings were made on acetate-covered aluminum disks that were polished to a high luster. The recording head cut the grooves into the disk as it spun, while the threaded screw moved the head across the disk. Recordings were made at either 33-1/3 or 78 RPM, starting either from the outside or inside. (Both, Bill Newbrough.)

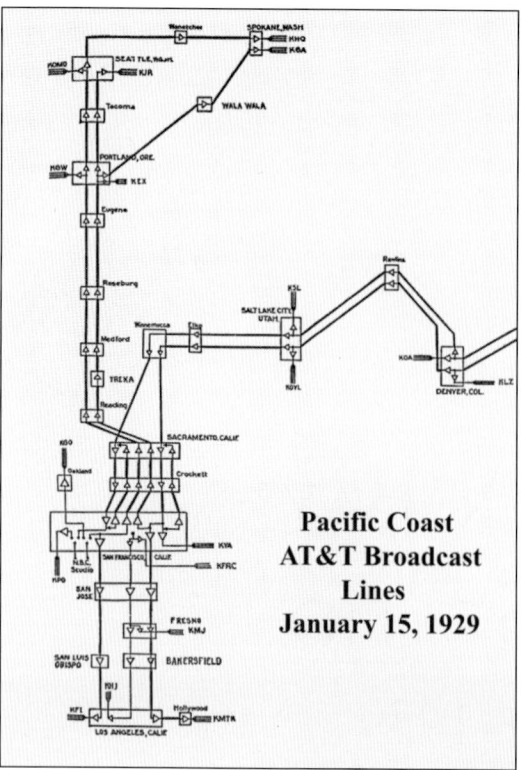

**Pacific Coast
AT&T Broadcast
Lines
January 15, 1929**

The Bell System diagram at left shows the broadcast program line connections on the West Coast in 1929. This clearly shows why NBC built its West Coast headquarters in San Francisco, as programs could be fed both up and down the coast. But eastward feeds required the complex process of "line reversal," where all amplifiers west of Denver reversed directions simultaneously. This limited the number of West Coast programs heard nationally. This all changed in 1937 with the completion of a second line to Los Angeles, allowing national network programs to be broadcast from Southern California. It also eliminated the need for "line reversal," as programs were now fed westward on the San Francisco line and eastward over the Los Angeles line. This new "round robin" line arrangement caused most programs and talent to move from San Francisco to Hollywood by 1942. (Both, author's collection.)

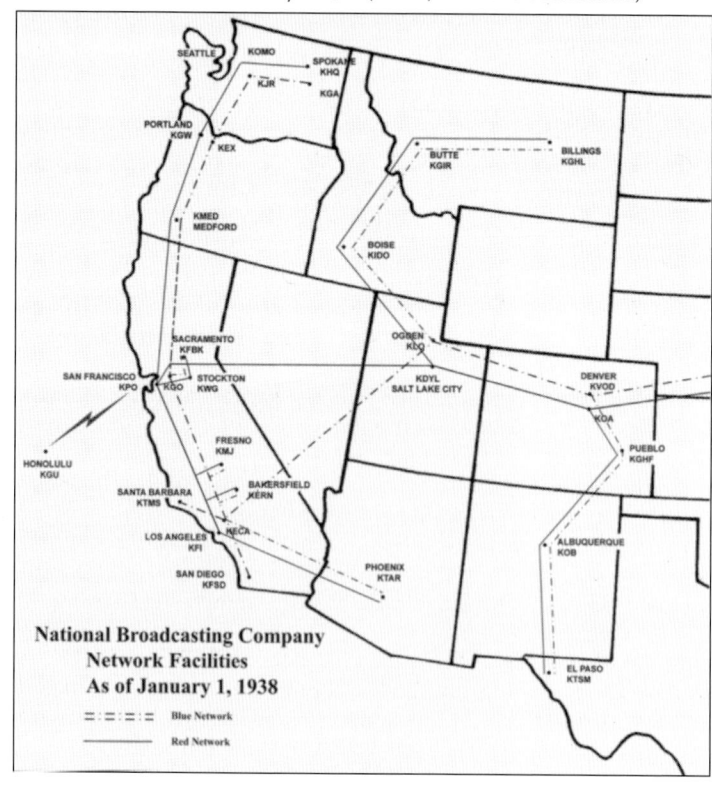

**National Broadcasting Company
Network Facilities
As of January 1, 1938**

=·=·:=·:=   Blue Network

————   Red Network

Four

OTHER BAY
AREA STATIONS
1930–1939

Looking back today on radio's golden era, the tendency is to focus upon the big national networks and their elaborate programs. However, a number of independent stations, both large and small, also made their mark on local broadcasting. To listen to the radio at that time was to hear a mixture of both national and local programs, so to understand early radio from the viewpoint of the listener it is also important to consider the contribution of those stations.

KSFO, KFRC, and KQW were San Francisco's biggest independent stations. All three stations took their turn being the local CBS outlet (CBS finally purchased KQW, which became KCBS in 1949). Nonetheless, even in the years when they were not network affiliates both KSFO and KFRC built tremendous local followings due to excellence in programming, with both stations employing large staffs of announcers, musicians, and technicians. KSFO, led by the visionary broadcaster Wesley I. Dumm, set the local standard for technology by constructing two large and elaborate studio complexes: first, for CBS in the Palace Hotel, and later, in an annex of the Mark Hopkins Hotel.

Two Bay Area newspapers also operated radio stations. KYA broadcast for nearly three decades from the Hearst Building as the radio voice of the *San Francisco Examiner*, and KLX operated from the Tribune Tower in Oakland.

Possibly the most interesting operations were the smaller radio stations, who served programming niches that were not covered by the big stations.

KJBS was the Bay Area's all-music "midnight to sunset" station, entertaining audiences with phonograph records and live announcers long before such programming became commonplace on radio. KJBS's Frank Cope, who hosted the morning show for 30 years, was one of the world's first disc jockeys.

A trio of small East Bay stations—KRE, KROW, and KLS—survived and thrived with a mixture of local shows and brokered programs, including foreign language, religious programs, and recorded jazz. KSAN specialized in broadcasting horse race results. All of them contributed to the patchwork quilt that was Bay Area radio in the thirties.

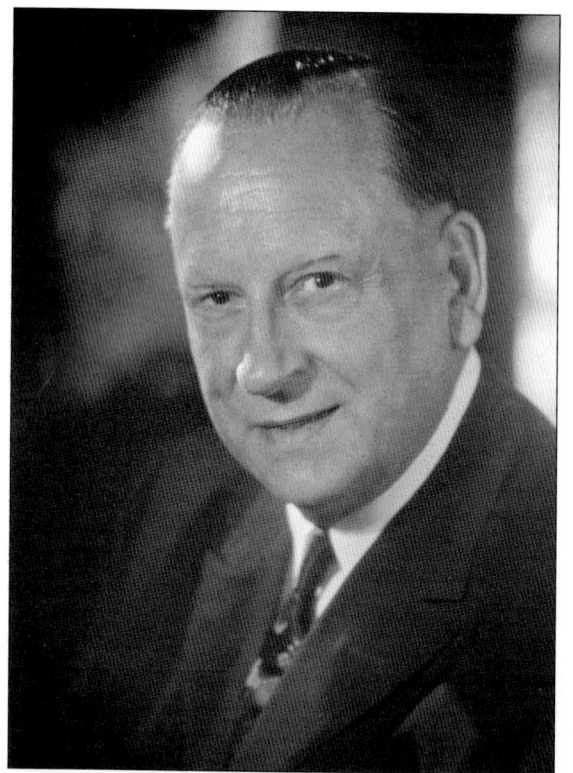

Wesley I. Dumm (left) was the president and majority owner of Associated Broadcasters in San Francisco for 20 years. He acquired KTAB from the Tenth Avenue Baptist Church in 1933, becoming its director and sole stockholder. He changed the call sign to KSFO and developed a new schedule of quality programming, turning it into one of the most important independent stations on the Pacific Coast. During the war years he constructed two powerful shortwave stations. After the war, he started the city's first television station, KPIX, which was sold to Westinghouse Broadcasting in 1954. KSFO was sold to Gene Autry in 1956, ending Dumm's radio career. Franklin Merrick Dumm (below), Wesley's older brother, was the man with his hands on the financial tiller at Associated Broadcasters—secretary-treasurer of the organization from 1938 to 1956. (Left, Penny Wilkes; below, Charles Dumm.)

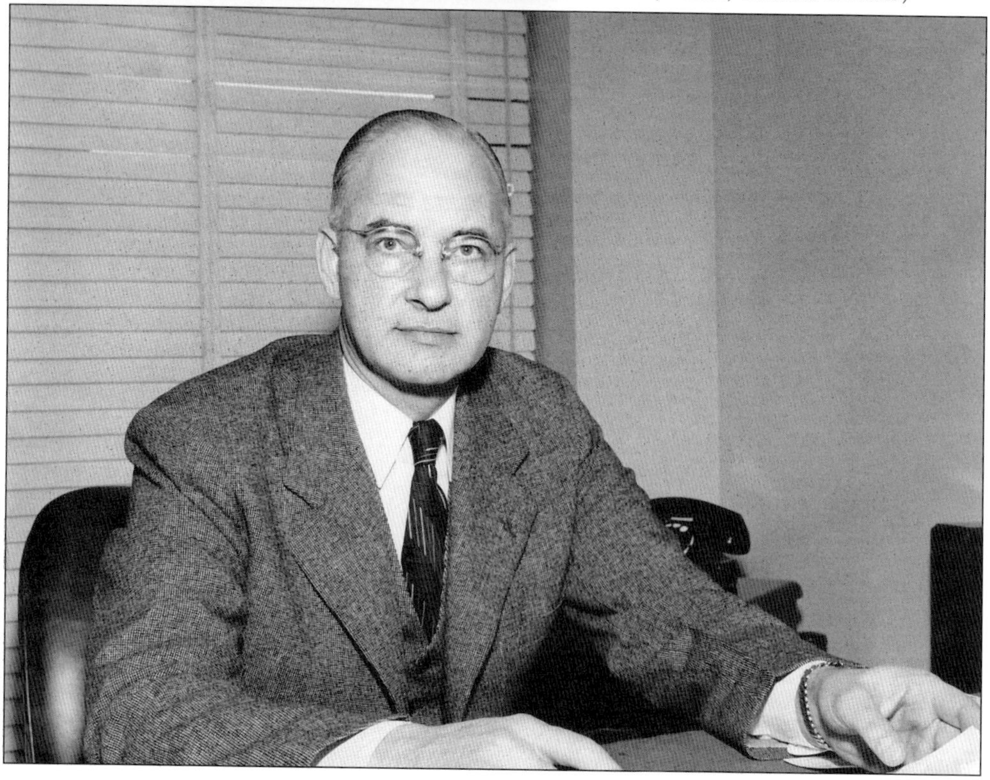

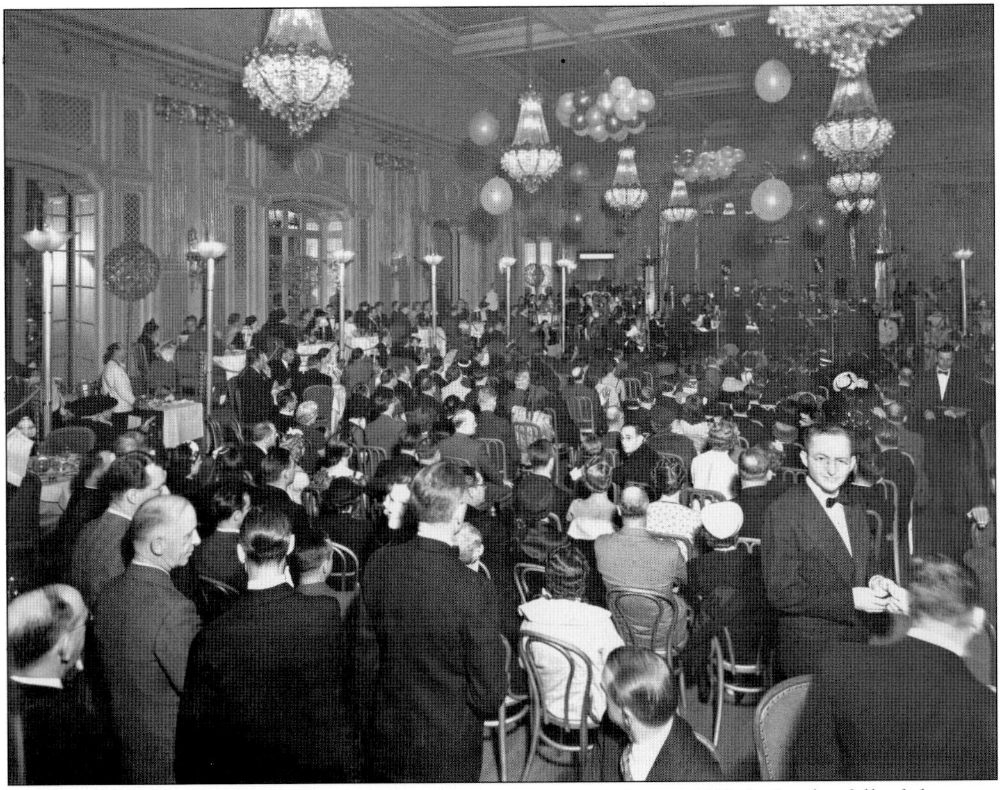

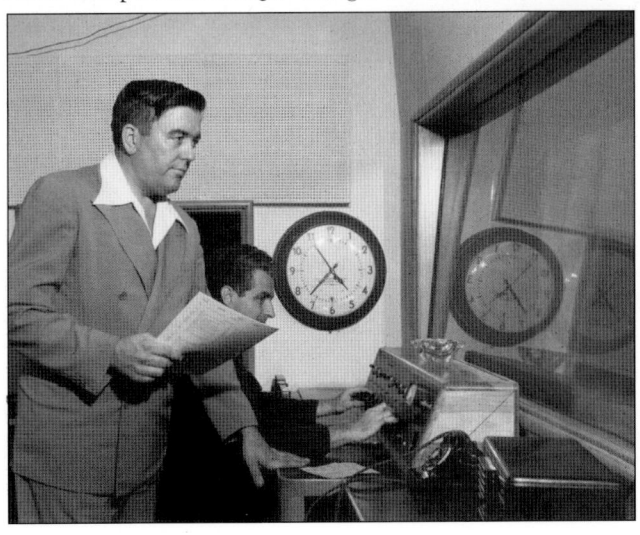

KSFO became the San Francisco CBS affiliate in 1936, replacing KFRC. In the fall of the next year, CBS opened its new quarter-million-dollar studios in the Palace Hotel, boasting no less than seven studios and 26 offices. In the photograph above, the ballroom of the Palace Hotel is decked out for a live CBS broadcast commemorating the inauguration of the new KSFO studio complex in the hotel. In the photograph below, a program producer and engineer oversee the broadcast of a CBS program from a control room in the Palace Hotel. In 1942, the Associated Broadcasters refused CBS's offer to purchase KSFO, which caused the network to transfer its affiliation to KQW, which moved into the studios. CBS purchased KQW outright in 1949. (Both, Penny Wilkes.)

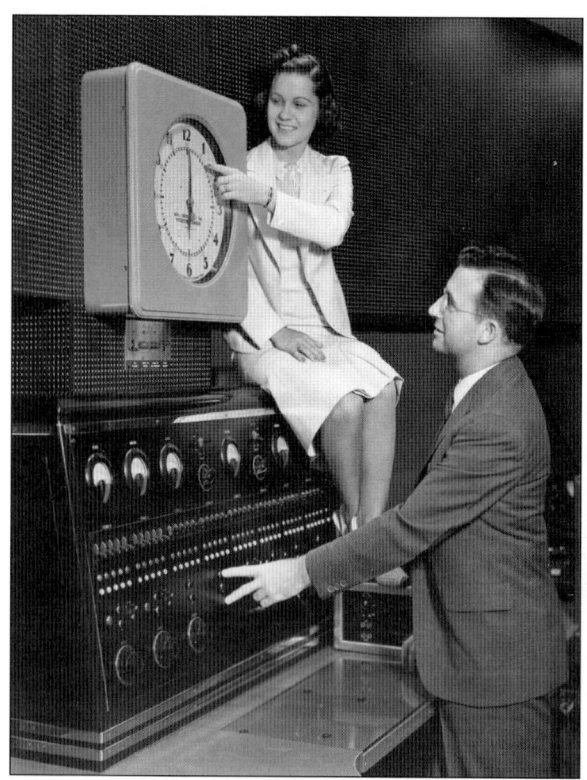

At left is a view of the KSFO master control console in its Palace Hotel studios. This console could feed programs from any of the seven studios and numerous remote lines to the CBS Pacific Coast network. The three volume knobs on the lower left are marked "north," "south," and "KSFO." The Western Union clock automatically corrected its time to hourly pulses sent from the US Naval Observatory over telegraph lines. These clocks were a standard feature of radio studios across the country for 40 years. Below, a KSFO studio engineer is shown in one of the many studio control rooms in the Palace Hotel around 1938. (Both, Penny Wilkes.)

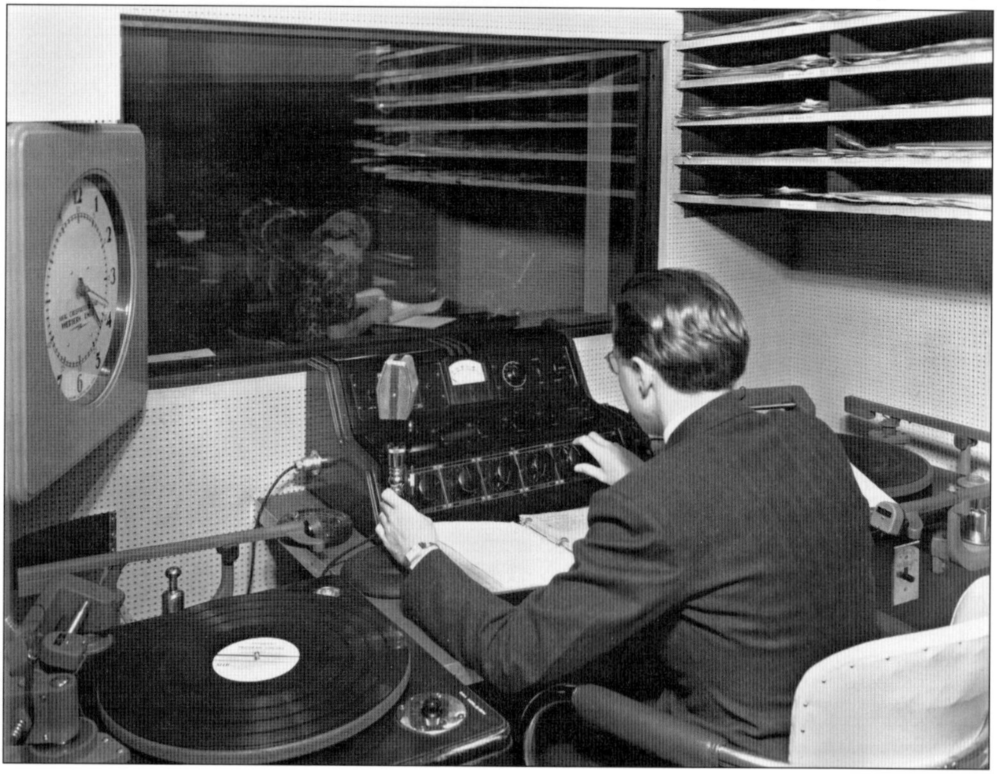

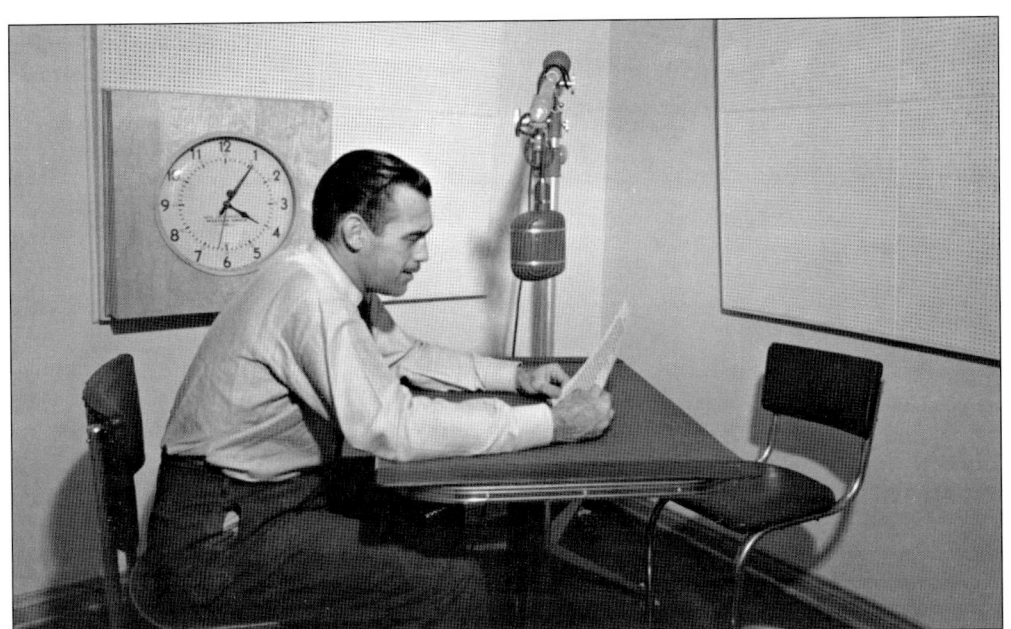

Above, a KSFO announcer broadcasts a news bulletin from one of the smaller studios in the Palace Hotel. Before eBay, there was KSFO's "Tonight's Best Buys" program, seen below, which was described by *Time Magazine* as "'Lots of bargains—YOUR bargains—the things YOU want to sell. We broadcast them absolutely free! Remember—it makes no difference what it is—as long as it's a bargain.' Thus on the air over 20 West Coast stations goes 'Tonight's Best Buys,' radio's big rummage sale. Six stenographers answer six constantly jangling telephones, type out names, descriptions, and prices of the items offered, providing an offstage, panic-on-the-stock-market sound effect. Wiry, fast-talking Narrator Sam Pierce offers the goods to the radio audience and tells how to reach the would-be seller. One-third of the odds and ends offered are bought." (Both, Penny Wilkes.)

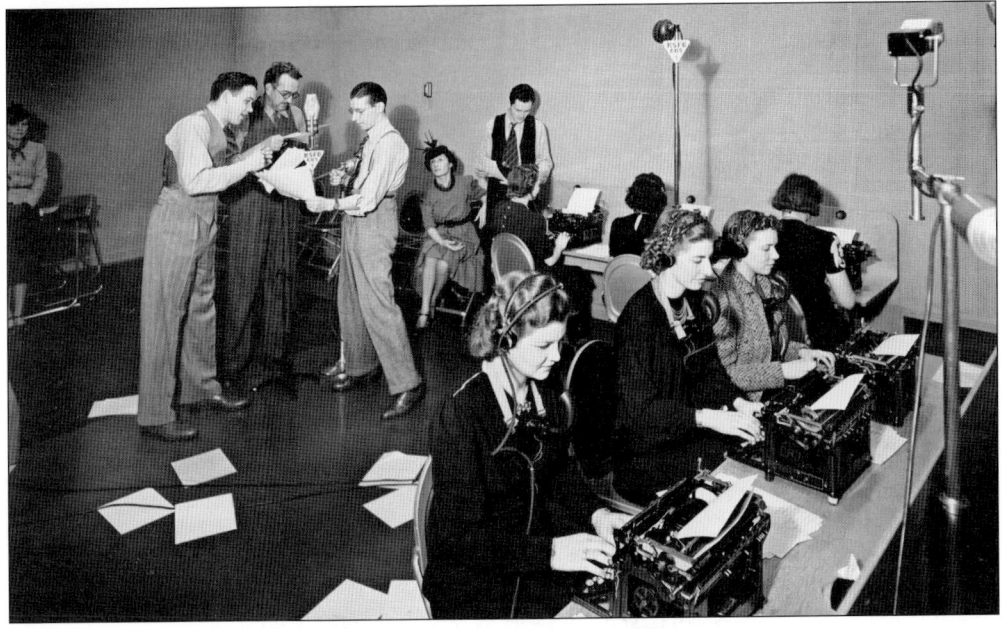

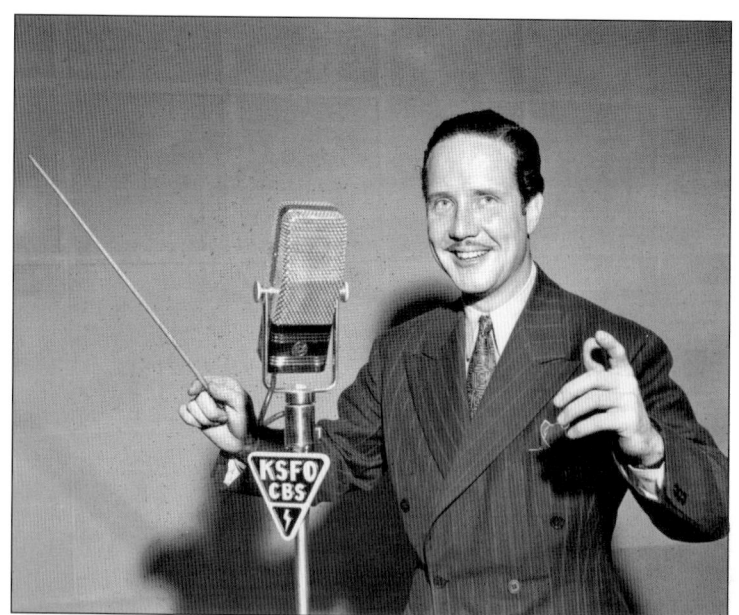

Local bandleader and organist Dick Aurandt started at KSFO as a staff organist and then became music director in 1940, replacing Jack Meakin. He later moved to Los Angeles where he had a successful career creating music for many of the popular network radio shows of the late 1940s and early 1950s. (Author's collection.)

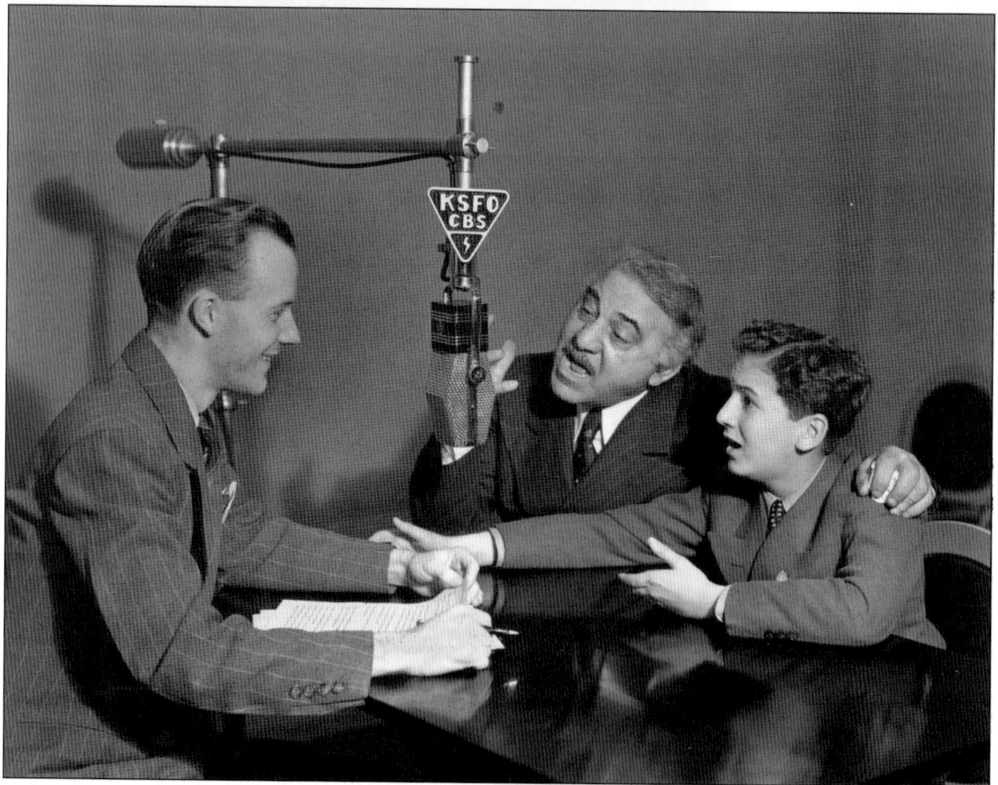

KSFO chief announcer Keith Kerby interviews Henry Armetta and Bobby Breen, stars of the new film *Fisherman's Wharf* in 1939. In the musical film, Breen played the adopted son of a San Francisco fisherman. Kerby's voice was heard frequently on KSFO from 1937 to 1949. He later became the program manager of KGO and then held radio positions in Los Angeles, San Bernardino, and Reno. (Penny Wilkes.)

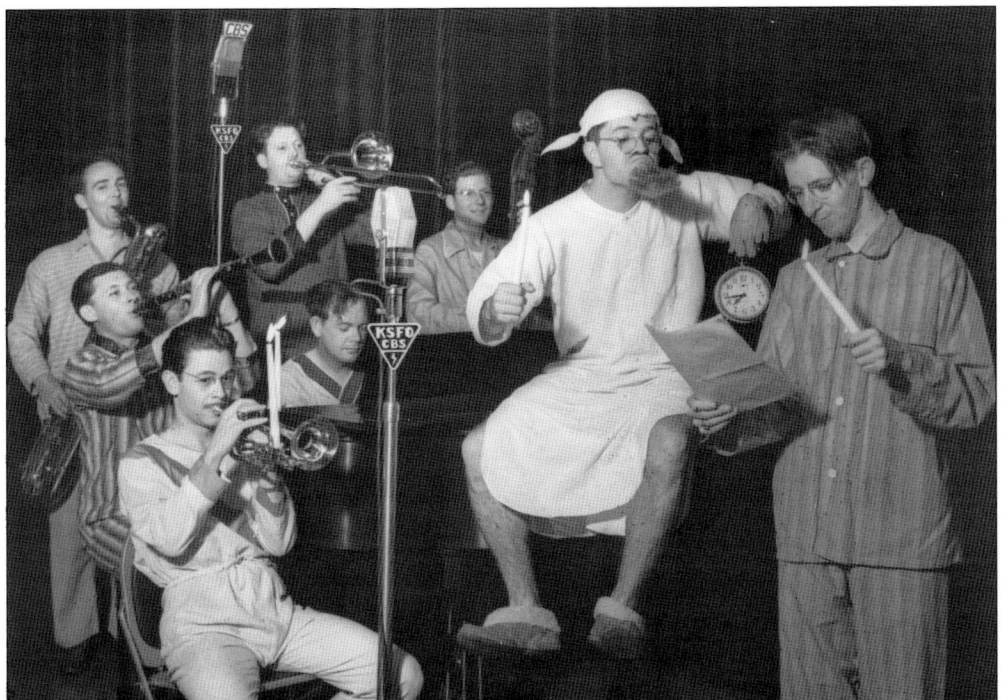

In 1939, KSFO's popular morning 7:00 to 8:00 a.m. "wake up" show was called the *Yawn Patrol*, hosted by announcer Bill Baldwin (seen here with the candle). It was said to be Northern California's only live talent show on the air before 8:00 a.m. Here, the staff is dressed in pajamas to emphasize the early morning hour of their broadcasts. (Penny Wilkes.)

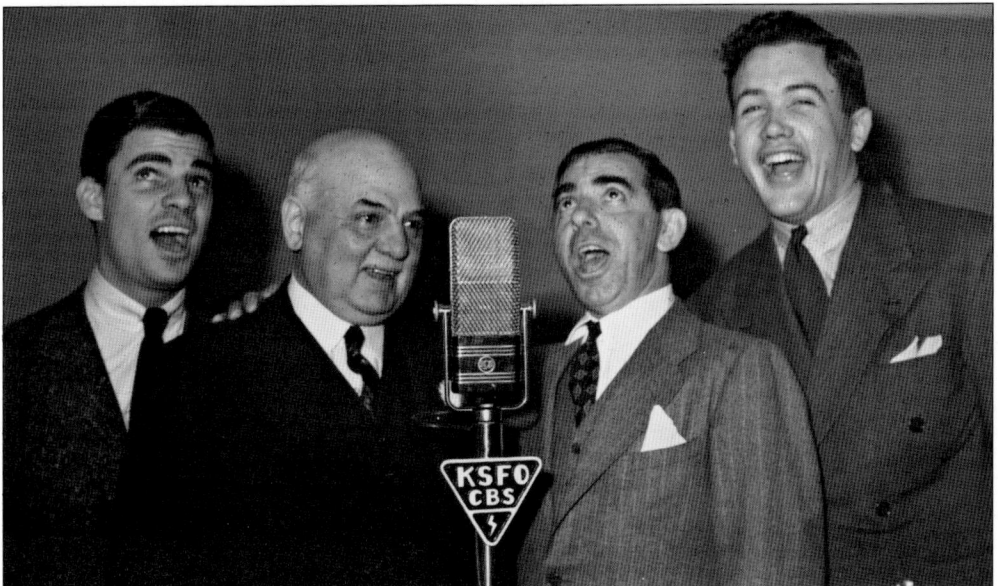

Eddie Cantor, one of CBS's biggest stars (third from the left), came to San Francisco in 1938 to promote KSFO's new affiliation with the network. Here, he sings barbershop harmonies with (left to right) Bert Parks, San Francisco mayor Angelo Joseph Rossi, and KSFO newsman Bob Garred. Rossi held the office of mayor from 1931 to 1944. (Penny Wilkes.)

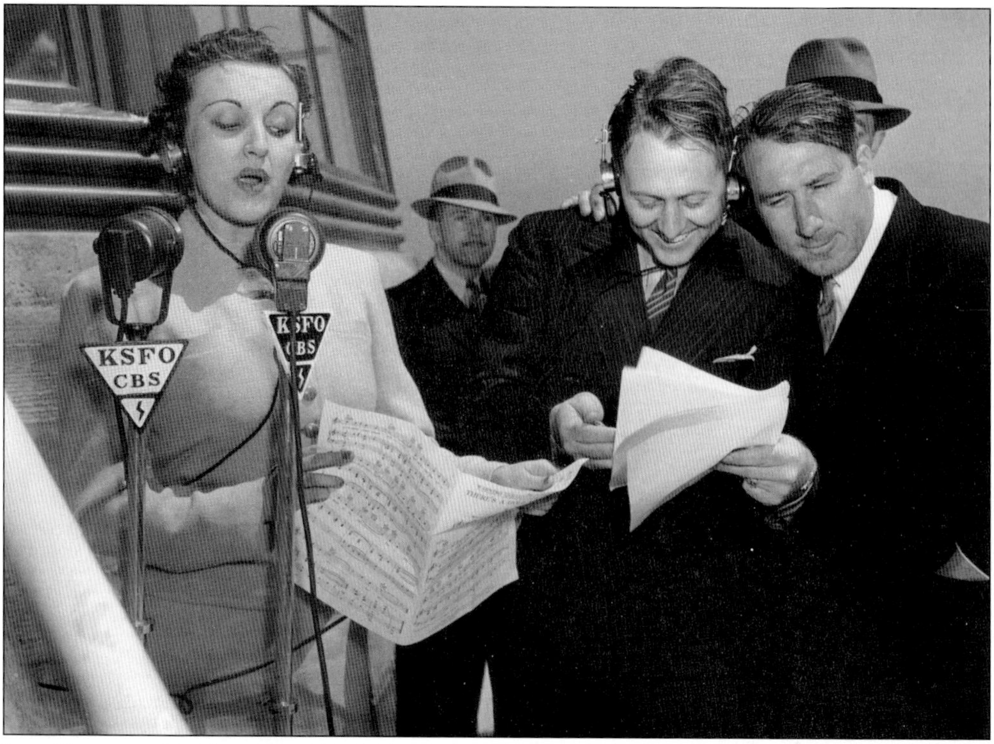

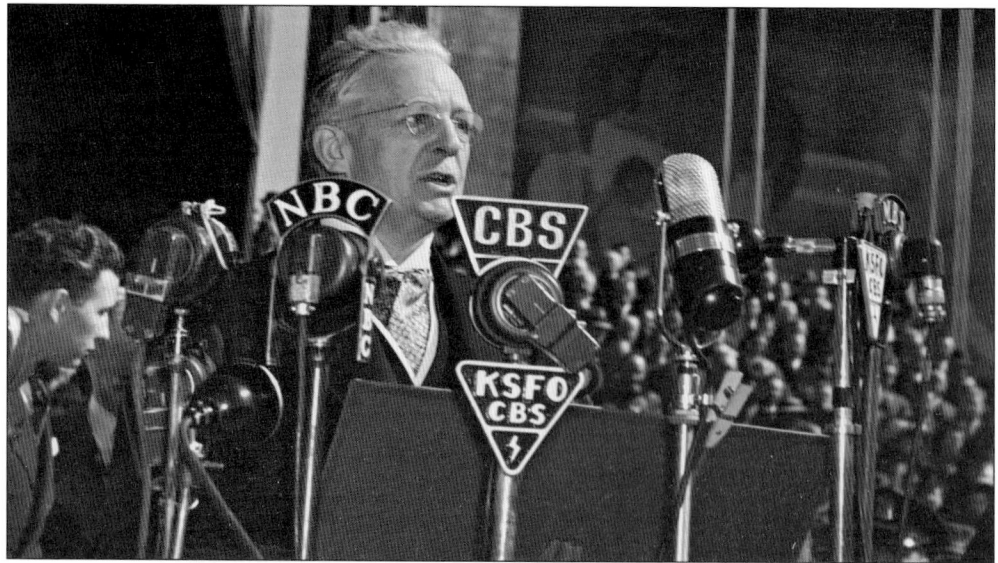

Jane Kaye, Art Linkletter, and Nick Kenny broadcast a salute to the Golden Gate International Exposition over KSFO in 1939. The Joe Sanders Nighthawks played "There's a Goldmine in the Sky" from an airplane flying over the fairgrounds, while Jane Kaye sang the lyrics on the ground. (Missouri Valley Special Collections, Kansas City Public Library.)

An address by California governor Culbert Levy Olson is picked up by KSFO for a CBS network broadcast. Olson, the 29th governor of California, fought bitterly with the legislature and the Catholic Church because of his liberal and secular beliefs. He was succeeded in 1943 by Earl Warren, to whom he said, "If you want to know what hell is like, just be governor." (Penny Wilkes.)

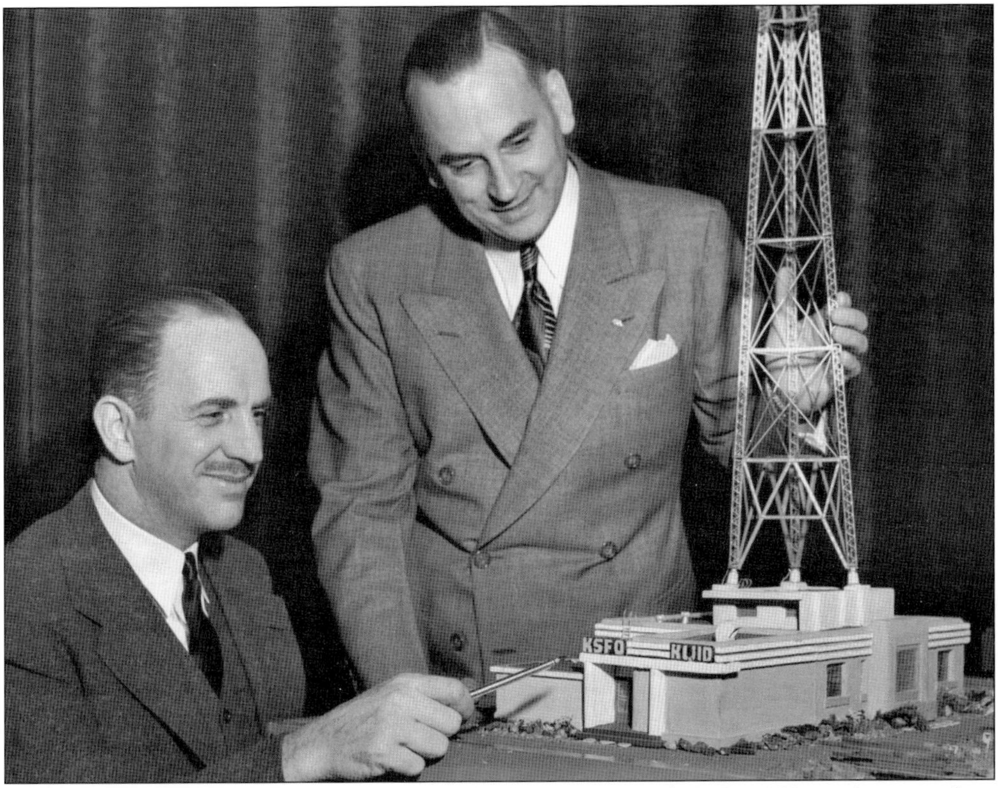

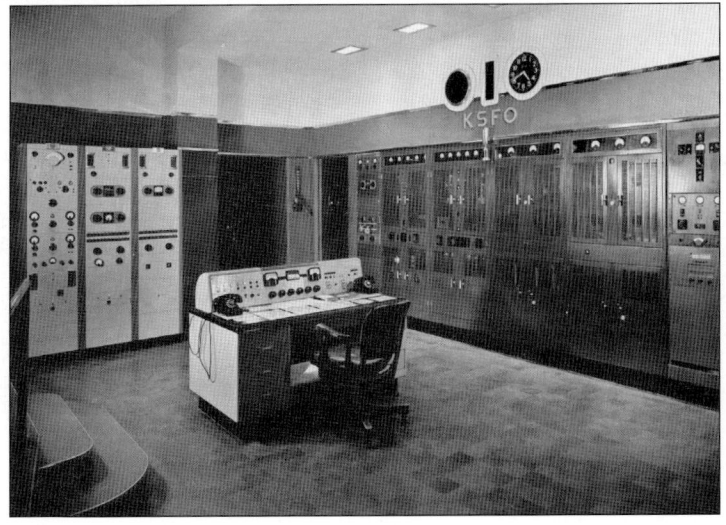

Above, KSFO president Wesley Dumm and chief engineer Royal V. "Doc" Howard review plans for the KSFO transmitter building on Islais Creek. The tower and building were constructed by CBS in 1937 on land leased from the State Harbor Commission on the San Francisco Bay seawall. KSFO purchased the building from CBS in 1941 after the network transferred its affiliation to KQW. These photographs were taken in 1942 when KSFO planned an expansion of the building to house its shortwave operations. KSFO still uses the building today. Below, an early 1940s interior view of the building shows the Western Electric transmitter and operator's desk. (Above, author's collection; below, Kevin Mostyn.)

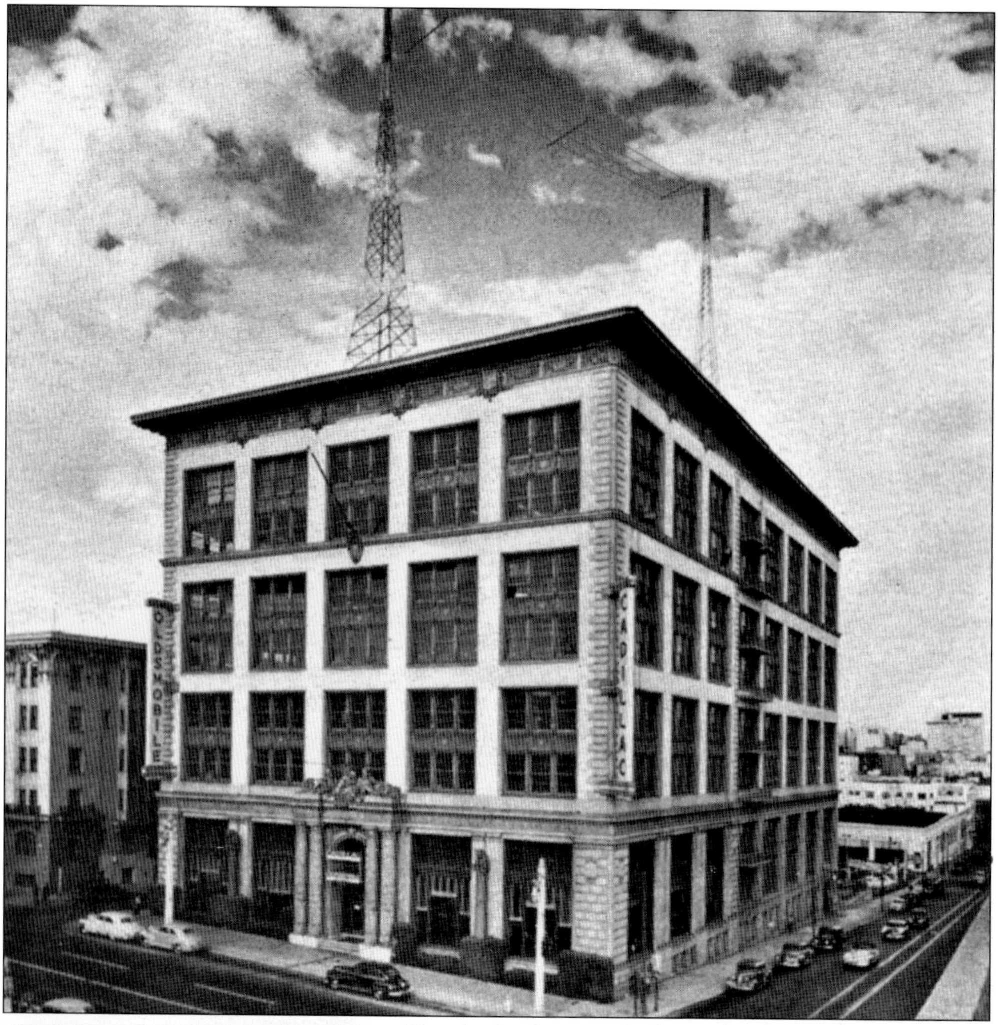

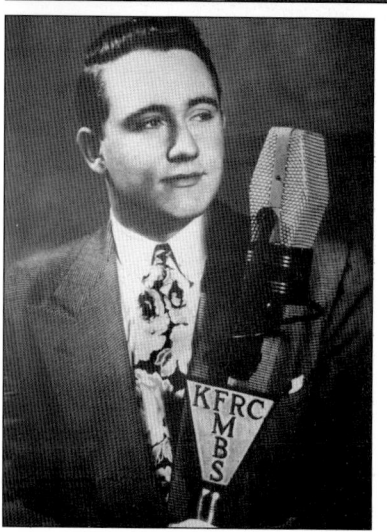

The above photograph shows the KFRC antenna on the roof of the Don Lee Cadillac building, located at 1000 Van Ness Avenue. It was a San Francisco landmark. There was fierce competition between Don Lee and Earl C. Anthony, who operated the Packard dealership across the street. Anthony owned KFI and KECA in Los Angeles, while Lee owned KHJ in Los Angeles and KFRC in San Francisco. Even though Anthony didn't have a station in San Francisco, he constructed two radio towers on his Van Ness Avenue dealership and hung a "KFI" sign on them. The never-used antenna stood proudly for nearly four decades. On the left, Merv Griffin (1925–2007) started his career at KFRC in 1945 as a singer and staff announcer, winning his job in an open audition. He stayed until 1949, when he joined the Freddy Martin Orchestra as a vocalist. (Above, from a 1940s KFRC booklet; left, George Zema.)

This is KYA's studio A in the Hearst Building during the 1930s. RCA velocity microphones and a portable turntable are visible, along with a grand piano. The main control room and its operator are seen through the window. KYA used these studios from 1934 to 1949, when the station moved to the Fairmont Hotel. (Kevin Mostyn.)

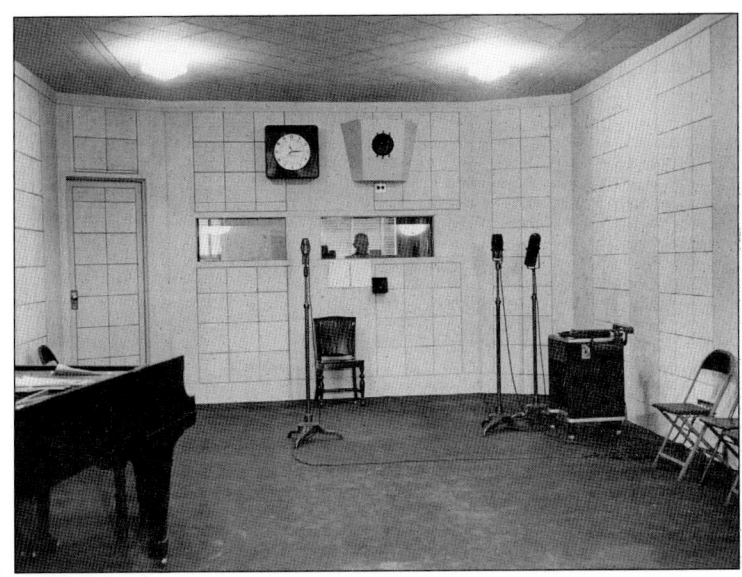

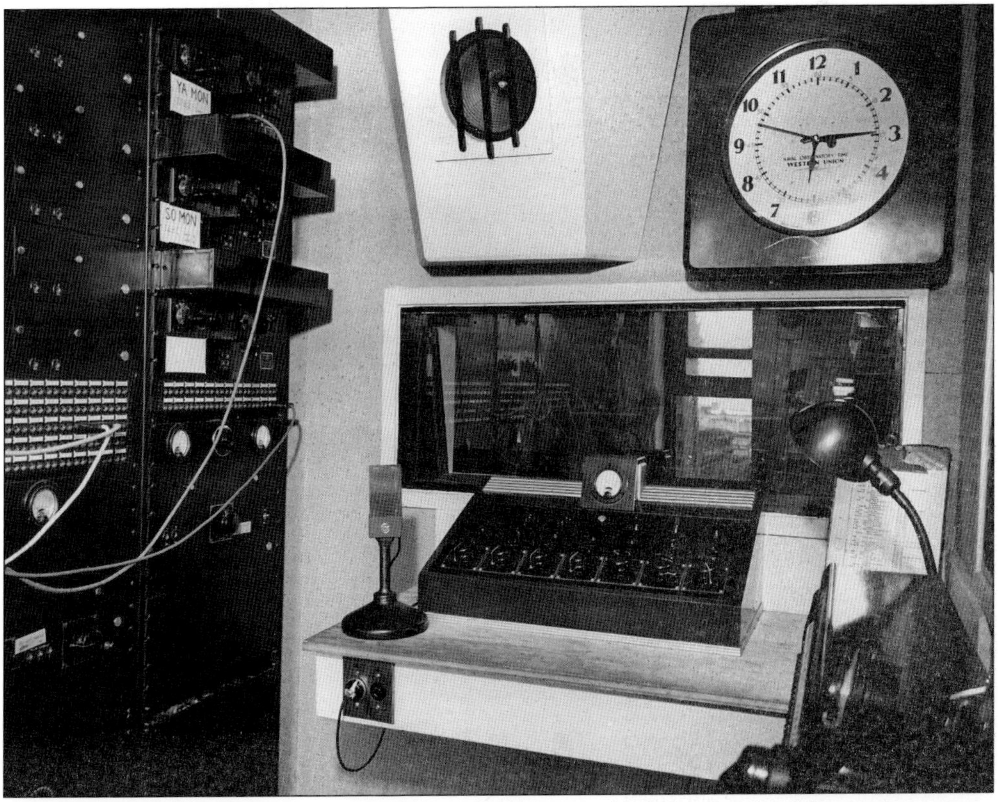

This was the KYA control room in the Hearst Building, on the opposite side of the window seen in the above photograph. The operator's desk housed the main audio console. The rack cabinets at the left hold the line amplifiers feeding telephone lines to the transmitter as well as line connections for outgoing network programs and incoming remote broadcasts. (Kevin Mostyn.)

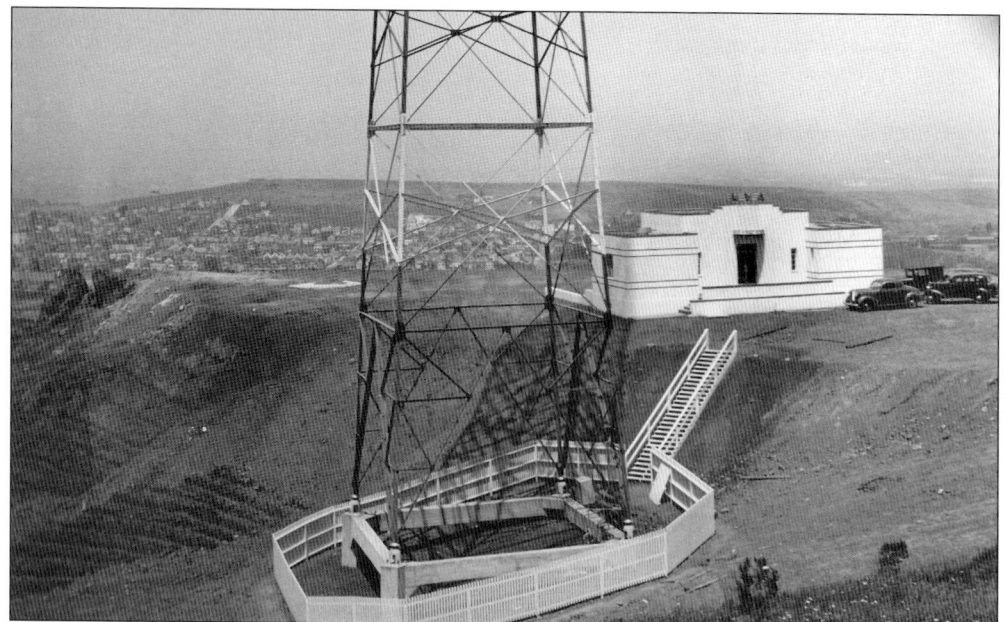

Hearst Radio, Inc., constructed this attractive new transmitter building for its station KYA on Candlestick Hill in southeast San Francisco. The modern Art Deco concrete structure housed a new 5,000-watt RCA transmitter, and a 450-foot self-supporting tower completed the installation. It went on the air on June 1, 1937, and is still in use today. (Kevin Mostyn.)

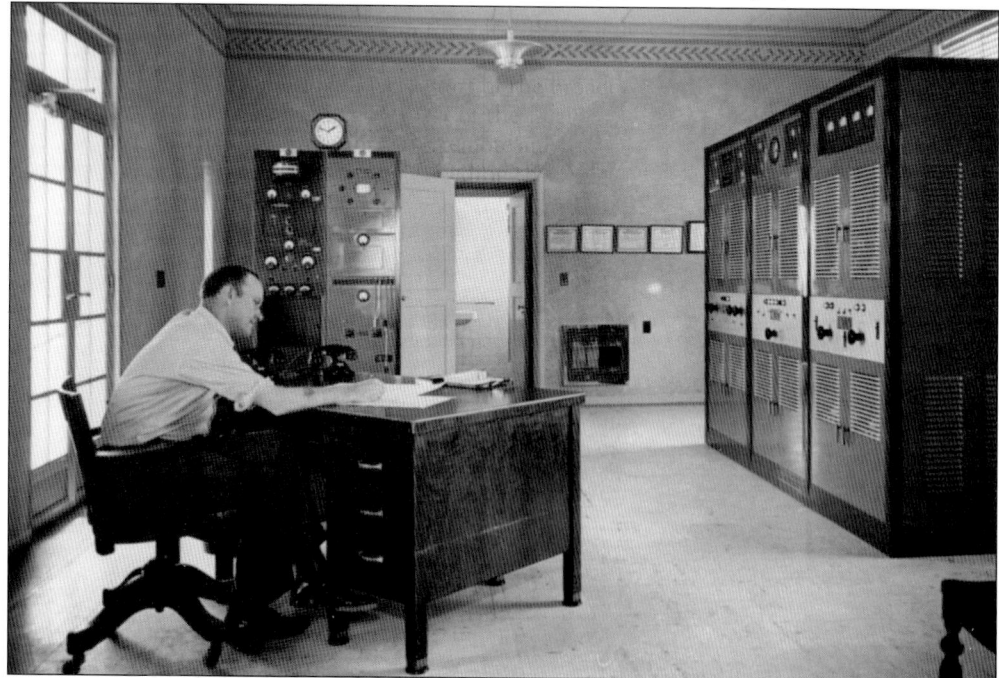

This is an interior view of the KYA transmitter building on Candlestick Hill in San Francisco, shortly after its completion in 1937. To the right is the RCA 5-C five kW transmitter. The speech input rack is to the left behind the operator's desk. The obligatory framed row of FCC operator's licenses lines the wall. (Kevin Mostyn.)

In 1936, Hearst Radio formed the California Broadcasting System. It was a loose-knit collection of stations organized mainly for sales purposes, but programs produced by its member stations were occasionally exchanged over the network. The Hearst station KYA offered the program *The Whirly Giggs*, broadcast at 10 p.m. on Saturdays. Florence Grimes played the character Mrs. Pearl E. Giggs. The network shut down in 1939. (Author's collection.)

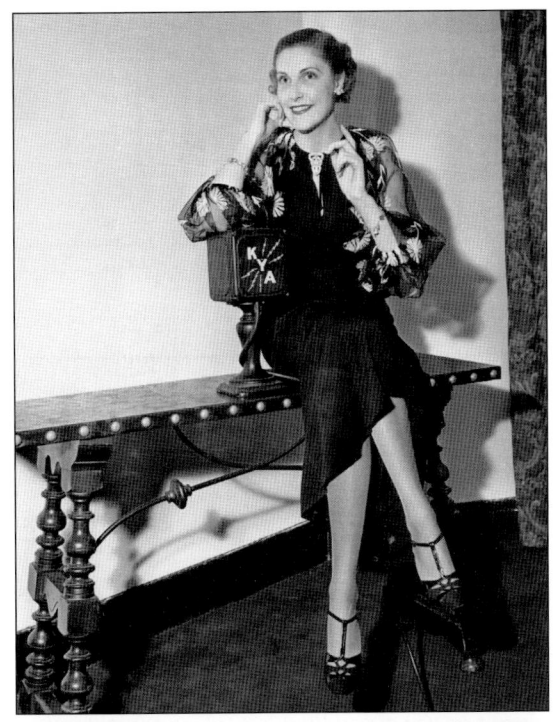

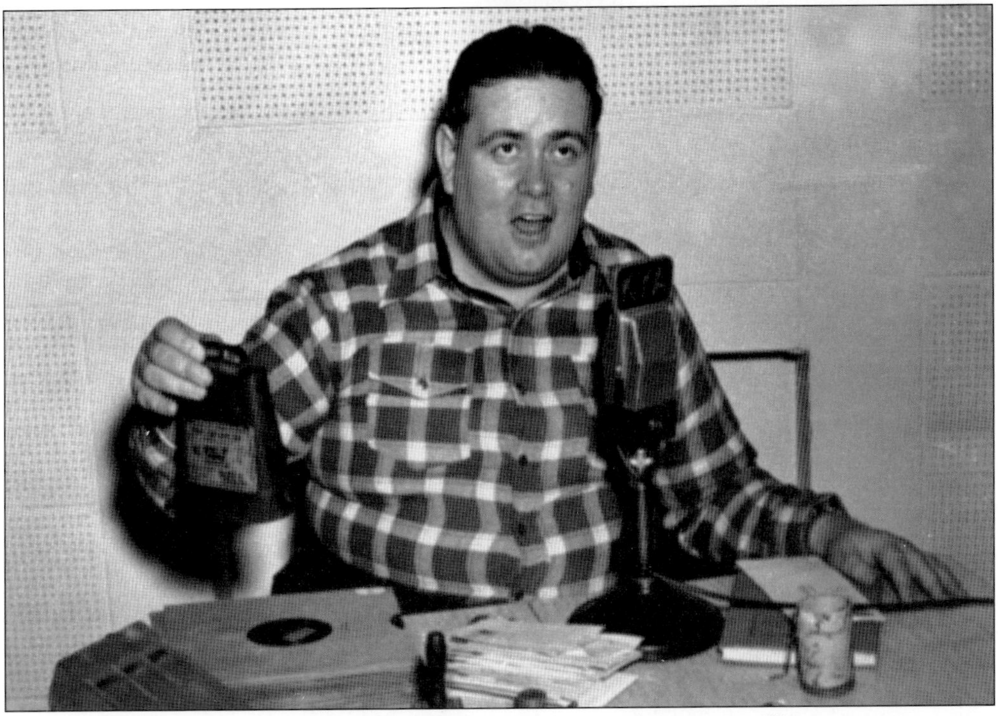

"Foreman Bill" Mackintosh hosted KYA's *Rhythm Rodeo*, a popular morning Western music program in the 1940s. Other local radio stations were also airing similar programs targeting the still-sizeable farm and agricultural community in the Bay Area. These included Dude Martin (KGO), Western Farm Home (KROW), and Sagebrush Serenade (KPO). (Author's collection.)

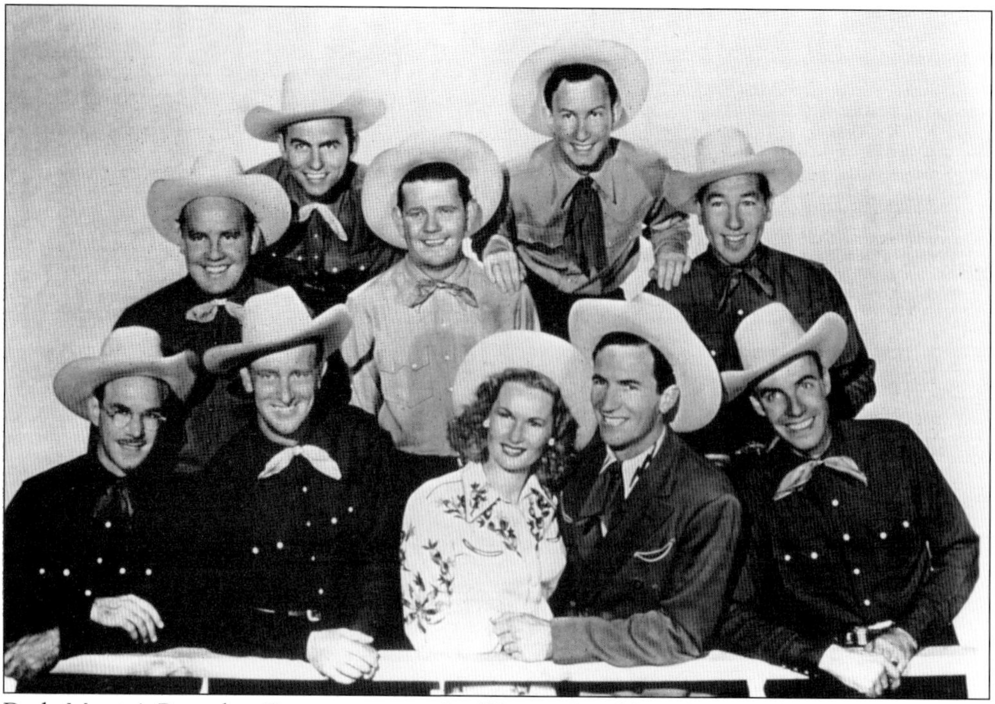

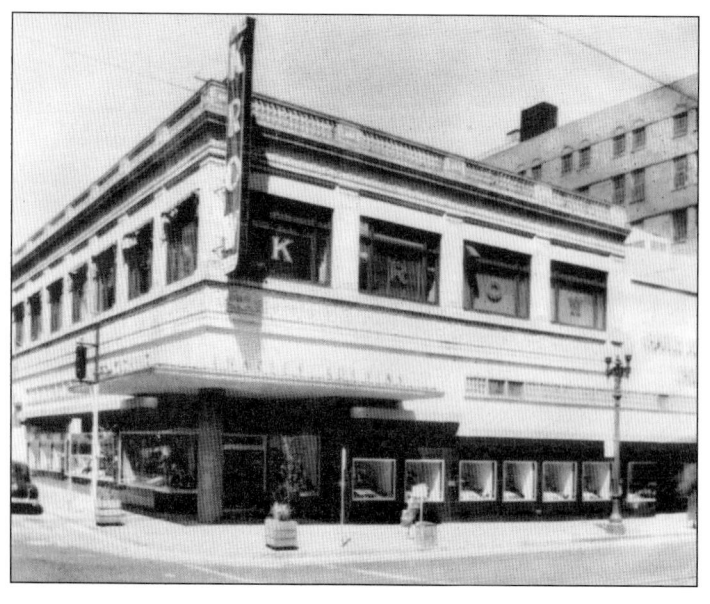

Dude Martin's Roundup Gang was a popular Western band heard on KTAB, KGO, KYA, and a few other stations during the 1930s, 1940s, and 1950s. He followed in the footsteps of Mac McClintock (KFRC) and Charlie Marshall (KPO), who were pioneers of Western music on local radio. Dude Martin (first row, second from right) went on to become a KGO-TV television host in the 1950s. (Author's collection.)

KROW debuted in 1925 as KFWM, operated by the Oakland Educational Society and located in an East Oakland church. In 1939, KSFO's Wesley Dumm and Phil Lasky combined with former KQW owner Fred Hart to buy KROW, and it became Oakland's "Home Interest Station." KROW's studios were on the second floor of Kushin's Shoe Store in downtown Oakland from 1936 to 1964. The station became KABL in 1959. (Author's collection.)

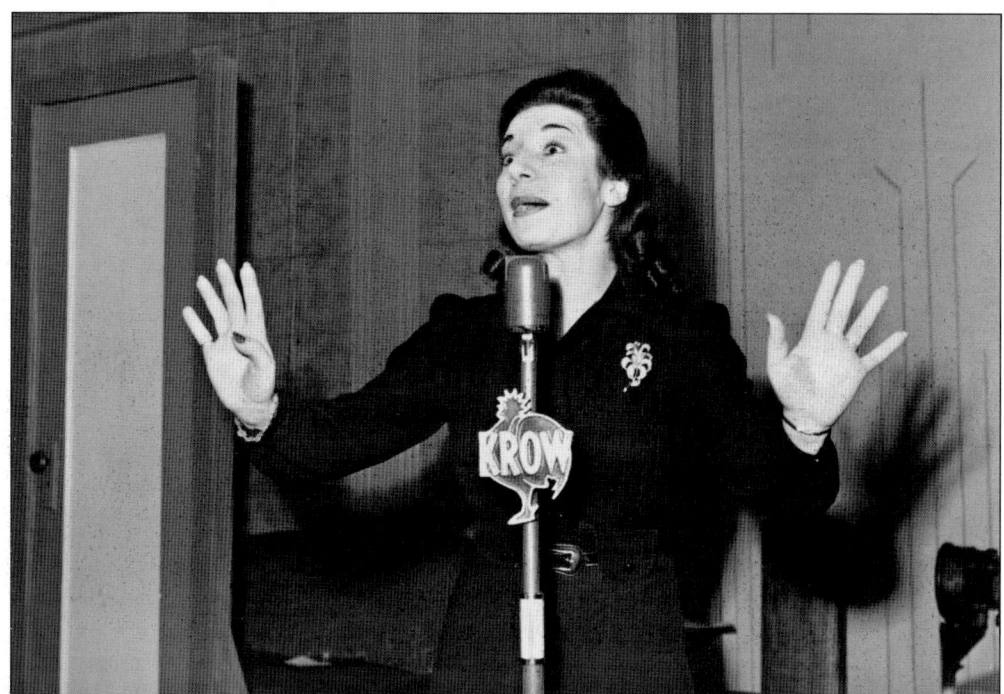

Foreign language broadcasts were the domain of small independent stations like KROW and KRE. Bella Sumares was part of a group of Portuguese entertainers that broadcast an hour each day over KROW in 1942. Sumares, born in Boston of Portuguese parents, sang on the program in both Portuguese and English. This is an Office of War Information photograph. (Library of Congress.)

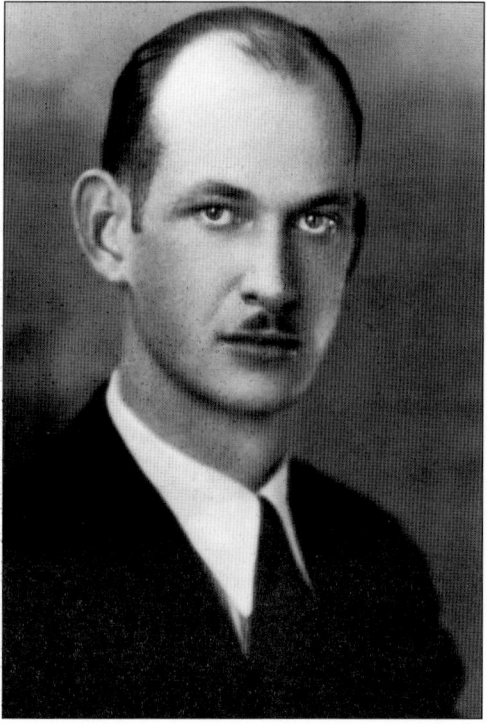

Frank Cope was probably the world's first bona fide disc jockey. His daily 5:00 a.m. to 8:00 a.m. Alarm Klok Klub on KJBS was San Francisco's most popular music program for nearly 25 years. After touring the country as a dance band musician, he started his radio career at KSL in Salt Lake City in 1927 and then joined the staff of KJBS in 1930. Except for a short hiatus from 1936 to 1938, he was a morning fixture of San Francisco radio until 1959. This KJBS publicity photograph is from 1931. (Author's collection.)

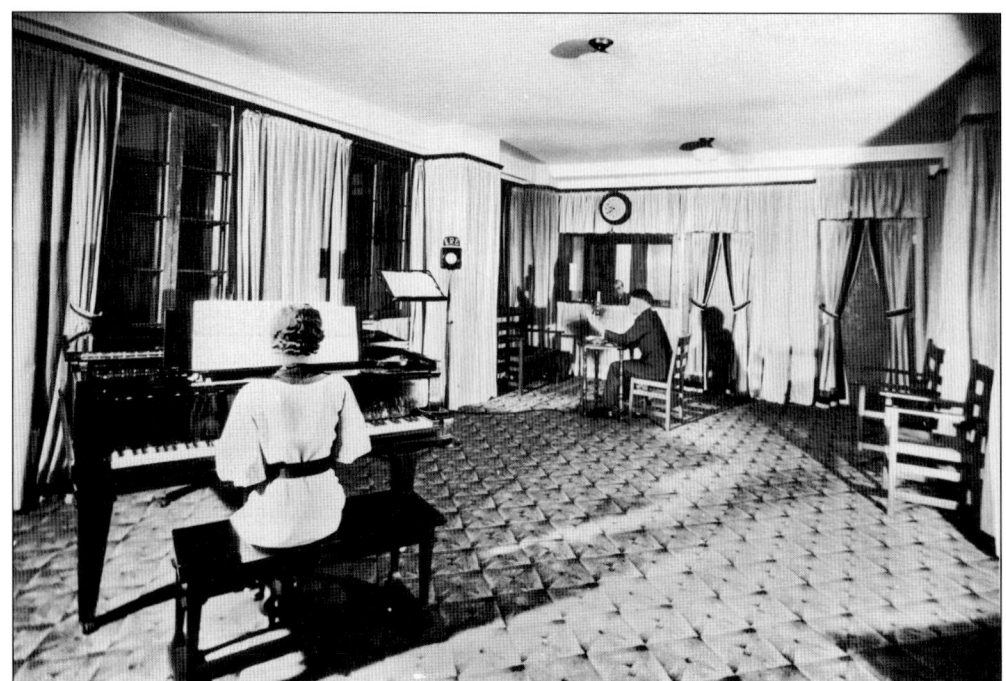

Arthur Westlund leased KRE from the First Congregational Church in Berkeley in 1930. He moved the studios to the Glenn-Connolly Building at 2337 Shattuck Avenue in Berkeley in 1933. The above photograph shows a view of studio A, looking towards the combination control room and announcers' booth. The smaller studio B was on the other side of the control room. The photograph below shows a small room in the church where KRE's transmitter room and backup studio were located. Shown are the station's 100-watt De Forest transmitter and its homemade 250-watt linear amplifier. The control desk has a small homemade audio mixer, two turntables, and a condenser microphone. On top of the console is a small set of hand chimes that were struck by the announcer when making station announcements. A new transmitter site was built at 601 Ashby Avenue in 1937. (Both, author's collection.)

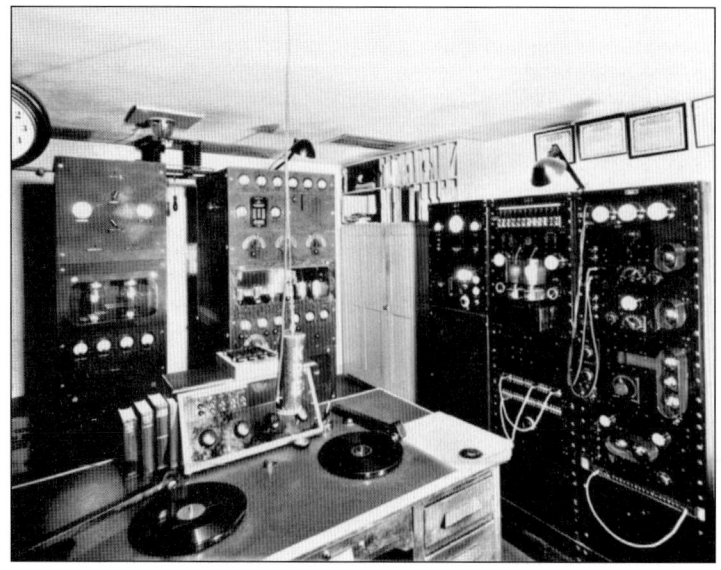

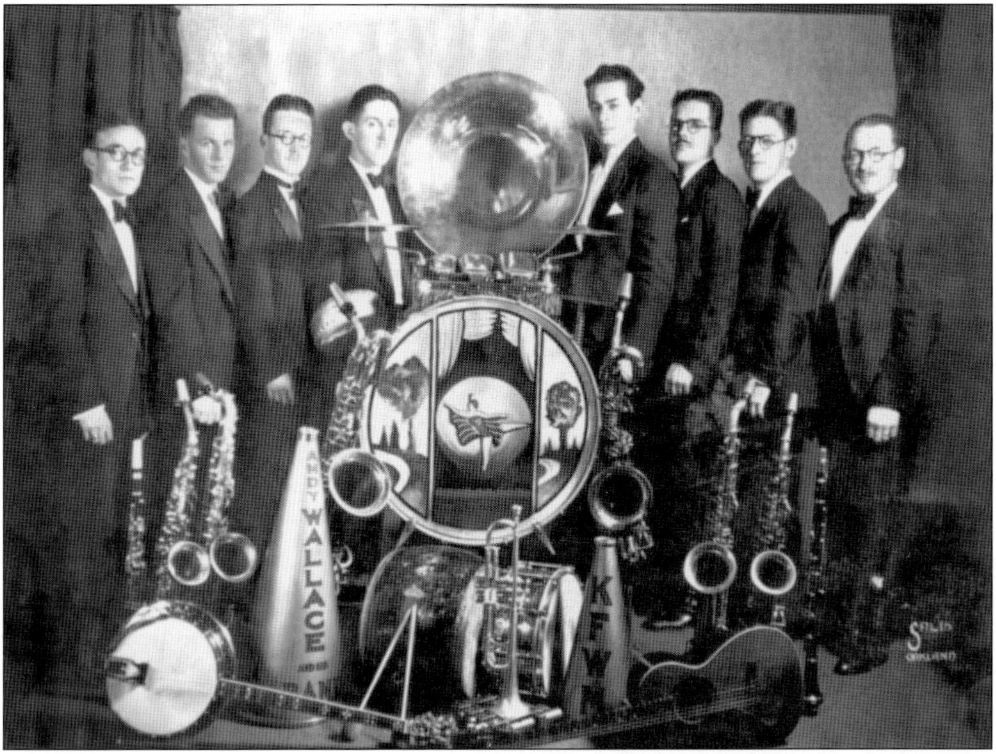

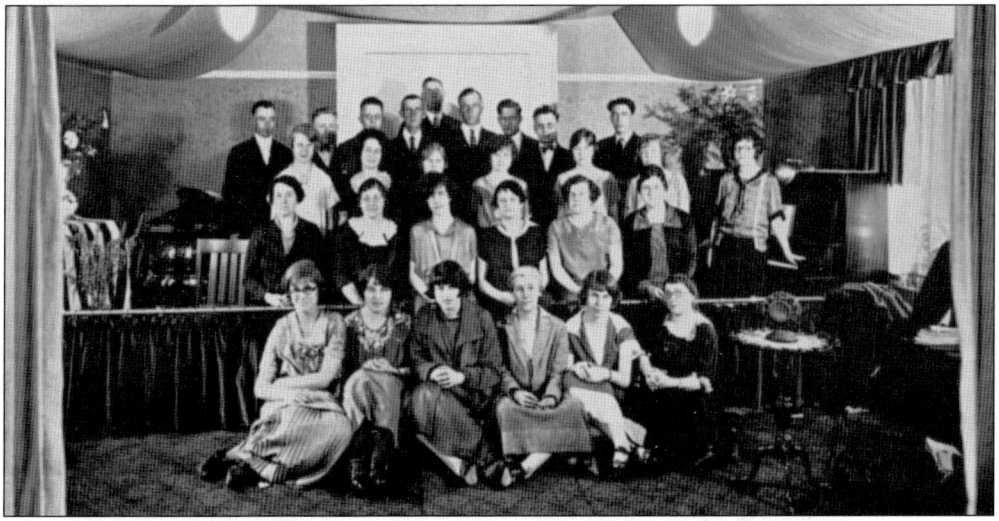

Above, the Andy Wallace Band was featured on KFWM in the late 1920s. KFWM became KROW in 1930. Below, Dr. Louis L. Sherman started KFUS in 1925, broadcasting from his home at 28th Street and Telegraph Avenue in Oakland. He also maintained a medical practice and taught classes in medicine at his home. KFUS's programming was an odd combination of medical advice and religious programming. Its license was revoked by the Federal Radio Commission in 1928 because of frequency stability violations, but Doctor Sherman continued broadcasting over KRE for the next several decades. In the photograph below, a class of students from Doctor Sherman's medical school poses in the combination lecture room and studio. (Above, author's collection; below, Dr. Lewis Sherman.)

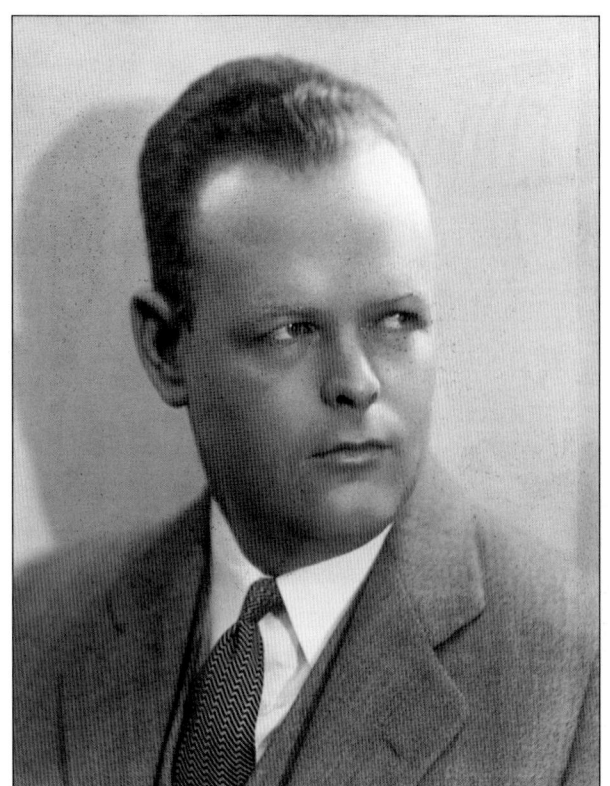

Charles L. McCarthy was the manager of station relations for NBC in San Francisco. In 1934, he joined with Ralph Brunton of KJBS to purchase KQW in San Jose from Fred J. Hart. McCarthy became KQW's manager and then was CBS's regional vice president and general manager after KQW affiliated with CBS in 1942. (Richard J. Rodriguez, McCarthy family.)

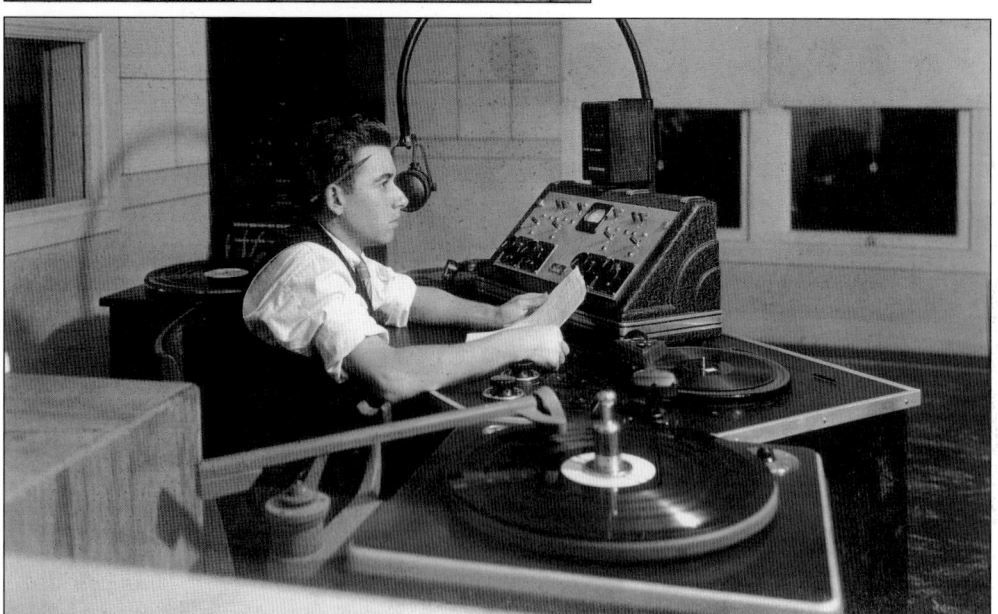

Small town radio stations have always been the place that aspiring young radio announcers "develop their chops." Here is John "Jack" Wagner beginning his career at KHUB Watsonville in 1937. Afterwards, he became the manager of KSYC in Yreka and KDB in Santa Barbara, then program director of KNBC (1953–1967), and finally was the director of broadcast operations at KCBS until 1981. Wagner died in 1988. (Mike Adams.)

Five

THE WAR YEARS
1939–1945

The 1939 Golden Gate International Exposition on Treasure Island put San Francisco on the international broadcasting map for the first time. RCA constructed a large radio studio at the fairgrounds and the big networks as well as small stations all took turns broadcasting from the fair. The exposition produced regular music remotes from the Guatemalan and Brazilian pavilions, feeding them free to any station that wanted them.

General Electric built its shortwave station KGEI on the fairgrounds. It was the West Coast's first international station, making daily broadcasts to Latin America and Asia. KGEI was built to be an international goodwill station and promotional vehicle for its owner, but the station suddenly took on strategic national importance when the Japanese attacked Pearl Harbor—it was the *only* American station that could be heard in the Pacific. William Winter, a news commentator heard on KGEI, became a crucial voice of information and encouragement to the Philippines during its conquest and occupation by the Japanese.

Answering an urgent plea from President Roosevelt, KSFO's Wesley Dumm built KWID in 1942. It was the West Coast's most powerful shortwave station. At the same time, the office of War Information (OWI) established radio studios in San Francisco and began producing round-the-clock programs for KGEI and KWID that were a vital link to both foreign citizens and US servicemen in the Pacific. This marked the beginnings of what later became the Voice of America, the government's international shortwave radio service.

San Francisco was also the headquarters for the gathering and dissemination of Pacific war news to an anxious nation. It was a fast-moving war, and the immediacy of radio for the first time gave radio an important edge over newspapers in the field of news reporting. CBS established a large news-gathering organization at KQW in the Palace Hotel and relayed live shortwave reports from its Pacific field reporters eastward to an eager audience. NBC and its spin-off network, ABC, both operated radio news bureaus from different floors of the Radio City building. KSFO also established its own large news organization and occasionally even surpassed the networks. It had its own reporter on hand for the Japanese surrender and carried live broadcasts of General MacArthur's arrival in San Francisco as well as all major events of the United Nations's organizational meetings.

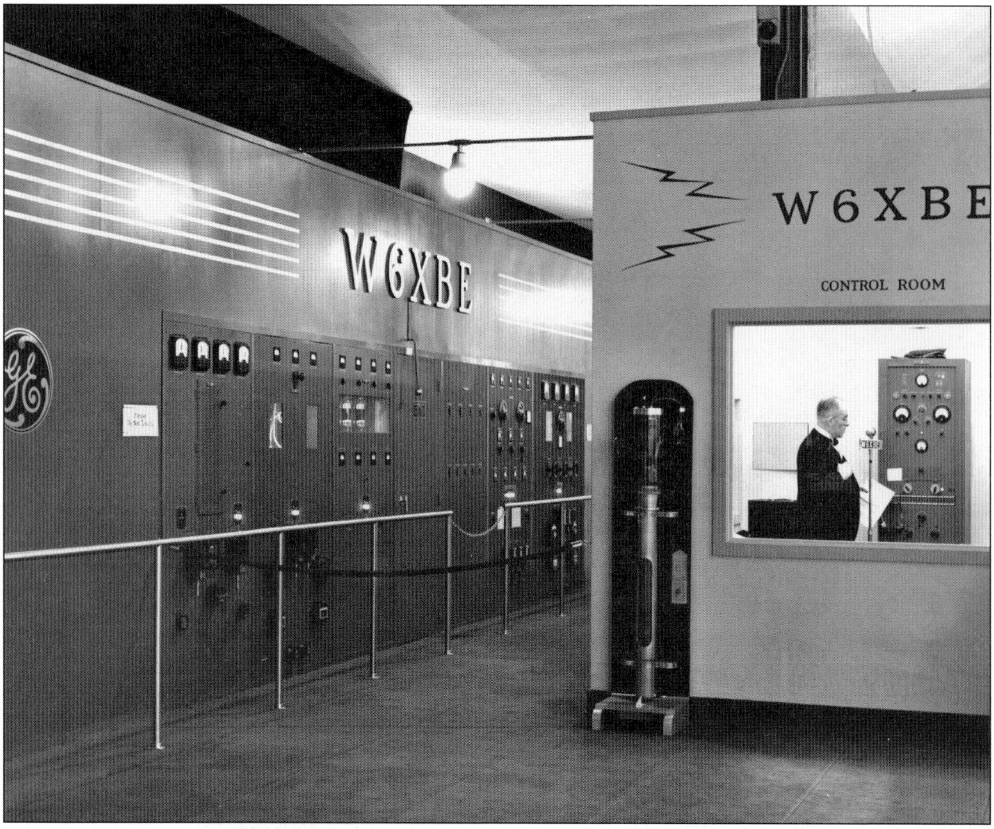

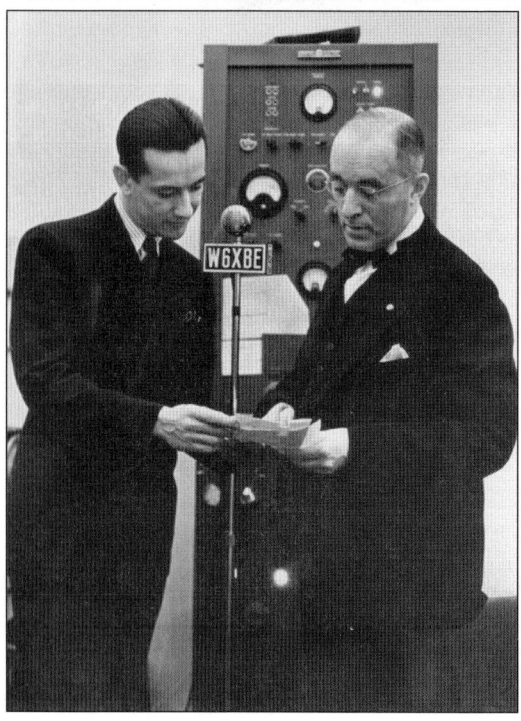

This photograph shows International shortwave station KGEI, which started broadcasting from the Golden Gate Exposition in San Francisco in 1939. General Electric built the station as a technological marvel, demonstrating the company's advanced industrial capabilities. It operated with the experimental call sign W6XBE before becoming KGEI in September. Above is GE's 20,000-watt transmitter with a cramped studio to the right. Between them is an example of a GE transmitting tube. More than four million fair attendees toured this exhibit and watched the live broadcasts through the studio's plate-glass windows. At left, Juan Trevina (left) and Carlos U. Benedetti (right), Spanish language announcers, prepare to broadcast a program on W6XBE. KGEI broadcasts were directed to Latin America in the evening and Asia and the Pacific during early morning hours. (Both, FEBC International.)

KGEI manager Buck Harris checks the INS press teletype in this 1939 photograph. The map shows the shortwave station's main beams, providing service to Latin America and the Asian Pacific. They were actually 180 degrees apart if viewed on a great circle map, and were aimed at Tokyo and Mexico City. The program schedule was timed to arrive at both target areas during local evening hours. (FEBC International.)

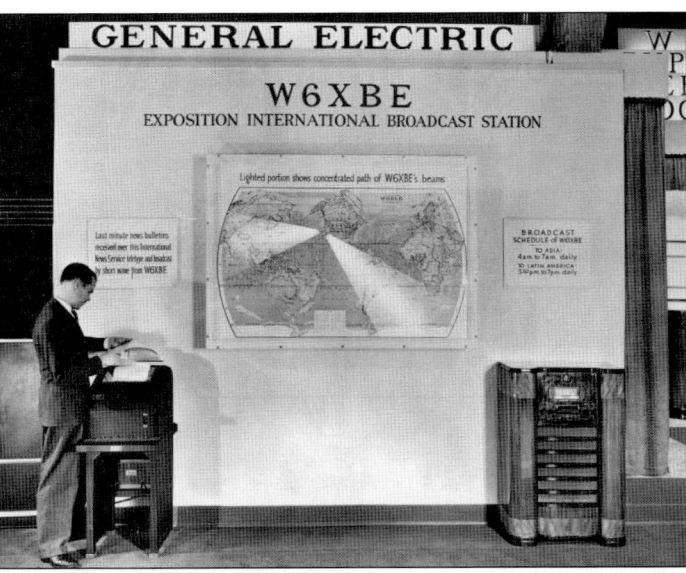

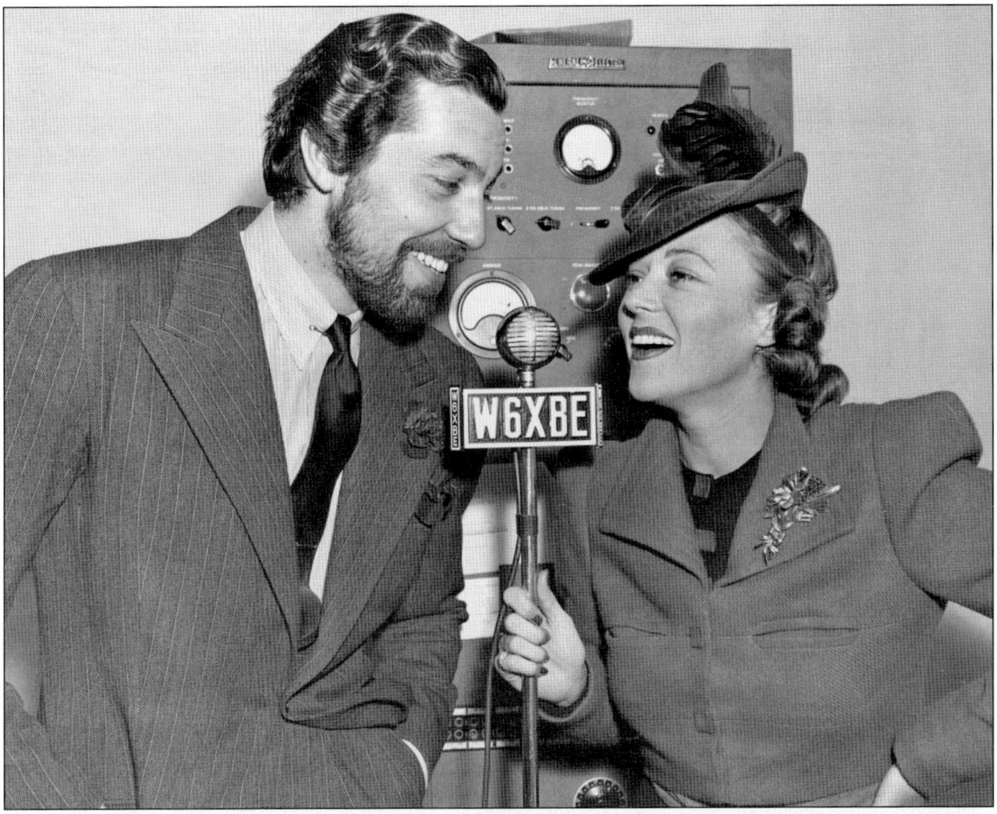

Hollywood stars Cesar Romero and Sally Eilers send greetings to Latin America in 1939 over W6XBE (later KGEI) at the Golden Gate Exposition on Treasure Island in San Francisco Bay. While originally focused on Latin America, it was the station's coverage of the Asian Pacific that would become of strategic importance during World War II. (FEBC International.)

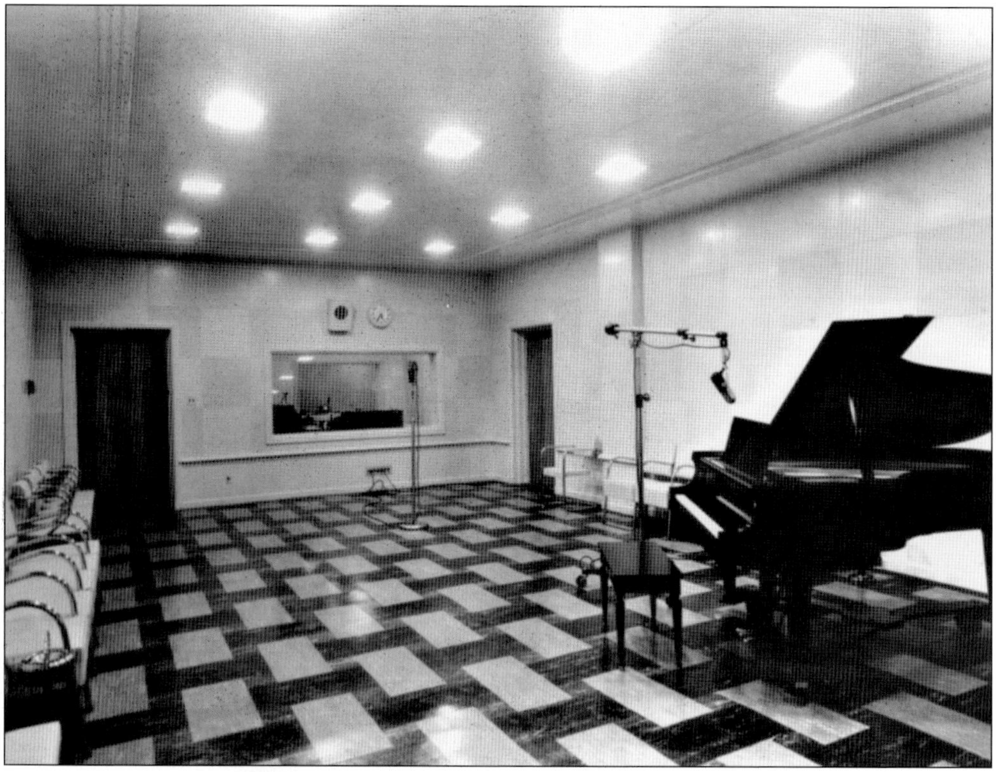

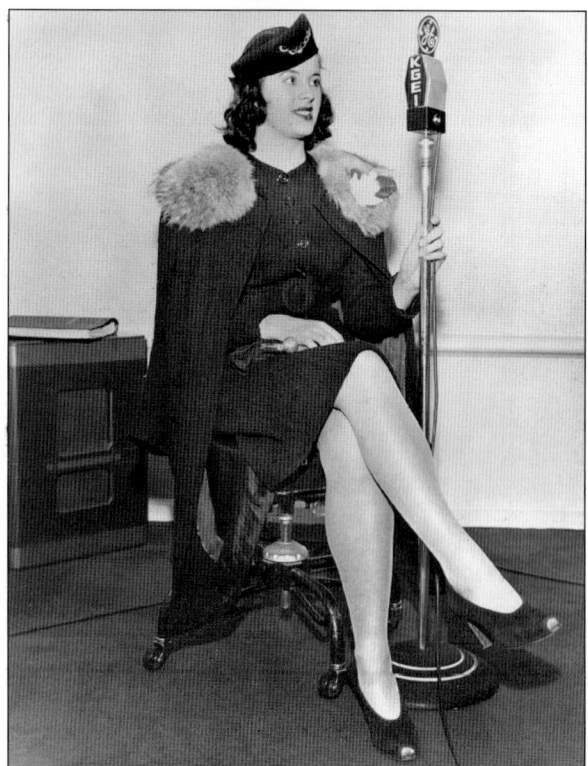

After the Golden Gate Exposition closed, KGEI moved to permanent studios in the Fairmont Hotel. Here is KGEI's studio A. During the Japanese invasion in the Pacific, radio commentator William Winter broadcast news bulletins and messages of hope and encouragement from this studio to America's allies and its servicemen in the Pacific. (FEBC International.)

Betty O'Lanie sends greetings over KGEI to her sweetheart, US Army private Richard Caum, who was stationed at Annette Island, Alaska. The weekly *Musical Mail Bag* program originated from the KGEI studios at the Fairmont Hotel in 1941 and was picked up and rebroadcast by KFAR in Fairbanks. It was directed at American servicemen stationed in Alaska, Hawaii, and the Pacific. (FEBC International.)

After the end of the Golden Gate Exposition, General Electric built this reinforced-concrete transmitter building for KGEI adjacent to the KPO antenna in Belmont. It would be KGEI's home until it signed off for the last time in 1994. After the early 1960s, when KGEI was operated by the Far East Broadcasting Company, this building also housed the studios. (FEBC International.)

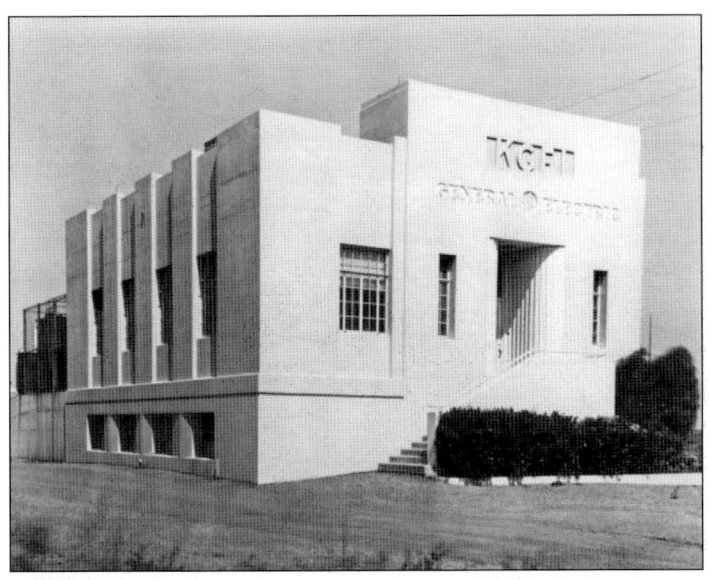

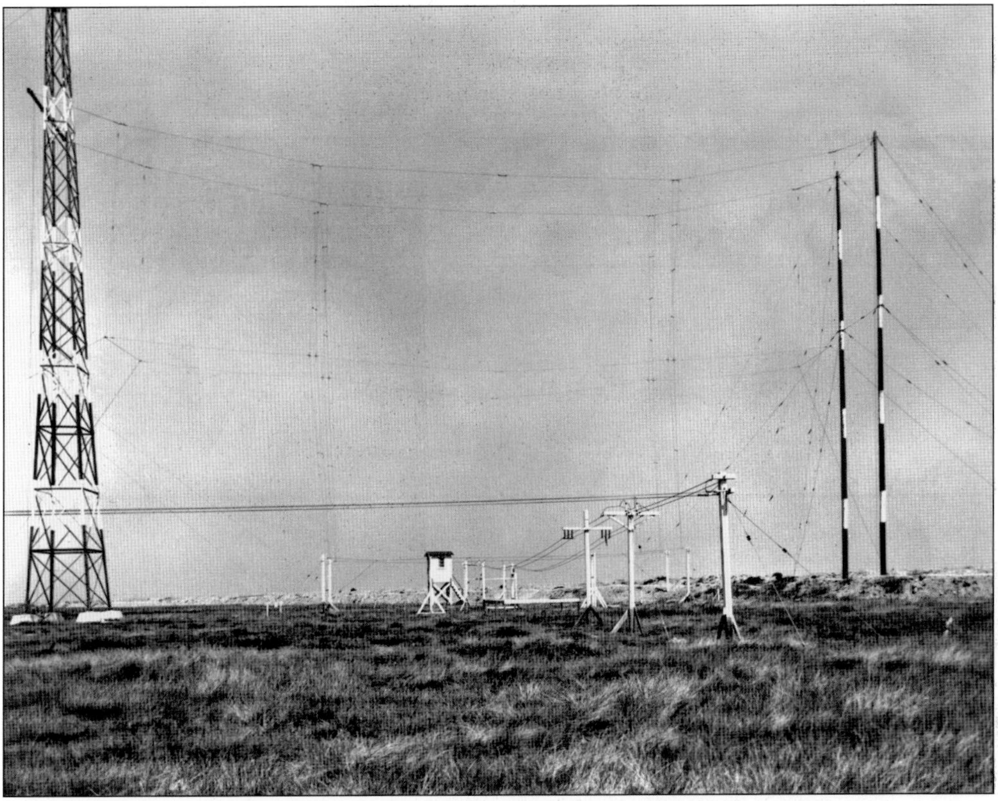

In this 1960s view, the KGEI 9 MHz shortwave antenna is almost exactly as GE constructed it in 1941. The tower on the left is part of the 11 and 15 MHz array, mostly out of view. Also visible is a guardhouse that was manned by the military during World War II. It was government policy during the war to protect all critical radio transmission sites. (FEBC International.)

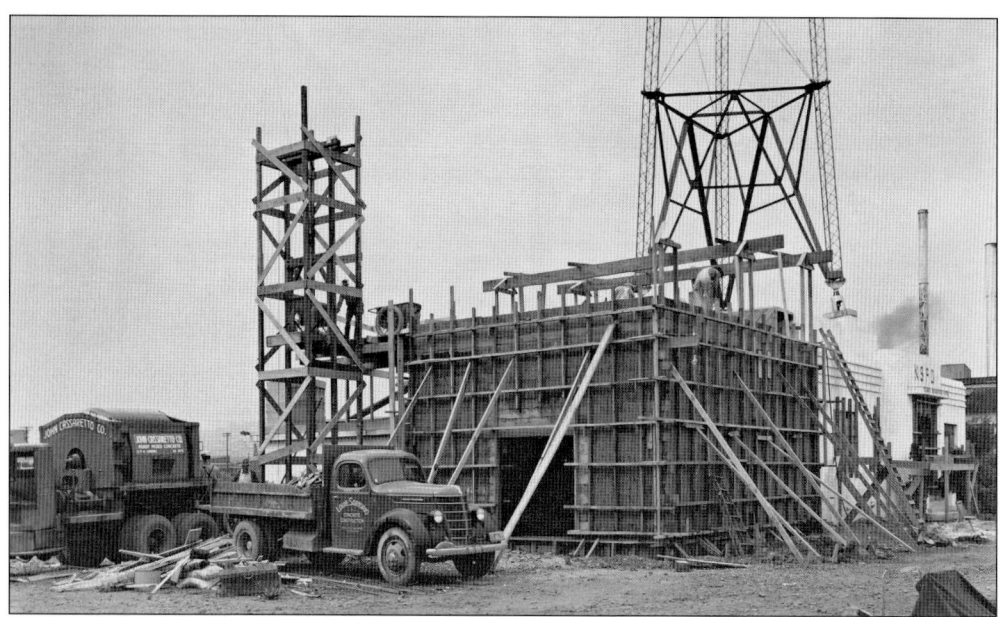

At the request of Pres. Franklin D. Roosevelt, KSFO built its powerful shortwave station KWID in 1942, supplying critically-needed additional American radio coverage of the Pacific. In the above scene, the transmitter building first constructed by KSFO at Islais Creek in 1937 is being enlarged to house the new shortwave transmitter. The KSFO AM tower on the roof of the building is still in use today. Seen below are some KSFO staff members and guests in front of the completed KSFO/KWID building. The wires at the upper left are transmission lines that feed the shortwave antennas. Longtime KSFO announcer Bob Hansen is third from the right. (Above, Kevin Mostyn; below, Penny Wilkes.)

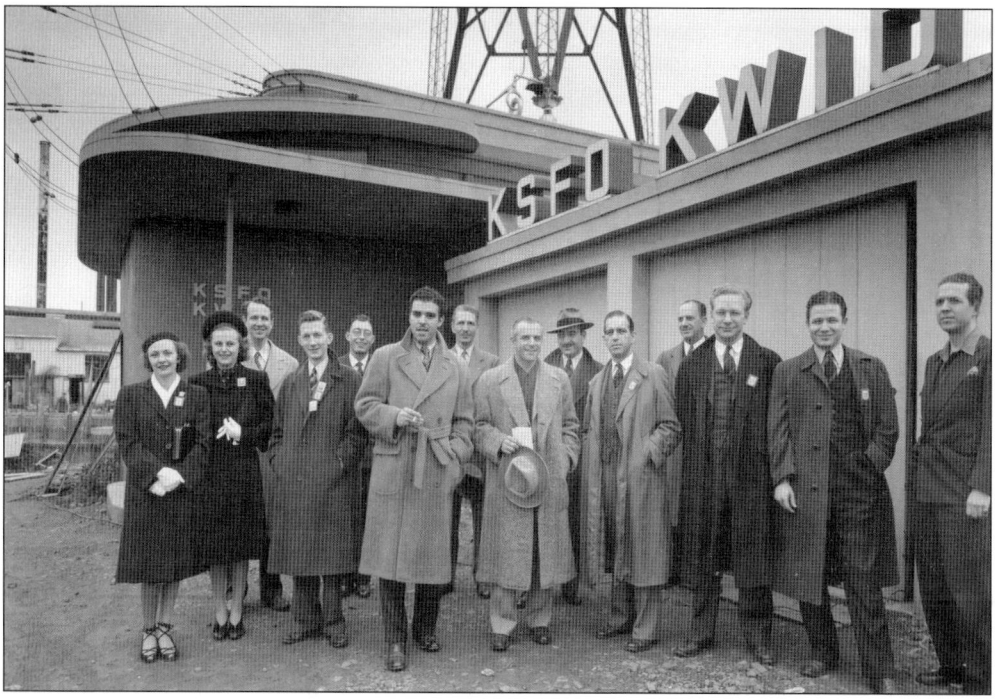

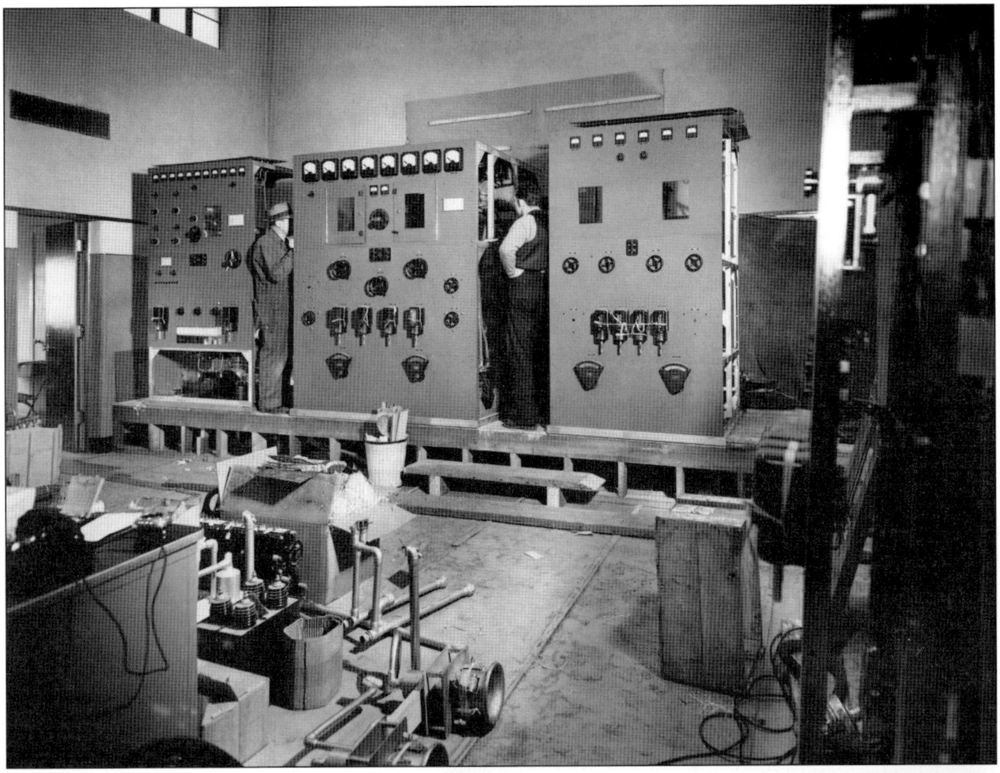

Engineers install KWID's 100 kW GE transmitter at the KSFO building on Islais Creek in 1942. During World War II, all programs were supplied by the Office of War Information from studios in San Francisco and after the war by the Voice of America. After KWID closed in 1953, this transmitter was acquired by Far East Broadcasting Company and later saw service in Okinawa and Saipan. (Kevin Mostyn.)

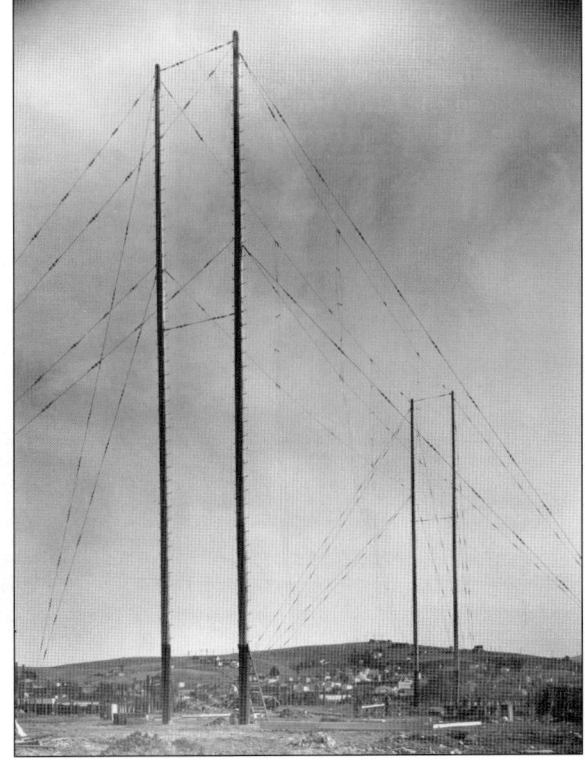

The KWID shortwave antenna is seen here under construction in early 1942. The station was already in the planning stages when Pearl Harbor was attacked, and KWID went on the air just five months later. This corner of San Francisco was then still fairly undeveloped, without the population density of today. The hill in the background is probably the present location of McLaren Park. (Penny Wilkes.)

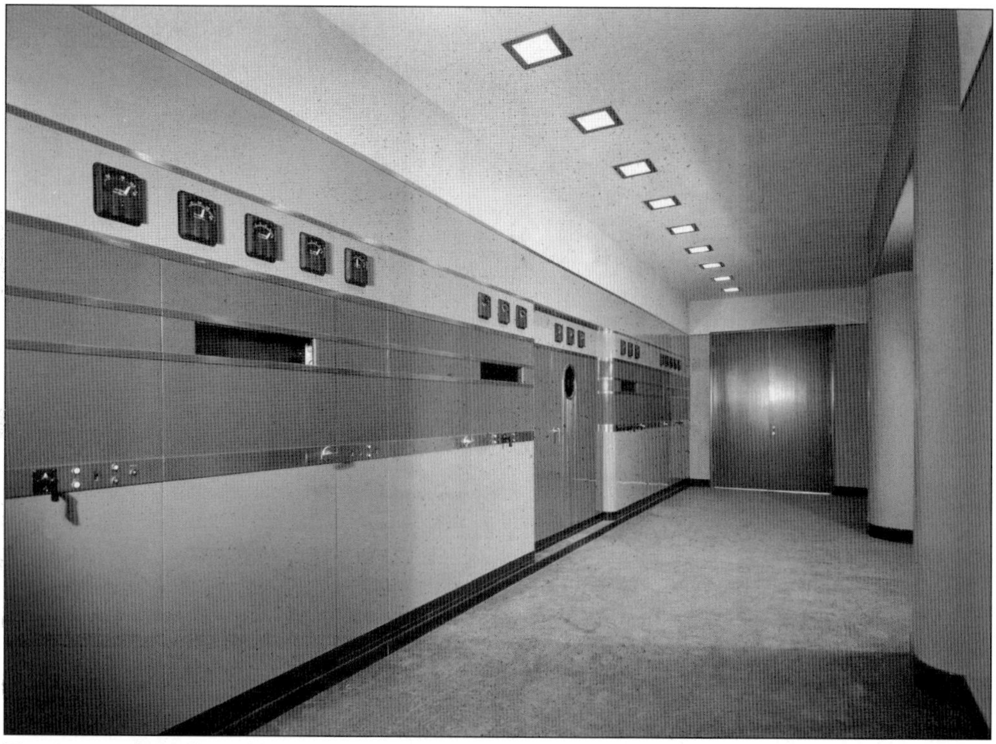

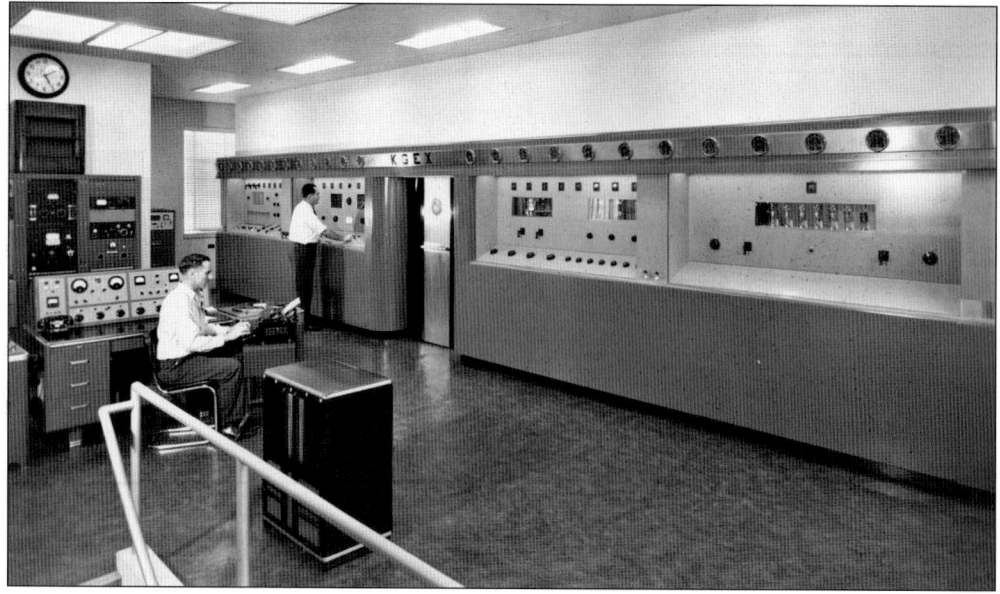

To augment the Office of War Information's shortwave broadcasting efforts, the federal government purchased 22 new transmitters in 1943. Above is the brand new 50 kW RCA transmitter, which it sent to KSFO and went on the air as KWIX. It was located in a north wing addition to the KSFO transmitter building seen on page 106. Below, this 100 kW GE transmitter went to KGEI and broadcast with the call sign KGEX. McKay Wireless and RCA also began operating OWI relay stations in Northern California. By the war's end, a total of 36 OWI frequencies were being aimed at Europe and the Pacific. (Above, Penny Wilkes; below, FEBC International.)

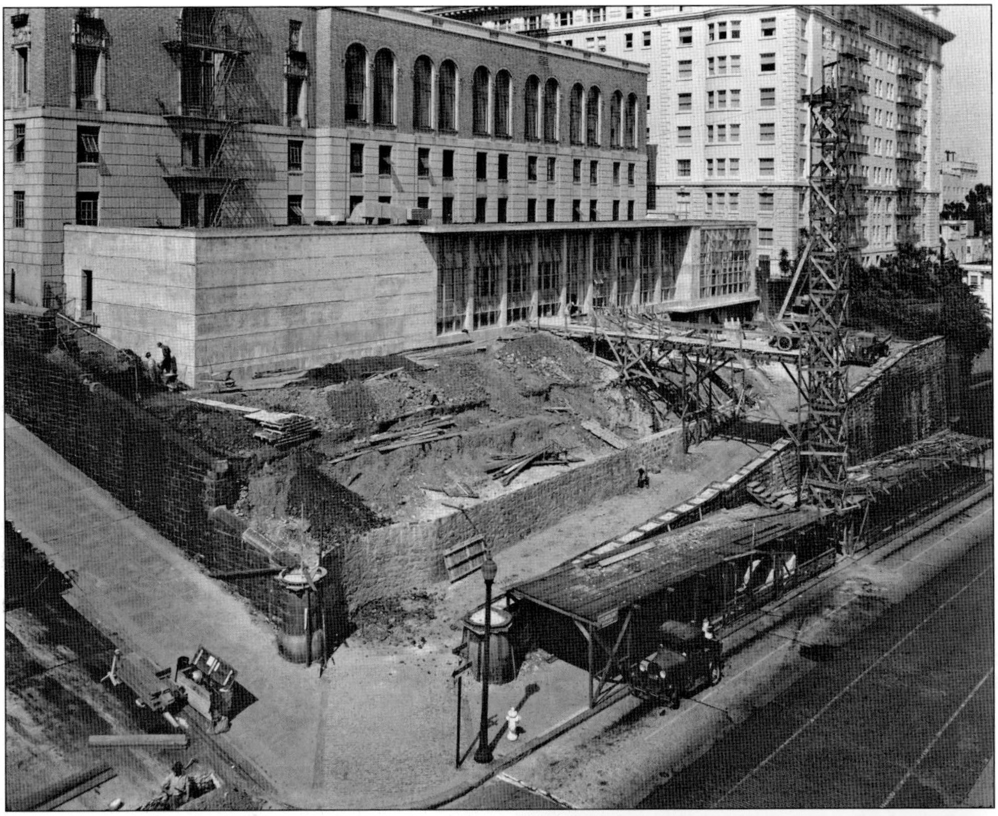

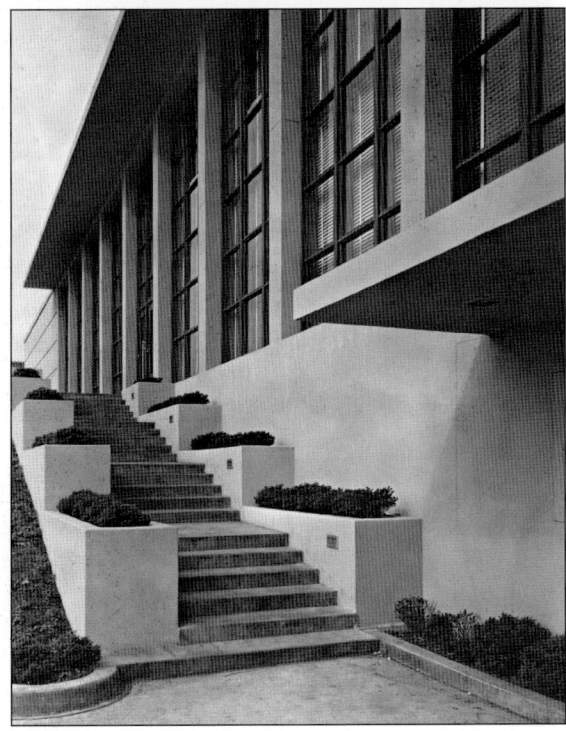

The Office of War Information's (OWI) growing operation quickly overwhelmed KGEI's modest studios in the Fairmont Hotel. Once again, the government turned to KSFO's Wesley Dumm, who built new studios for both KSFO and the OWI in an annex to the Mark Hopkins Hotel. Known as "Number One Nob Hill Circle," the studios were located in the hotel's former parking garage, felt to be safe from enemy bombs. Completed in 1943, this elaborate facility became the source of most programming for KSFO, KGEI, KGEX, KWID, and KWIX. After NBC moved to Radio City in 1942, its former studios at 111 Sutter Street were also taken over by the OWI. After the war, KSFO used this entire building until moving out in 1954. The building later was the home of KYA from 1958 to 1979. (Both, Kevin Mostyn.)

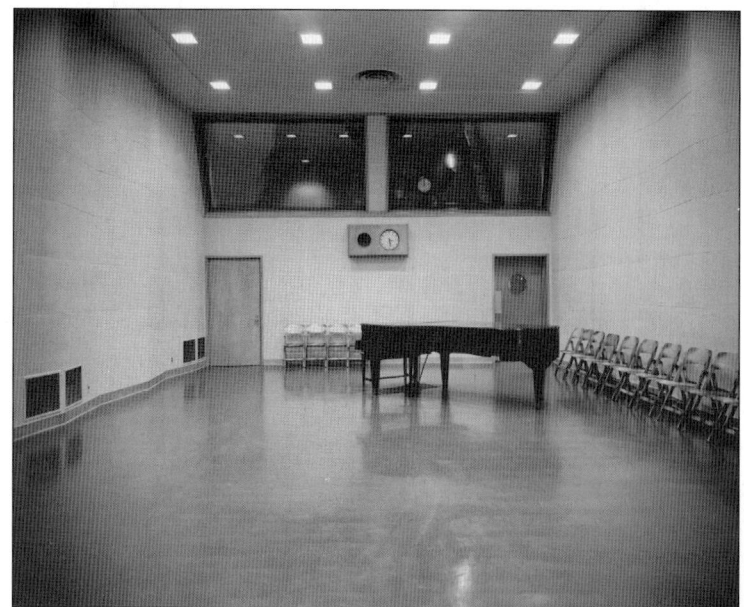

KSFO's studio 11 was the main performance studio at Number One Nob Hill Circle. Large musical ensembles could broadcast from this spacious two-story area. One of the glass windows above was the studio control room, and the other was the sponsors' booth, where advertisers could enjoy a private view of the programs they sponsored. (Kevin Mostyn.)

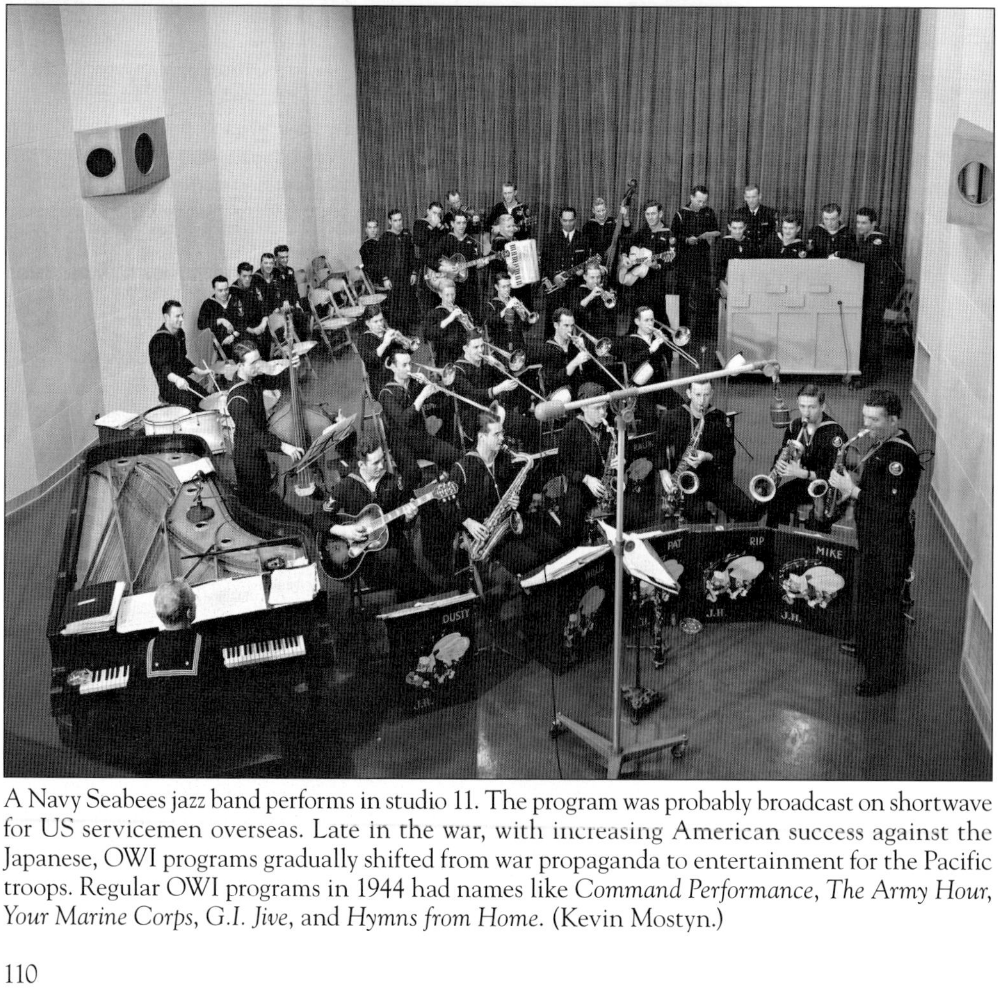

A Navy Seabees jazz band performs in studio 11. The program was probably broadcast on shortwave for US servicemen overseas. Late in the war, with increasing American success against the Japanese, OWI programs gradually shifted from war propaganda to entertainment for the Pacific troops. Regular OWI programs in 1944 had names like *Command Performance*, *The Army Hour*, *Your Marine Corps*, *G.I. Jive*, and *Hymns from Home*. (Kevin Mostyn.)

This was the studio 11 control booth. Each studio had its own control room, responsible for mixing the microphones and other audio sources that originated in the studio. The programs leaving these control rooms then went to the master control room (below). There were also several small announcers' studios in the 11-studio complex. (Kevin Mostyn.)

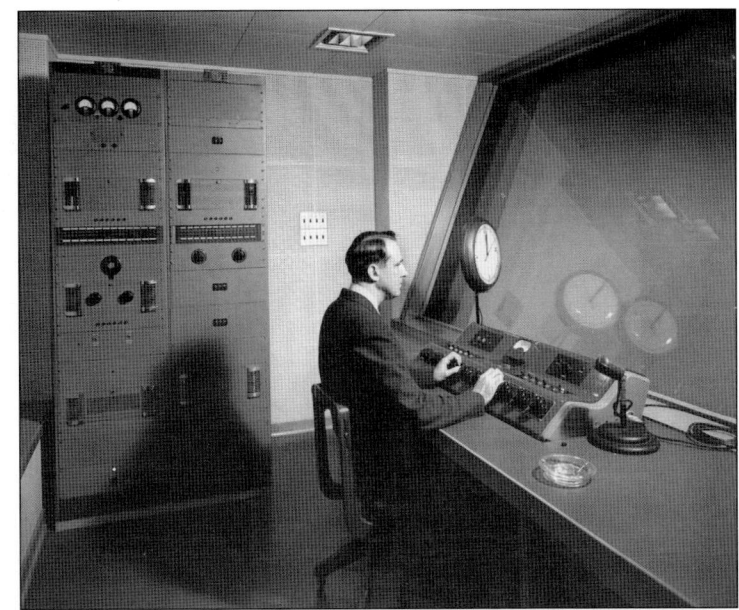

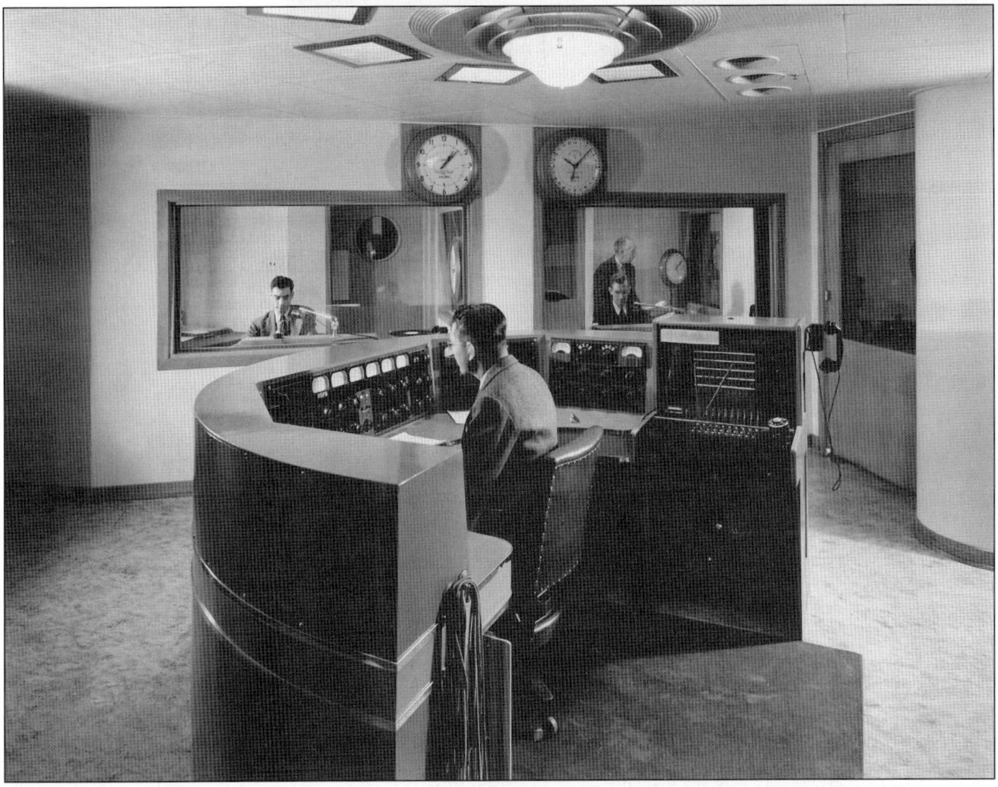

This was the KSFO master control console at Number One Nob Hill Circle. It was in the center of the operation, surrounded by windows looking into the different studios and control booths. From this operating position, one engineer simultaneously oversaw all the audio for broadcasting, auditioning, recording, and rehearsing in each of the studios. Network connections and remote broadcasts were also managed from this desk. (Kevin Mostyn.)

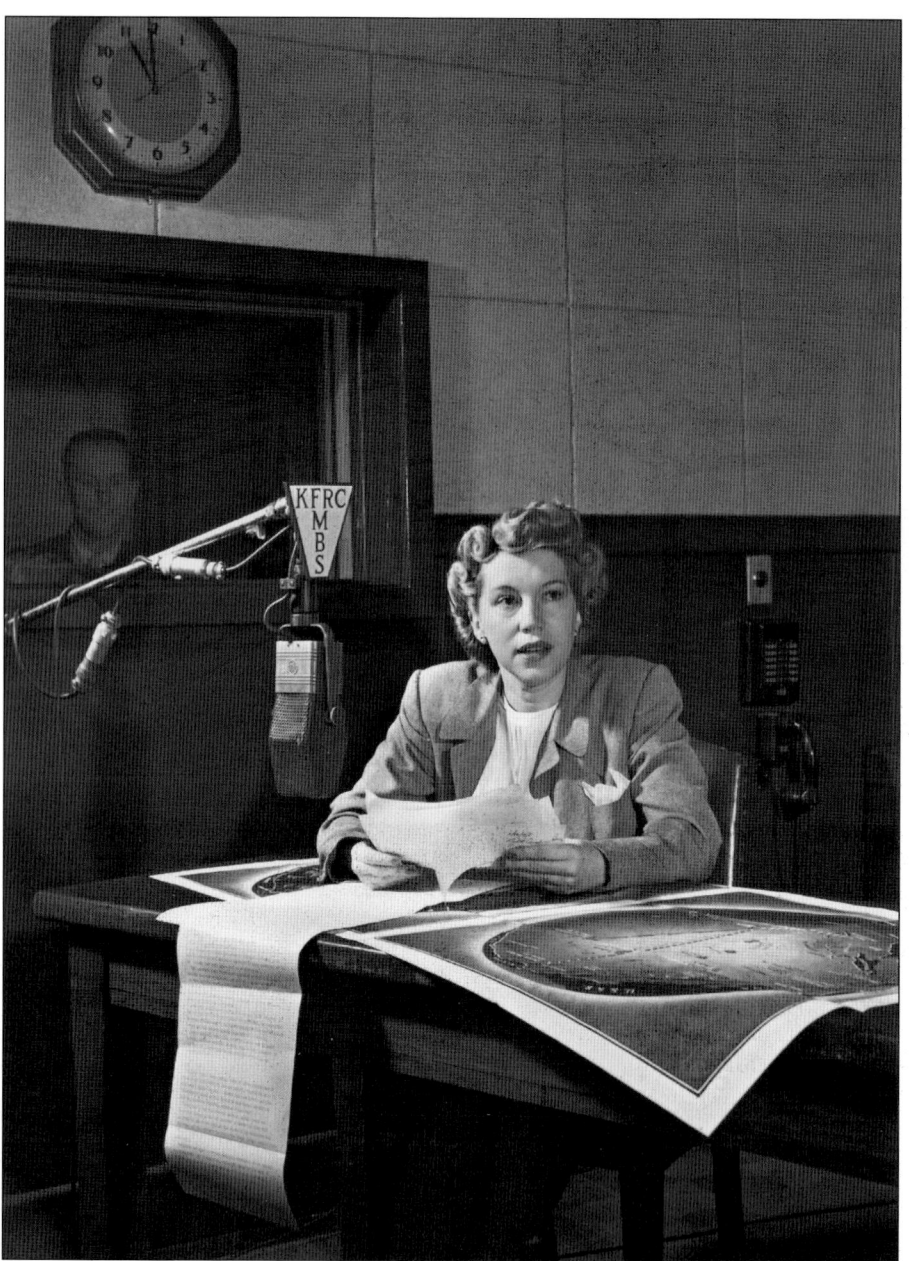

Most women in early radio were either actresses, musicians, or secretaries. The choice positions of announcer, news reporter, or commentator were always reserved for men. However, in the early 1940s, many of the country's best announcers and commentators were taking leaves of absences to fight in the war. As with other critical services, some women stepped in to take their places. Ruth Anderson (pictured) at KFRC was the city's only female news reporter. A graduate of radio soap operas, she started editing, preparing, and reading her own newscasts in October 1942. Her 15-minute program *Last Minute News* was heard six days a week, sponsored by a San Francisco department store. Women were heard more frequently in such roles after the war, but it would still take decades for them to achieve parity with their male counterparts on the air. This is a Farm Security Administration/OWI photograph. (Library of Congress.)

Six

THE DISC JOCKEY ERA
1945–1960

The radio industry went through great upheaval in the years following the war. After the introduction of television, the old-style entertainment and variety shows were no longer sought by radio listeners, so radio successfully reinvented itself as a music entertainment medium. The disc jockey, whose domain in the past had been limited to smaller, independent stations, was suddenly the new king of radio. The stilted, scripted music announcements of past years were abandoned in favor of a casual ad-lib style that established a personal connection with each audience member. Recordings of popular mainstream adult music were soon joined by early rock 'n' roll music and the first top 40 stations. KEWB and KOBY were the first Bay Area stations to adopt the new format in the late 1950s, followed by KFRC and KYA in the 1960s.

Even as there was uncertainty over the future of radio, there was no shortage of new entrepreneurs who wanted to get into the radio business. Once the FCC lifted its wartime freeze on licenses for new radio stations, the number of AM stations more than doubled nationwide in just a few short years. Locally, many new stations took to the airwaves: San Jose had KEEN, KSJO, KLOK, and KXRX, as well as San Rafael's KTIM and KSMO in San Mateo. Existing stations also took advantage of the opening to expand their coverage. KGO raised its power in 1947 to 50,000 watts, and KCBS followed in 1951. New FM stations also appeared, and many believed FM would quickly supplant AM radio. In reality, the transition would take nearly 40 years. KALW, the first local FM station (1940), was followed after the war by a half dozen other stations, but the anticipated FM boom never occurred when the public demand for FM receivers failed to materialize. Some FM stations hung on—mostly those owned by the established AM stations—but the majority of independent stations quickly folded. A second FM wave would take hold more gradually in the 1960s.

Early television, on the other hand, met with immediate success. Wesley Dumm's KPIX, the first Bay Area television station, came on the air from the Mark Hopkins Hotel on Christmas Eve 1948, when there were just 3,500 television sets in Northern California. ABC's KGO-TV and the *Chronicle's* KRON-TV followed in 1949.

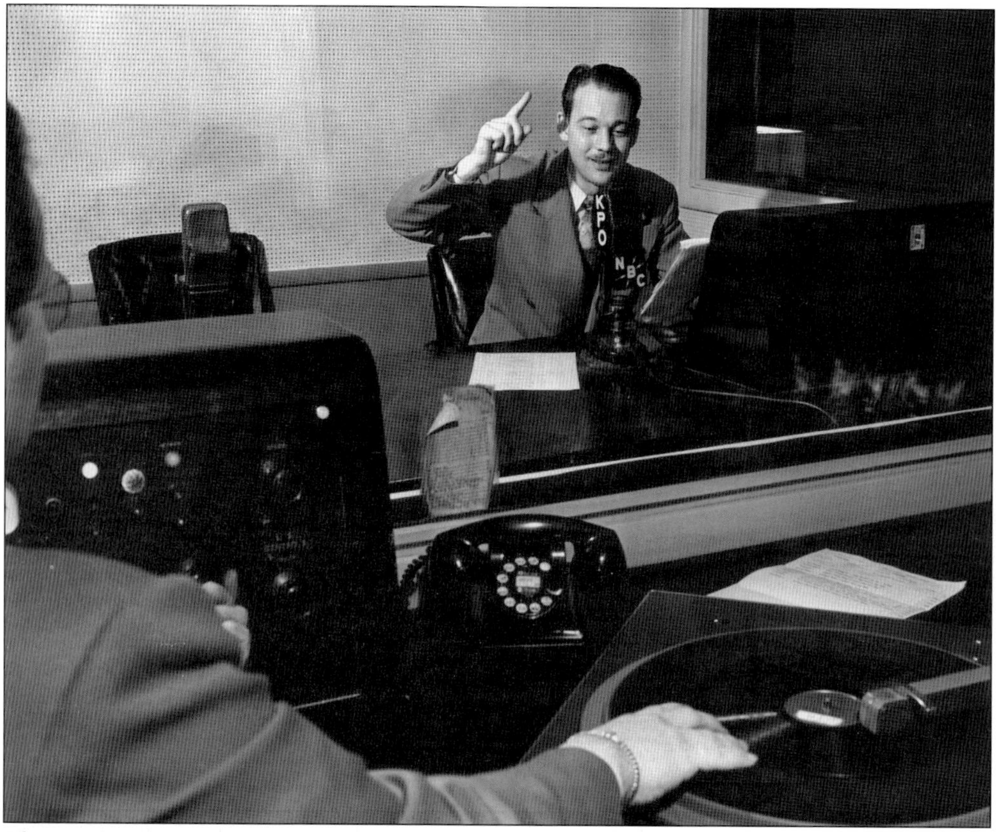

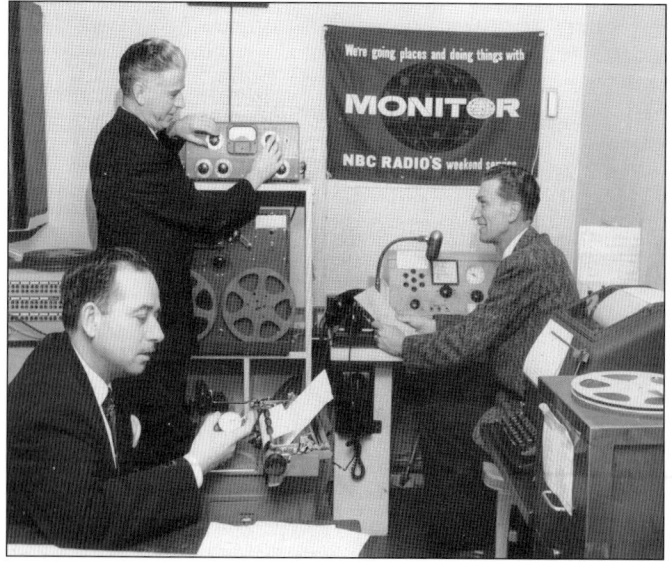

This is Your Home was a popular KNBC show in the late 1940s and 1950s. It featured historical San Francisco documentaries written by prolific radio writer Samuel Dickson and narrated by Budd Heyde. Here, Heyde announces one of the programs and cues engineer Russ Butler to fade in a musical bridge. The show was later heard on KNBR under the name *The San Francisco Story.* (Caryl Heyde Saunders.)

Monitor was a weekend NBC network show that began in 1955 and ran for 20 years. It was a "magazine of the air," conceived at a time when old-style radio formats were dying. It originated in New York, but network stations around the country also contributed feature material. Here (left to right) are Jack Wagner, Alan O'Neill, and Clarence Leisure recording a Monitor feature at KNBC in the 1950s. (Mike Adams.)

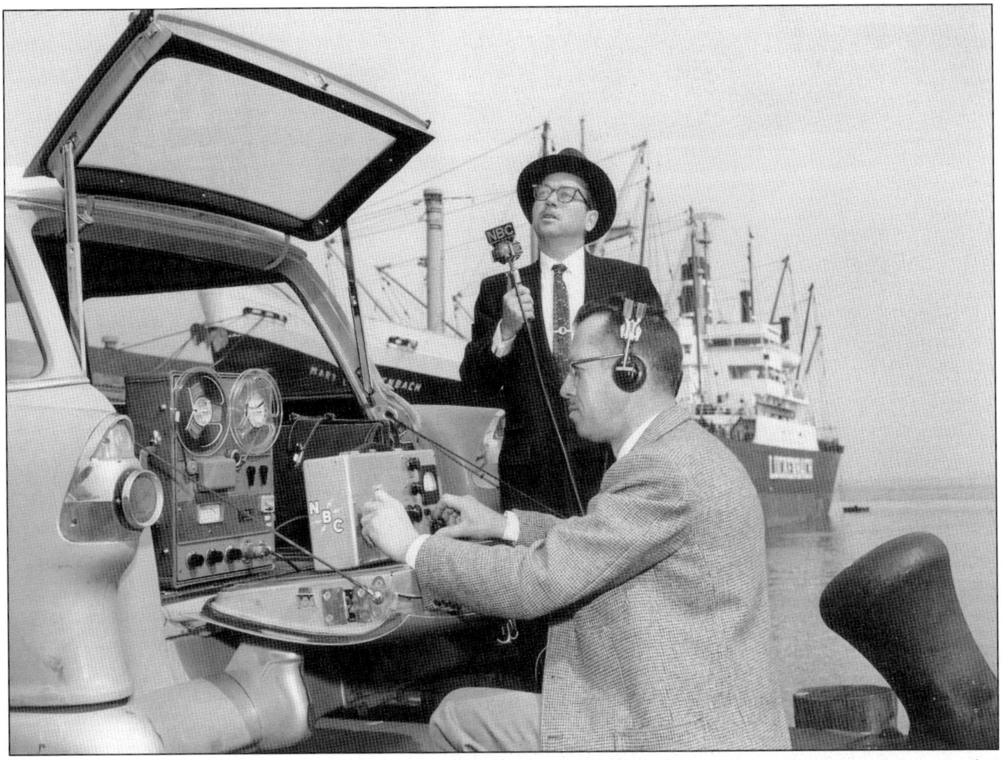

KNBC announcer Jack Wagner records a broadcast from the San Francisco waterfront in the mid-1950s. An engineer runs the microphone mixer. (Union rules prevented NBC announcers from operating their own equipment.) The tape recorder is the famous Ampex 601 professional suitcase portable that was a radio-industry workhorse into the 1960s. (Mike Adams.)

A KNBC remote broadcast truck transmits from Telegraph Hill in San Francisco sometime in the early 1950s. Shown are announcer Gayne Whitman and Glenn Hall Taylor of the N.W. Ayer Co. The vehicle is the iconic 1948 Pontiac "Woodie." Another icon, San Francisco's Coit Tower, is seen in the background. (Author's collection.)

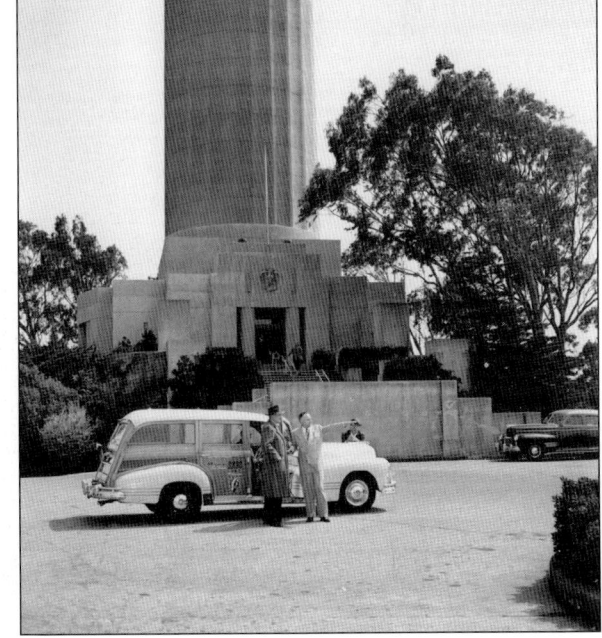

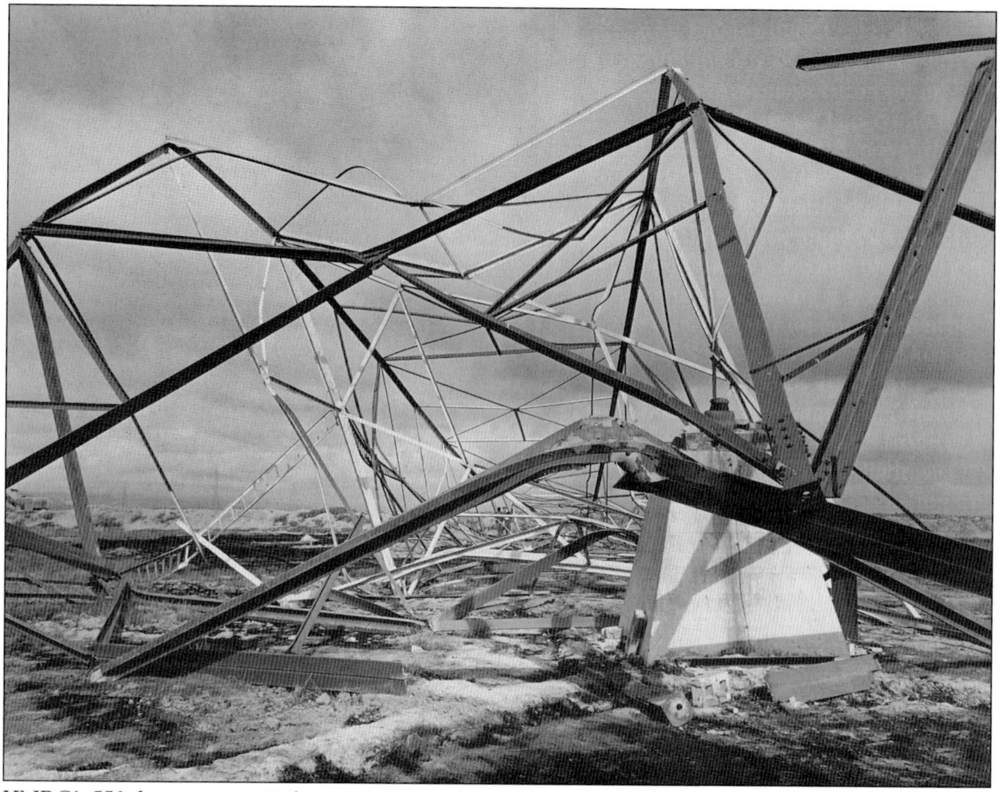

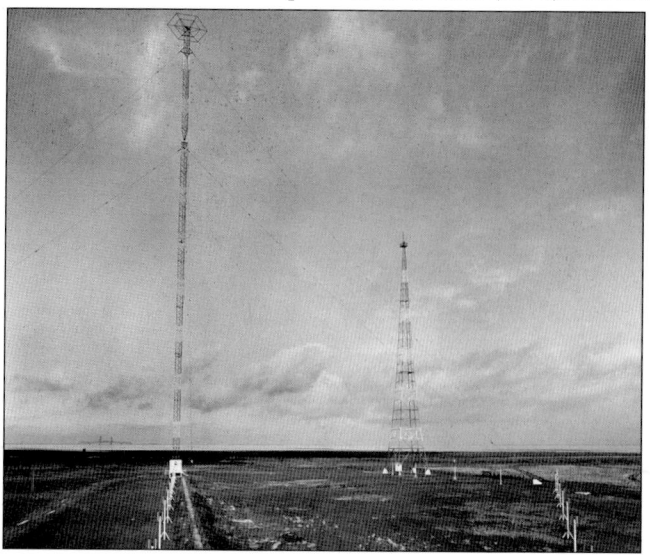

KNBC's 550-foot tower in Belmont was completed in 1949 and still serves KNBR today. The tower is easily visible to motorists crossing the San Mateo Bridge. It uses a unique two-section design, separated in the middle by a porcelain insulator. The framework at the top is called a "top hat," which increases the electrical height of the antenna. Above, the old KPO west tower comes down to make room for the new tower. Below, the big tower stands proudly soon after its completion. The old KPO east tower is to the right. It was kept as a backup antenna and is still standing today. The first KNBC-FM antenna can be seen at its top in this 1949 view. (Both, Bill Newbrough.)

KNBC's Joe Baker climbed to the top of the new tower upon its completion in 1949. The unidentified man at right is a member of the construction crew. The framework that forms the "top hat" of the tower is clearly visible, but it is hard to see Baker's white knuckles as he holds on to the tower beacon. (The person with the most courage is the one who took the photograph!) (Bill Newbrough.)

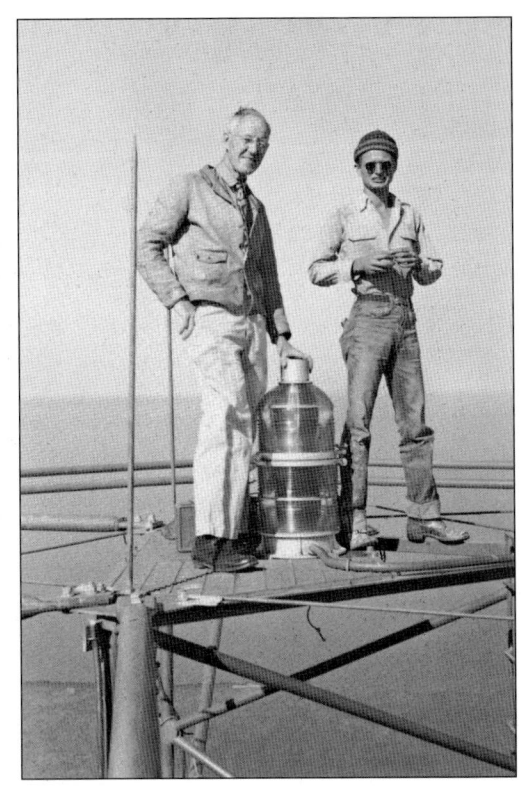

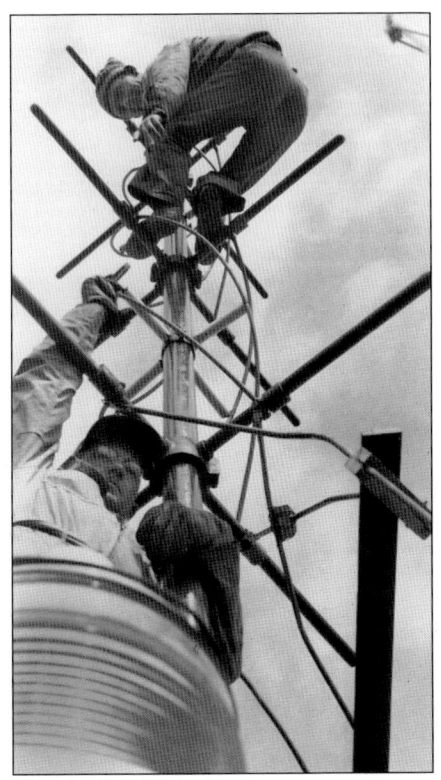

FM radio first came to the Bay Area in 1940, when KALW, signed on as the first FM station west of the Mississippi. By 1947, there were eight local stations, including KNBC-FM. Its antenna was temporarily mounted on the old KPO east tower in Belmont until a permanent site could be completed on Mount San Bruno. This scene shows a "crossed dipole" antenna being installed on the tower. (Bill Newbrough.)

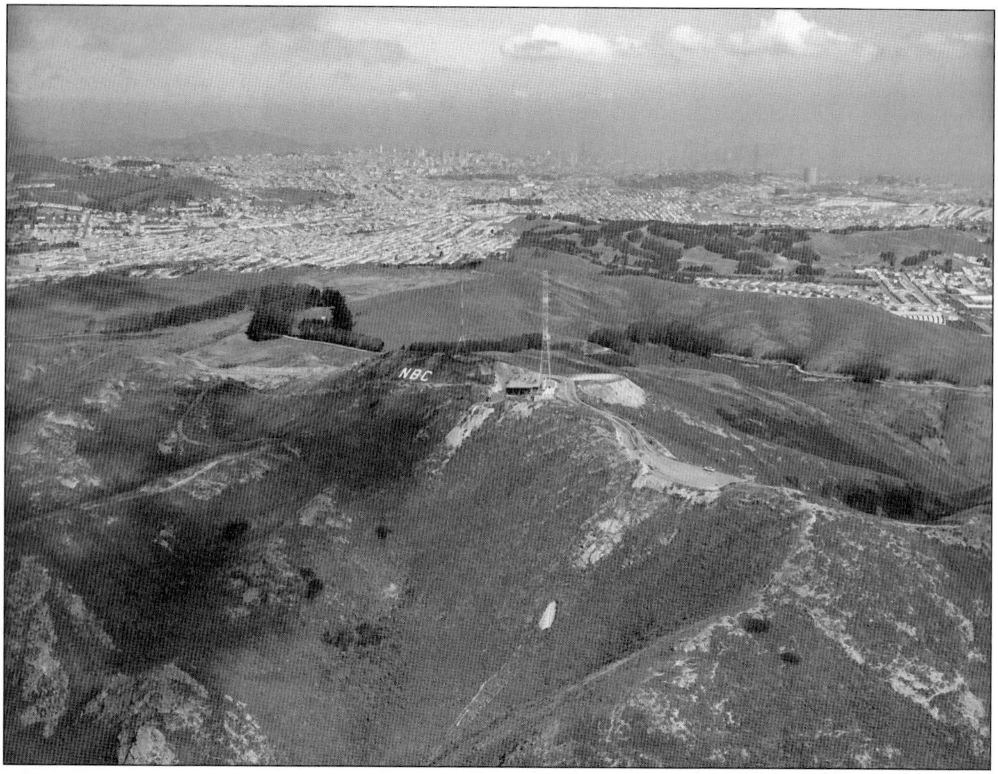

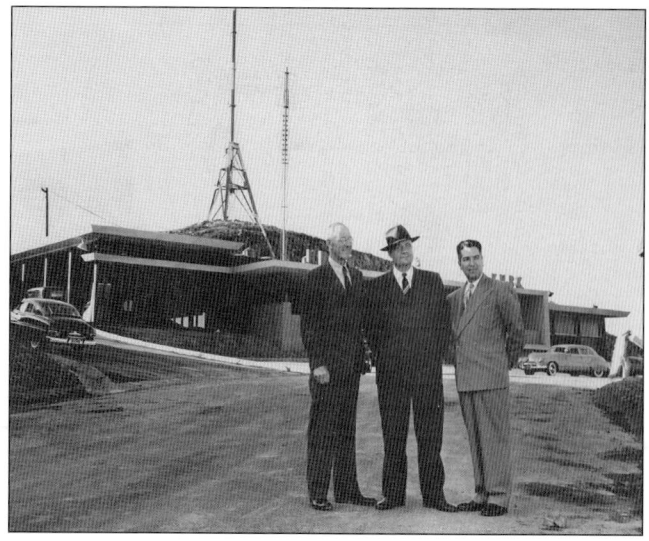

Above, KNBC-FM moved to its permanent location on Mount San Bruno in South San Francisco in 1949. KNBC-FM's tower is at the left, and KRON-TV's tower is at the right. These were the first two broadcast installations on the mountain, which today bristles with radio and television towers. Below, KNBC's Joe Baker, Curtis Peck, and George Greaves stand outside the new KRON/KNBC transmitter building on Mount San Bruno in 1949. The *Chronicle*'s KRON-TV occupied the left side of the building, and KNBC-FM had the right side. KNBC-FM's tripod tower is in the background, next to KRON-TV's "batwing" standby antenna. The main KRON-TV antenna is out of view to the left. (Both, Bill Newbrough.)

KPIX-TV was San Francisco's first television station, built by KSFO's Associated Broadcasters. It signed on December 22, 1948. The antenna was atop the Mark Hopkins Hotel on Nob Hill, seen here being hoisted into place. The transmitter was on the top floor, and KSFO's studio 11 on the ground floor became its first television studio. Competitors KGO-TV and KRON-TV joined the airwaves the following year. (Penny Wilkes.)

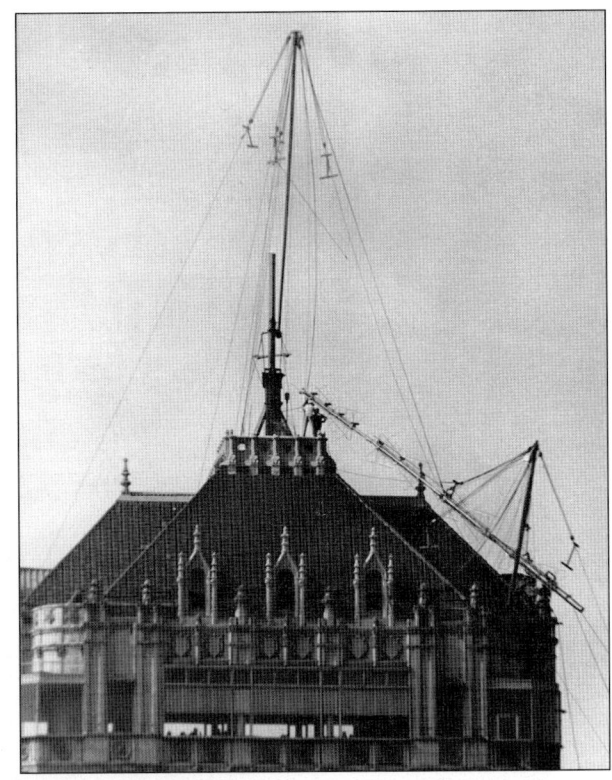

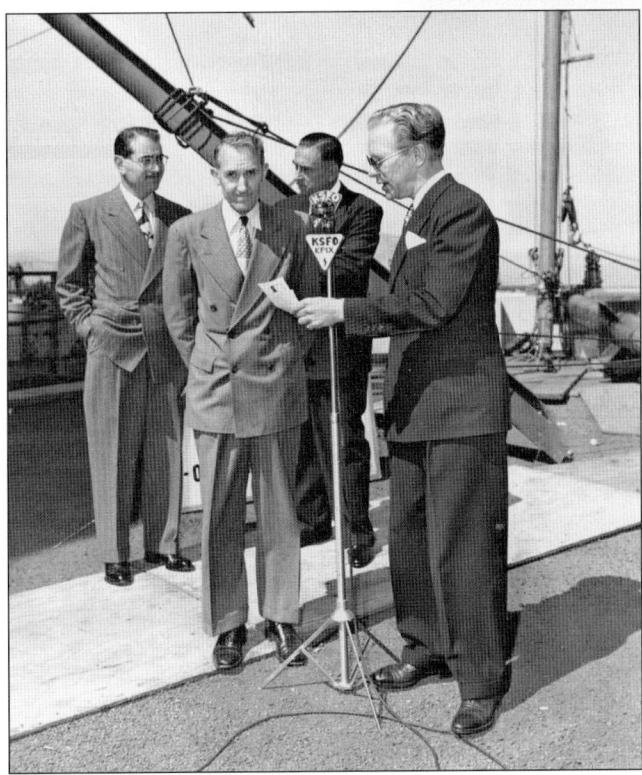

Al Towne, the KSFO-KPIX chief engineer, is interviewed by announcer Bob Hansen on KSFO for a live broadcast celebrating the installation of the KPIX-TV antenna on the roof of the Mark Hopkins Hotel on Nob Hill. Executives Philip G. Lasky and Wesley I. Dumm are seen in the background in this 1948 photograph. (Penny Wilkes.)

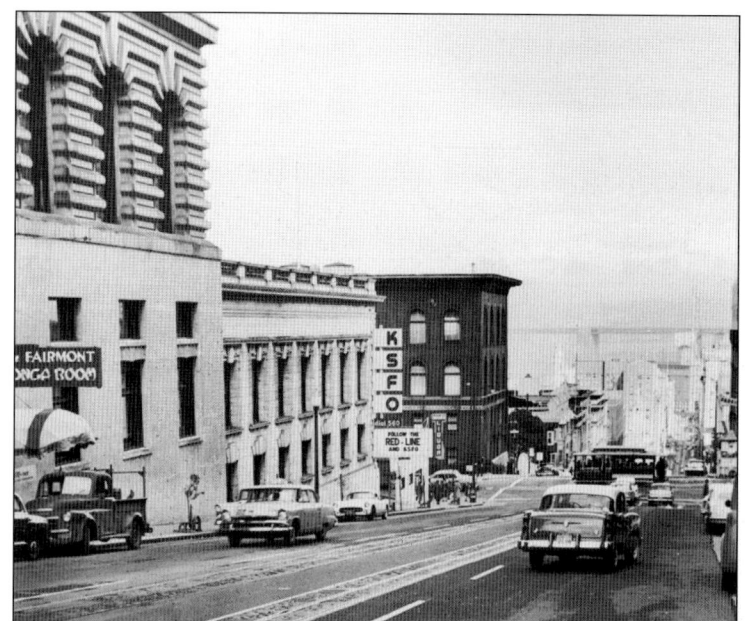

The Associated Broadcasters combined KSFO and KPIX-TV operations into a single building on Van Ness Avenue for a few years, until it sold KPIX-TV to Westinghouse Broadcasting in 1954. KSFO moved into this annex of the Fairmont Hotel the following year, which would be the home of the station for the next two decades. KSFO was sold to Gene Autry's Golden West Broadcasters in 1956. (Author's collection.)

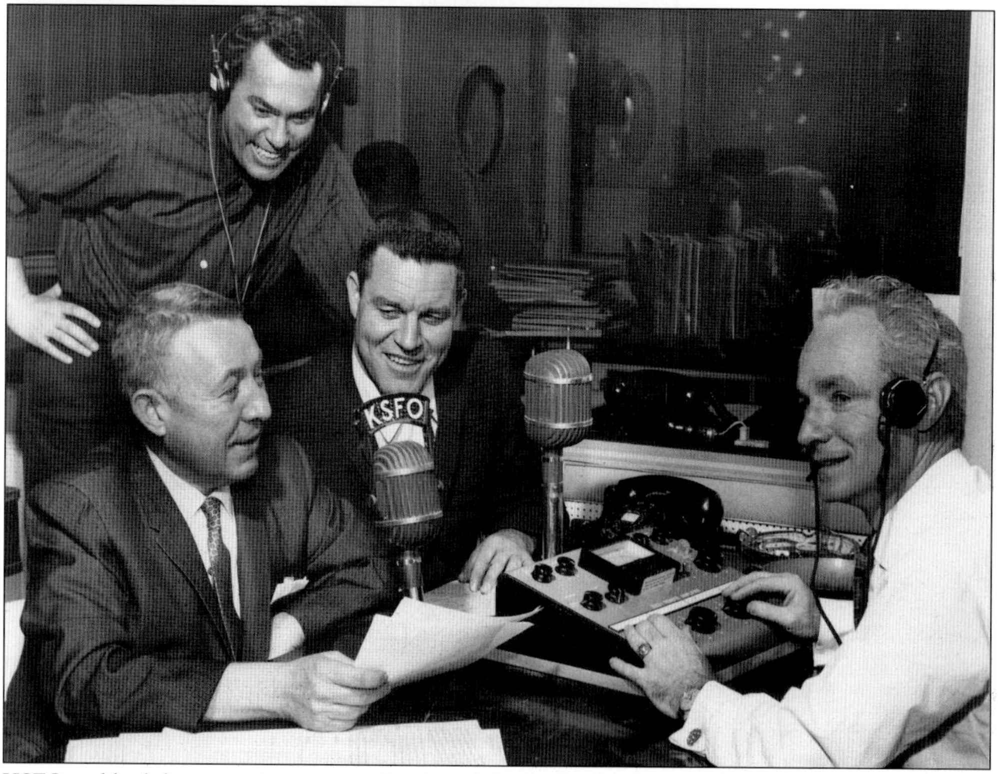

KSFO grabbed the top ratings spot under Autry's leadership and stayed there for decades. It became the key station for baseball's Giants when the team moved to San Francisco in 1958. Seated here are the Giants's crack sports-casting team of Russ Hodges (left; 1910–1971) and Lon Simmons (center; 1923–). Gene DeAlessi is standing, and technician Richard Schmale is at right. Hodges and Simmons are members of the Bay Area Radio Hall of Fame. (Kevin Mostyn.)

United Broadcasting's KEEN Radio in San Jose went on the air in 1947 with 1,000 watts at 1370 kHz. Partners George Mardikian, Floyd Farr, and George Snell first became friends at NBC in San Francisco and they decided to invest together in the new San Jose station. Here is KEEN's transmitter building, located in an orchard on the Old Oakland Highway near Wayne Avenue, close to the Milpitas town limits. (Keith Farr.)

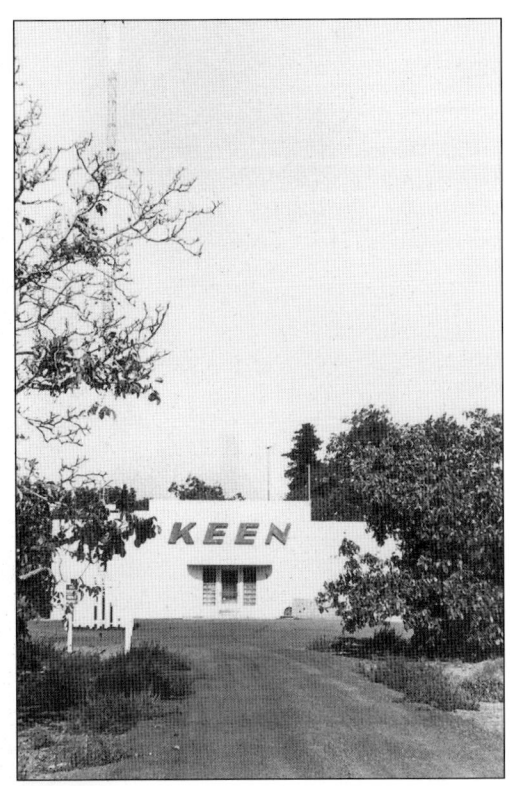

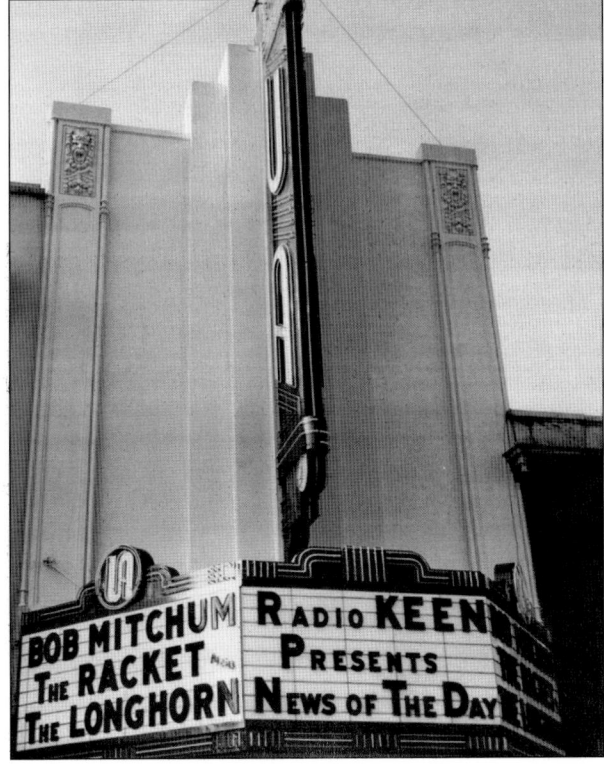

A KEEN publicity announcement appears on the marquis of the United Artists (UA) Theatre at 263 South First Avenue in San Jose in the early 1950s. Built in 1919, the Art Deco theater (formerly known as the Hippodrome) was demolished in 1975 as part of a downtown redevelopment project. (Keith Farr.)

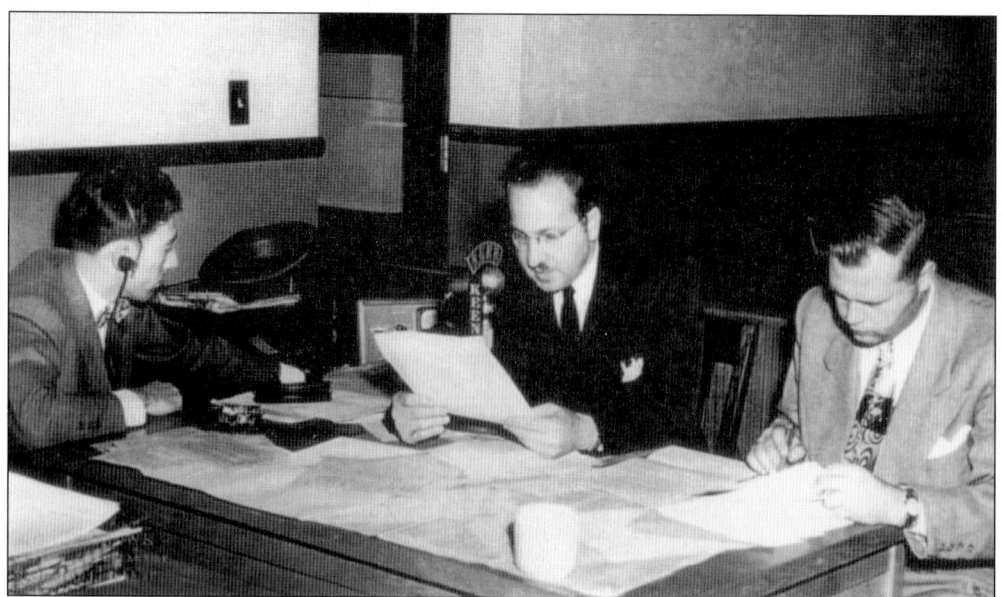

Here, KEEN signs on from its studios in the DeAnza Hotel in San Jose on June 21, 1947. General Manager Floyd Farr is the announcer. KEEN struggled for the first few years before adopting a country-western music format, which proved successful. The formula was later applied to the development of KBAY, KVEG, KFIG, KFOA, and KAHU under the parentage of the United Broadcasting Company. (Keith Farr.)

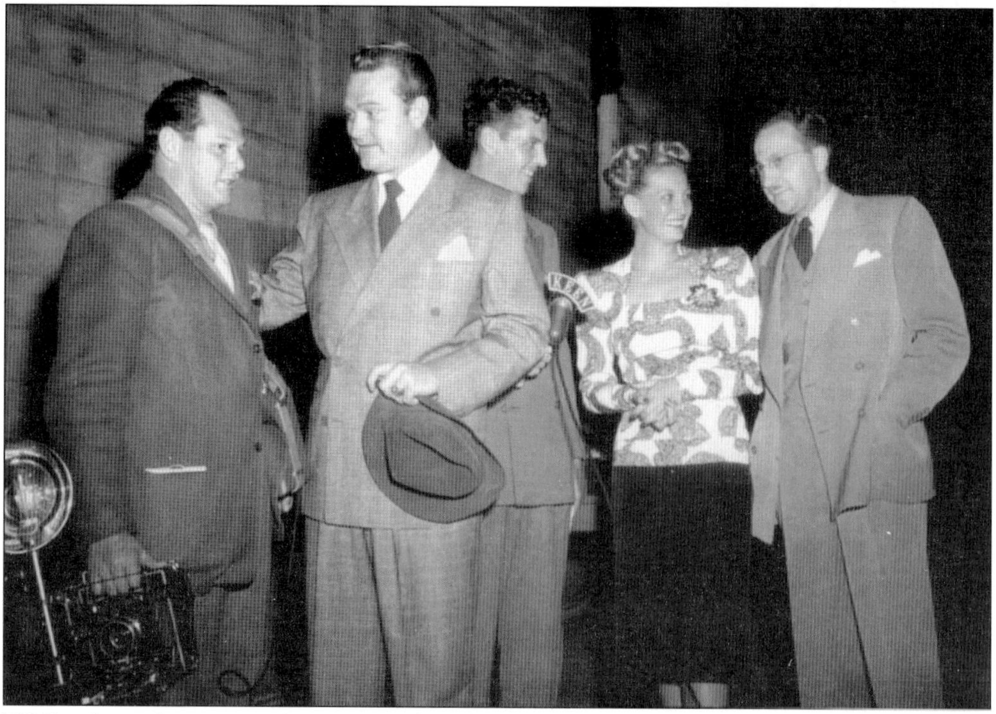

NBC radio and motion picture star Red Skelton (1913–1997), second from left, makes a guest appearance to help celebrate the grand opening of radio station KEEN at San Jose's Hotel De Anza on June 21, 1947. Floyd Farr, KEEN's general manager, is at the far right. (Keith Farr.)

This is a scene from KEEN's second anniversary celebration in 1950. Included are owners Floyd Farr (front row, second from left), George Mardikian (back row, second from left) and George Snell (back row, fifth from left). Mardikian hosted his own program, *The Rubaiyat of Omar Khayyam*, at noon each Sunday on KEEN into the early 1950s. (Keith Farr.)

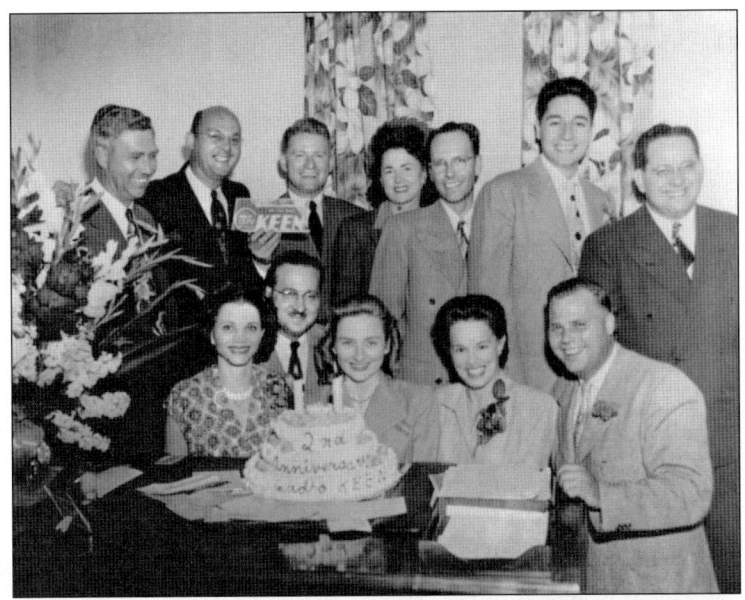

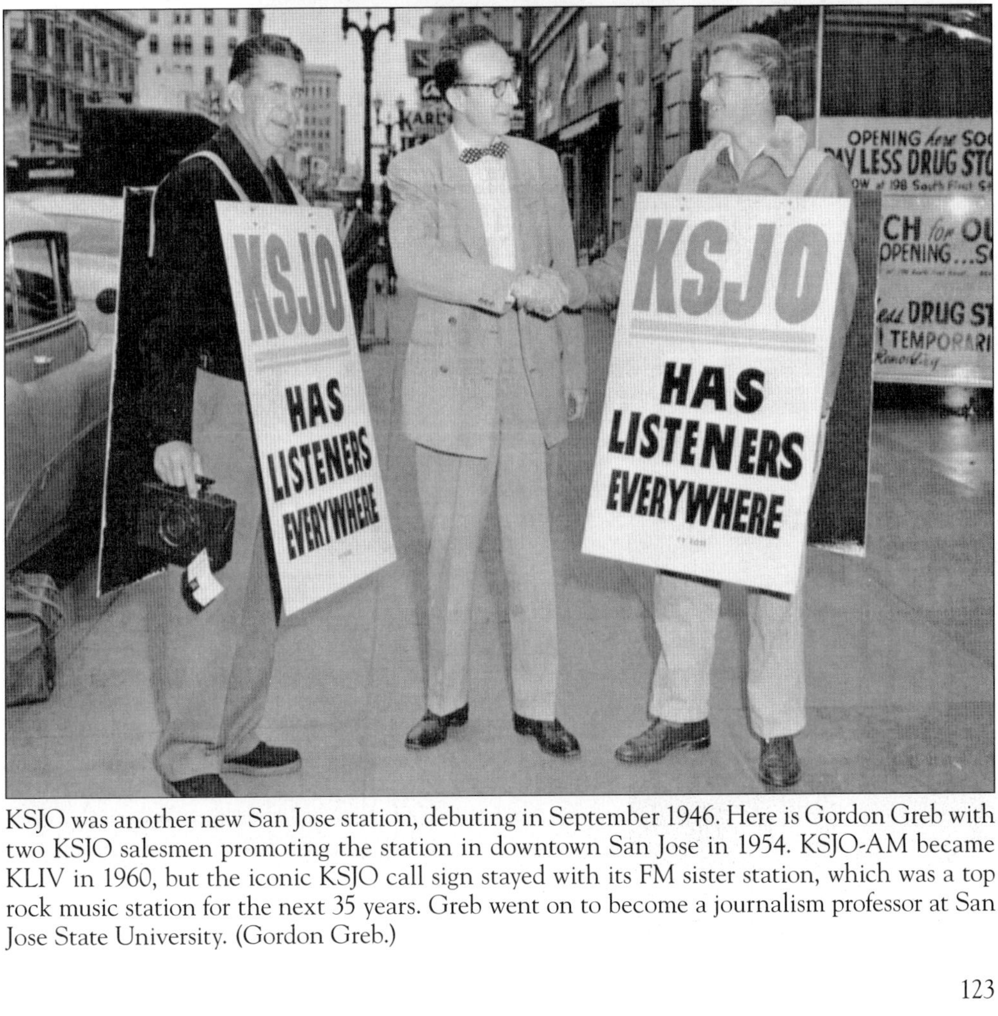

KSJO was another new San Jose station, debuting in September 1946. Here is Gordon Greb with two KSJO salesmen promoting the station in downtown San Jose in 1954. KSJO-AM became KLIV in 1960, but the iconic KSJO call sign stayed with its FM sister station, which was a top rock music station for the next 35 years. Greb went on to become a journalism professor at San Jose State University. (Gordon Greb.)

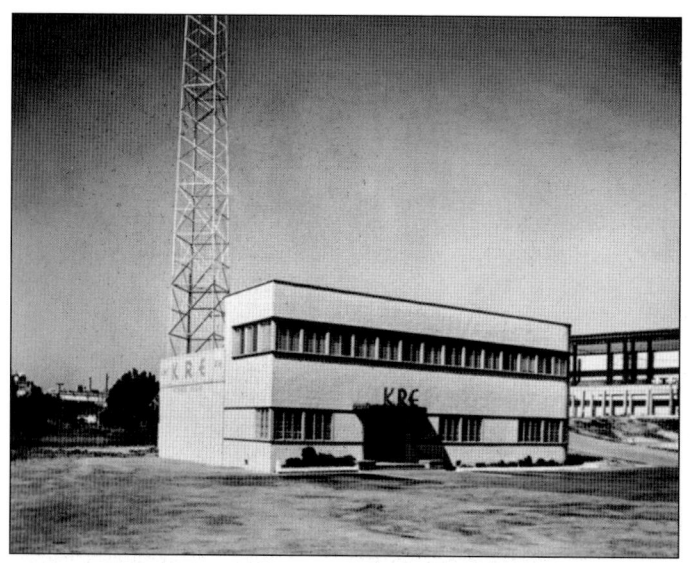

This was KRE's Art Deco studio at 601 Ashby Avenue in Berkeley. It was built in stages—the transmitter building was expanded to incorporate studios in 1938, and then upper story offices were added in 1948. This photograph was taken before 1957, when this 178-foot tower collapsed in a windstorm. The building is now the headquarters of the California Historical Radio Society and its Bay Area Radio Museum. (Author's collection.)

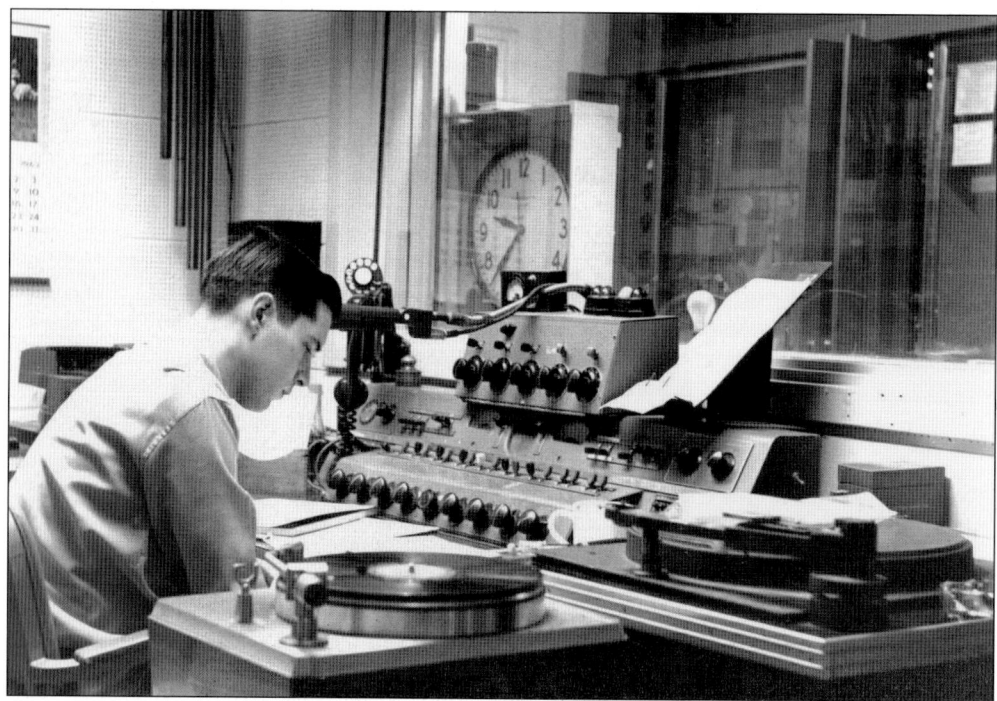

Here is San Francisco's beloved disc jockey Carter B. Smith, seen early in his career while working at KRE in Berkeley. His first big break was when he became the straight man for KSFO's legendary disk jockey Don Sherwood, and he went on to become a familiar voice on KSFO, KNBR, KFRC, and KABL. Smith passed away in 2011 after more than 40 years in Bay Area radio. (CHRS Archives.)

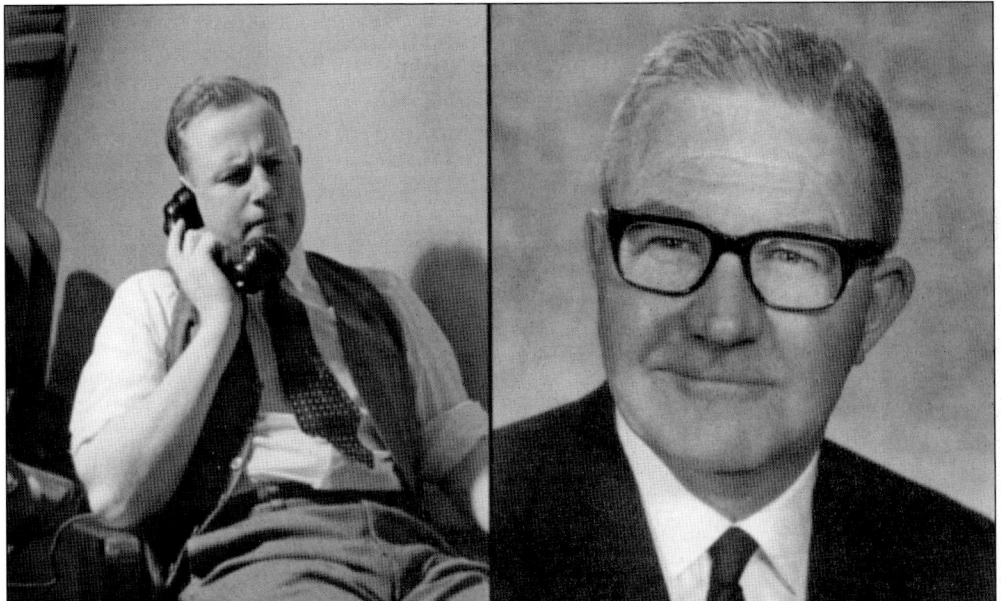

Arthur Westlund (left) and Don Hambly (right) were the principal hands on the KRE rudder for more than 30 years. Westlund managed the Chapel of the Chimes mausoleum, an early KRE advertiser. He leased KRE from the First Congregational Church in 1930, acquiring it outright in 1936, and was its owner and manager until 1963. Hambly was the station's commercial and program manager for most of those same years. (CHRS Archives.)

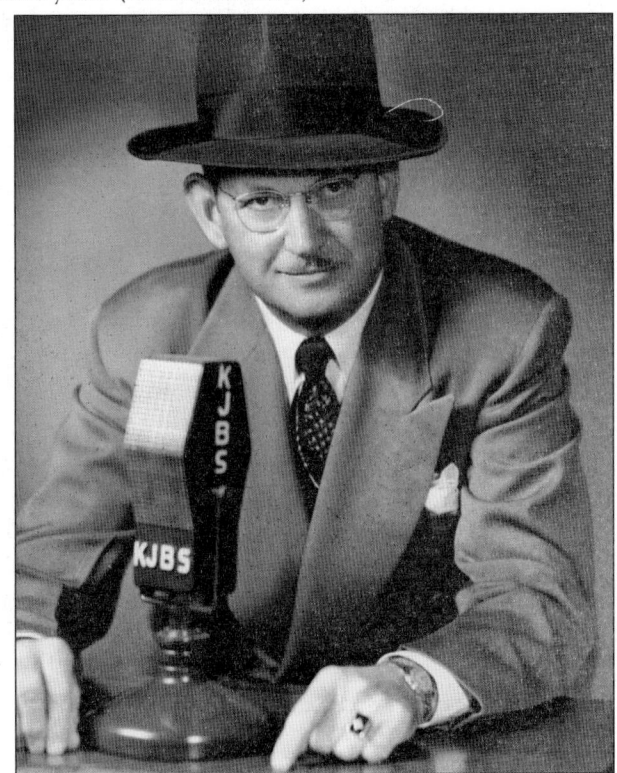

Here is a later photograph of the popular KJBS disc jockey Frank Cope, taken in 1954. Cope began his career in 1929 at KLO in Ogden, Utah, and came to San Francisco the following year. Cope's *Alarm Klok Klub* was a popular early morning staple over KJBS from 1930 to 1959, earning him the title of the World's Oldest Disc Jockey. Cope passed away in 1974 at the age of 72.

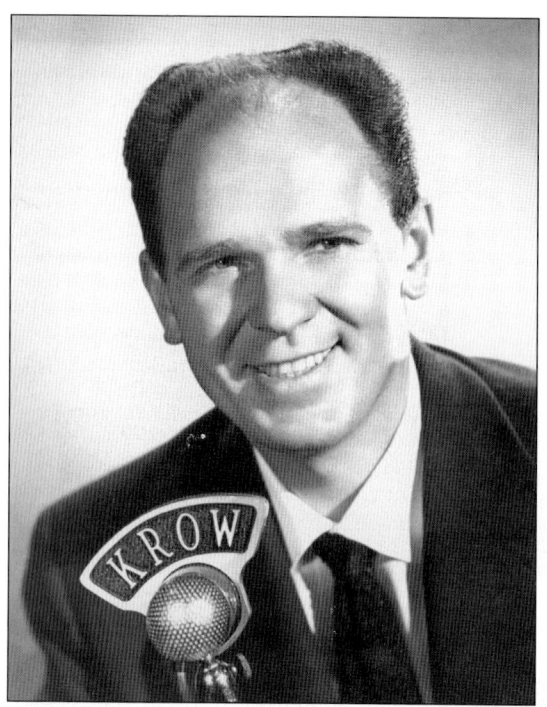

Walt Jamond was a stalwart and friendly Bay Area radio voice for more than three decades. He is seen here on the air at KROW in Oakland in the 1950s. In later years, his distinctive voice was heard on KQBY, KRE/KPAT, KABL, KNBA, and KMPX. (Dr. Suzanne S. Teuber, Jamond Family.)

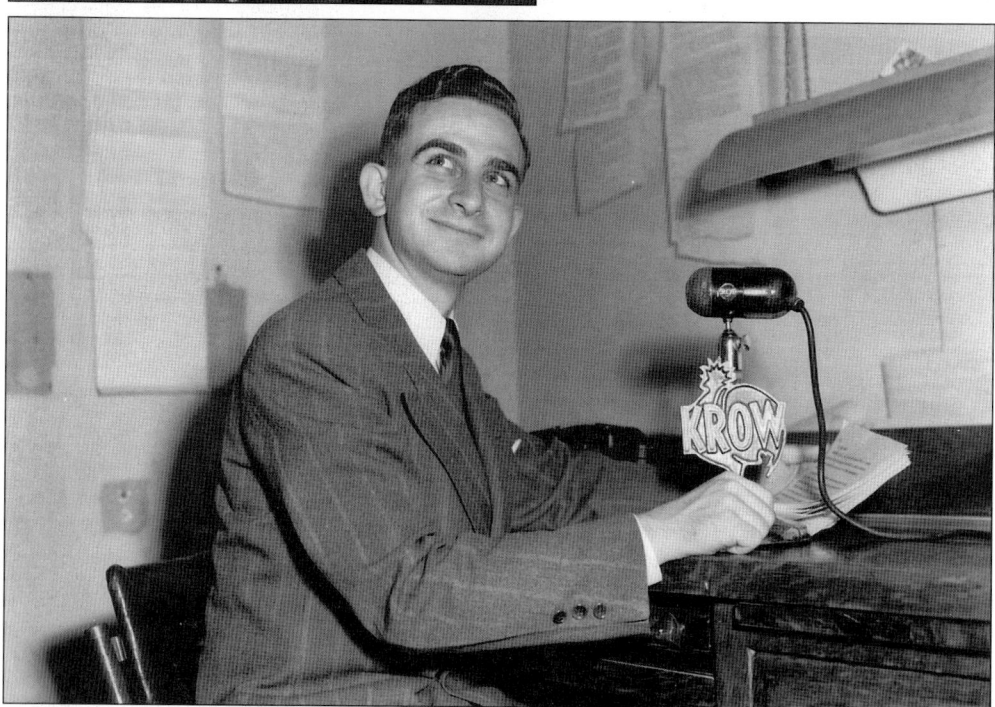

Bruce Sedley was heard on KROW in Oakland from 1947 to 1957. He announced programs throughout the day and did his own show in the evening called *Sedley's Medleys*. Other KROW voices were Don Sherwood, who was half of the morning team *Nick and Nudnick* before becoming the top local personality on KSFO; Pat Henry, who later started his own jazz FM station; and newscaster John K. Chappel. (Bruce Sedley.)

KPEN (now Star 101.3), one of the Bay Area's first popular FM stations, was founded in 1957 by Stanford students Jim Gabbert and Gary Gielow. Each invested $3,000 to build the first new local FM station in eight years. They emphasized quality adult music and high fidelity when most AM stations were abandoning adults in favor of top 40 formats. Pictured at right are Gielow (left) and Gabbert in their KPEN studio in the Whitcomb hotel in 1959. Below is KPEN's first transmitter/studio site on Kings Mountain behind Stanford University. This 125-year-old adobe building was moved to Skyline from Menlo Park, and KPEN operated from here for a year with just 1,500 watts. After moving to Menlo Park it was the first local station to use a microwave link. Here is Jim Gabbert moving the microwave dish at the Skyline site. (Both, Jim Gabbert.)

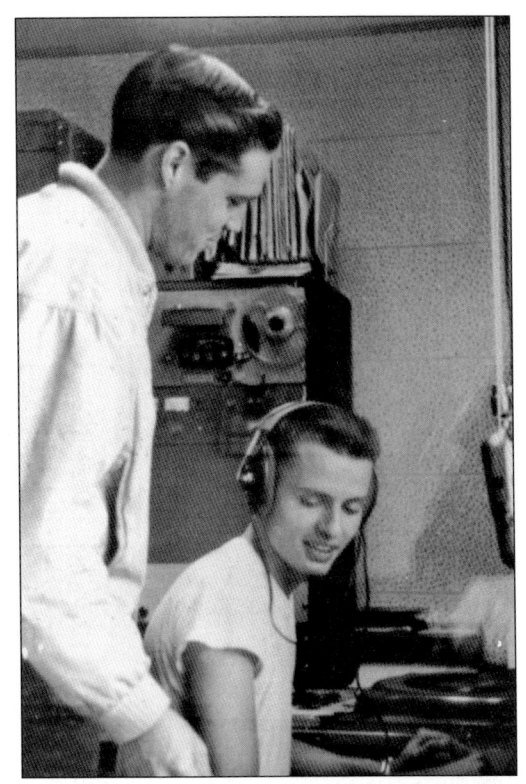

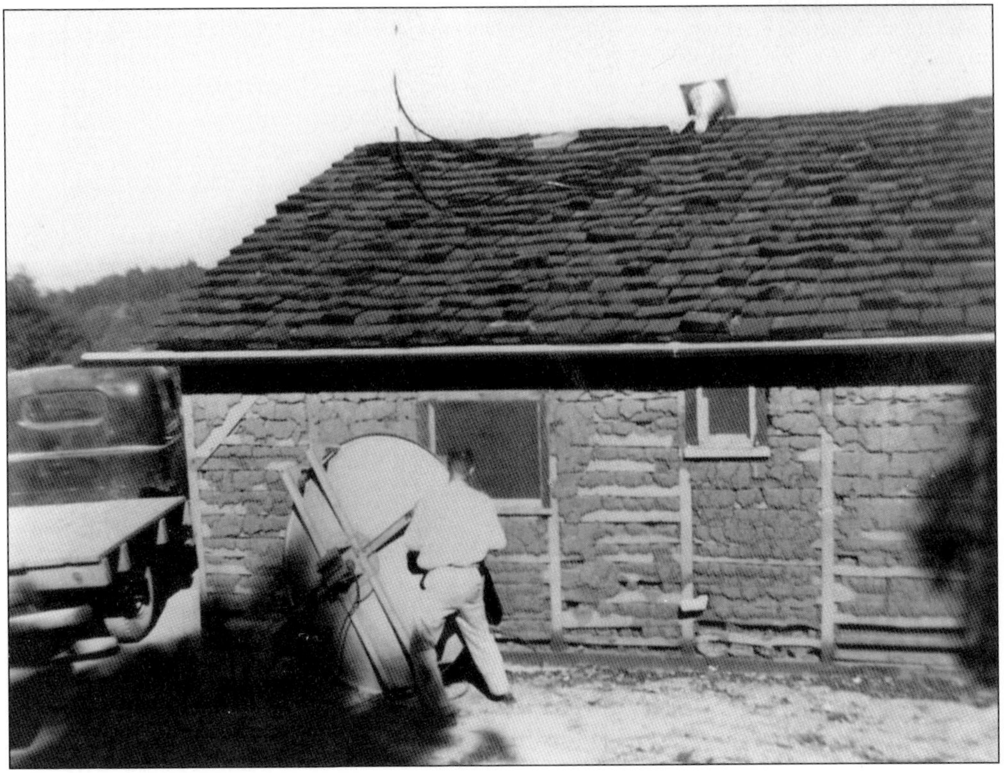

DISCOVER THOUSANDS OF LOCAL HISTORY BOOKS FEATURING MILLIONS OF VINTAGE IMAGES

Arcadia Publishing, the leading local history publisher in the United States, is committed to making history accessible and meaningful through publishing books that celebrate and preserve the heritage of America's people and places.

Find more books like this at
www.arcadiapublishing.com

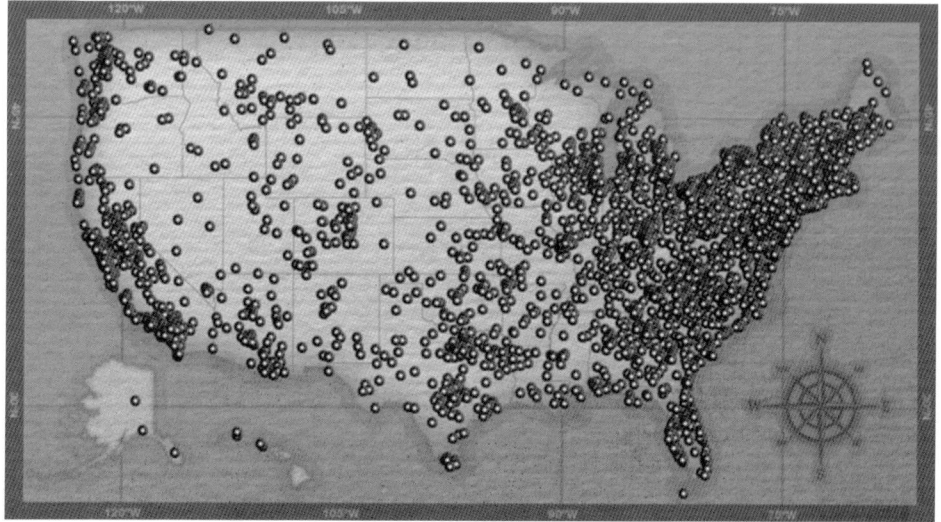

Search for your hometown history, your old stomping grounds, and even your favorite sports team.

 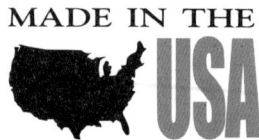